DANCING WITH THE FIRE

Dancing
WITH THE
FIRE

TRANSFORMING LIMITATION
THROUGH FIREWALKING

Michael Sky

foreword by Peggy Dylan-Burkan

BEAR & COMPANY
PUBLISHING
SANTA FE, NEW MEXICO

LIBRARY OF CONGRESS CATALOGING-IN-PUBLICATION DATA

Sky, Michael, 1951-
    Dancing with the fire: transforming limitation through
firewalking / Michael Sky.

        p.   cm.
    Bibliography: p.
    ISBN 0-939680-56-4

    1. Fire walking.   2. Fire walking — Psychological aspects
3. New Age movement   I Title
BL619.F57S59 1989
133 — dc19   88-32624
                                                    CIP

Bear & Company
Santa Fe, New Mexico 87504-2860

Cover photo: Marie Favorito, © 1988

Handtinting of photo: Kelley Kirkpatrick, Media Resource Group

Cover & interior design: Angela C Werneke

Editing: Gail Vivino

Typography: Buffalo Publications

Printed in the United States of America by R.R Donnelley

9 8 7 6 5 4 3 2 1

This is for Penny,
my partner at the Dance.

SPECIAL NOTICE TO THE READER

This book is a reference work and as such is intended solely for use as a source of general information and not for application to any individual case. The opinions expressed are not necessarily those of the publisher; nor can the publisher certify that the use of the procedures or recommendations contained herein is safe or will produce the responses or results described. The information contained herein is in no way to be considered as a substitute for guidance or consultation with a professional firewalking teacher Therefore, before attempting to follow any of the procedures mentioned in this book, it is suggested that the reader seek the expertise of a trained firewalking instructor.

CONTENTS

DANCING WITH THE FIRE

ACKNOWLEDGMENTS

With Gratitude:

to all the firewalkers, firedancers, fireplayers, and firefearers; to all who have joined in this ongoing celebration — your courage is the whole story

to Tolly Burkan and Peggy Dylan-Burkan for opening the gate

to Sydney Cooke, Phoebe Reeve, and Ken Cadigan for teaching me how to dance

to Bear & Company for being so willing, and so easy to play with

to Peter Kevorkian, Stephen Stern, and Garret Whitney for gentle review of the early manuscript

to Marie Favorito, John Michaelson, and Rob Cooper for catching it all on film

to Jeff Volk for producing the movie version of the book, and to Michael Johnson and Cathy Gallo for their starring roles

to my mom, who, when I first told her I was walking on fire, said, "Well, if you can do that, then you can do anything."

and to a small Circle of friends 'back home': for actually coming to the first walk; for all the magic in my life; for so many years of steady support

FOREWORD

I had never heard of firewalking — at least not in the context of anything I considered real. It was something fakirs did in exotic lands, along with climbing ropes suspended in midair and lying on beds of nails. Definitely not part of my Western reality, which did include the mystical as long as there was a distinction between it and my life. Heaven versus Earth. You know, Earth, the physical plane, something to be transcended, overcome, detached from, and when that was attained, there was the remote possibility of enlightenment, nirvana, heaven.

Here I was, never having heard of firewalking, standing in front of a fire which had burned fiercely for a few hours and was now being raked out so we could walk on it. Walk on it? The thought was preposterous. Those coals were glowing orange-red, and even from where I was standing, I could feel the heat. The man raking the coals was Tolly Burkan, later to become my partner in introducing the Western world to firewalking. Putting the rake down, he walked to the head of the glowing path of coals and easily strolled across.

The sight of my right foot descending onto those orange coals is indelibly imprinted in my mind. I crossed the fire. I felt no heat, no pain. I left the workshop in Tolly's hands, staggered out to the orchard and sat on a tree stump. My mind was reeling. I had just done something I had believed to be impossible. Not just impossible because of my personal limitations, but something humanly impossible.

In that moment, I had to question every belief I held about reality, about human beings, about myself. I had demonstrated to myself irrefutably that I could firewalk, and that somehow here within this ancient ritual, the mystical and the physical joined, allowing me to transcend my beliefs about reality. Heaven and Earth merged, the body/mind connection became demonstrably clear, and I gave up my absurd denial of spirit's presence in physical reality.

This is how my dance with the fire began. This dance led me to understand more and more deeply why mystics and spiritual adepts have danced and walked on fire since before recorded history. As the healing powers of the firewalk became more and more evident, Tolly and I began to introduce the public to firewalking. Eventually it became necessary to teach others how to lead this experience. Michael Sky came to our first instructor's training.

Tolly and I were both struck by Michael's courage: he had never walked on fire and yet, through some inner prompting, knew that it was his path. This same courage and attunement has distinguished him as a teacher and is felt throughout his book. Michael and I have since become friends. His sensitivity and insightfulness have often been a blessing to me, and I know that his scientific mind and scrupulous research have greatly contributed to this book. In *Dancing with the Fire* lies the possibility of glimpsing the reality which underlies the firewalk and therefore of absorbing some of its magic — allowing heaven and Earth to come one step closer.

Peggy Dylan-Burkan
Twain Harte, California
November, 1988

Peggy Dylan-Burkan is the co-author of Guiding Yourself into a Spiritual Reality *and the author of* Guiding Your Self. *She is the co-founder of the American firewalking movement.*

PREFACE

Since the spring of 1984, I have been leading small groups of people through the ancient practice of walking on fire. This involves burning a large wood fire down into a path of glowing, red, hot embers and then walking on the coals: barefooted, for several steps, and, for the most part, without burning or experiencing pain. I have now led more than a hundred firewalks, throughout the United States, with over three thousand participants.

For the first two years of my experience, I was something of a skeptic. Even as I motivated others to walk on fire, with encouraging speculations about the human condition and the 'true' nature of reality, I wrestled with some rather persistent doubts. I was very put off by the pop-sensationalism that many brought to the firewalk. I worried that it was all an ego-trip, an unhealthy fascination with 'special powers,' and a likely distraction from the truly important work before us.

Most disturbingly, I questioned the presumed significance of firewalking. Watching groups of people simply and joyously crossing paths of glowing embers, I wondered if we were in fact doing anything extraordinary. Maybe the coals just *looked* hot enough to burn; maybe there was no real danger to the walkers; maybe the powerful lessons of the firewalk all rested on essentially faulty evidence.

Gradually, my doubts have been, quite literally, burned away. For at times the experience of firewalking is not so simple, is not at all joyous, and does in fact *hurt* a great deal. The coals are hot enough to burn, beyond doubt. All that I have witnessed around so many fires has led me to conclude that the deciding factor — Will I burn or will I not burn? — is in some way a function of my individual consciousness. Sometimes I am burned, and sometimes I am not, and the difference lies somewhere and somehow within me. Furthermore, I have learned that I can to some extent *consciously* affect the outcome — *through the special medium of human consciousness I can alter a primary relationship between fire and flesh.*

Simple though it may sound, this is a radical conclusion for

Western culture. The notion that human consciousness can creatively impact objective reality is an abrupt departure from classical scientific thought, with profound implications. My purpose in writing is to explore these implications in depth, with the firewalk serving as a central sounding board, a data-rich example of humans interacting with their environment in a nonordinary way.

Firewalking is quite special in that it is a *somewhat* controllable physical demonstration which sheds light across a wide spectrum of human studies. The act of walking on fire imparts lessons in walking through all of life — lessons in biology and psychology, lessons in ecology and theology, lessons in taking risks, lessons in group dynamics, lessons in singing, dancing and breathing, lessons in the conscious co-creation of reality. Most urgently, I believe, *firewalking is a model for the positive experience and expression of the energies of fear;* Dancing with the Fire *is a metaphor for living with spontaneity, joy and creative excitement during these troubled, fearsome times.*

I would like to see the firewalk become a common ritual — a community celebration — accessible to all who are drawn to its special possibilities. I have included a lot of detail in this book to support that vision. I also want to explore the lessons of firewalking with those who may never actually participate in a firewalk, and thus have attempted to paint as clear a picture as possible of the whole event.

As a final note, understand that this book is *not* intended as a 'how-to' book for the would-be firewalker. As I make very clear, firewalking is potentially dangerous, and should only be approached with the assistance of an experienced guide.

Michael Sky
November 1988

one

FIRST WALKS

*Where will this take us? If even some of my speculations are
proved right we are in store for a whale of a trip — provided we
keep the planet together. I foresee medical advances involving
consciousness not only of organs and cells but even molecules,
electrons, and, perhaps, the ultimate — photons of light ... By
consciously manipulating whether a particle, such as a protein
molecule in a neural membrane, is a wave or not, I expect that
we will be able to change our bodies at will. I expect that with
that gain in sensitivity and consciousness new messages will be
received and our evolution will be speeded up so fast that it will
make our heads spin. Perhaps we will be able to heal ourselves
simply by thinking positively about ourselves. Perhaps we will
be able to regenerate new limbs, increase our intelligence, and
even live for 500 years or more.*

*If we can learn to live together as a species, we will not just
survive this world, we will create it as well as other worlds beyond
our present dreams. The intelligence of the body quantum is
absolutely unlimited.*[1]

*Alice laughed. "There's no use trying," she said, "one can't
believe impossible things."*

*"I dare say you haven't had much practice," said the Queen.
"When I was your age I always did it for half-an-hour a day.
Why, sometimes I've believed as many as six impossible things
before breakfast."*[2]

It's a mystery to me why people are drawn, or even compelled,
along different paths in life. From the very first time I became
aware of the possibility of firewalking, I knew that somehow,
someday, I would be doing it myself. I could not have explained
my attraction to such a strange practice, but this attraction was
enough to have me thinking about it from time to time; to have

me looking for 'firewalk' in the indexes of likely books; to have me trying, so hard, to imagine and really feel what it must be like to place my bare feet on a bed of glowing, red, hot embers and through whatever magic it entails, not to burn.

Living in Boston, I could only assume that my firewalking would have to wait until I was able to travel off to some exotically primitive locale where such irrational activities were the norm. Meanwhile, the same part of me that was drawn to the firewalk had also been drawn to an exploration of unconventional healing practices. This eventually led me to teaching about such things, which in turn led me to regularly telling small groups of people about firewalking and what I saw as its special lessons. I had come to view the firewalk as a graphic example of how the mind and body might better interact, and as a way of inspiring the belief in and pursuit of human potential. And, I suppose, talking about the firewalk was a very sensible alternative to actually doing it.

In early 1984, I was leading a weekend workshop and was feeling frustrated by the end of the first day. I thought to myself that if I could light a candle in the middle of my talk and hold my hand in the flame, unburning, this would prove what I was teaching and greatly boost what we were trying to achieve. That very evening a good friend called and asked if I had seen the latest issue of *New Age Journal*, for, believe it or not, someone out in California (where else?) was leading people through firewalks! I would eventually come to read that article a dozen times, my mind spinning around and around its implications, for this man named Tolly Burkan totally upset all of my theories and expectations. Where I had always assumed and taught that firewalking was the province of the high adepts of advanced metaphysical practices, Tolly was taking groups of mostly middle-class Americans, unscreened and unprepared, and successfully leading them across the coals in just four hours. And, as far as I could glean from the article, the techniques he was using were unbelievably simple.

Needless to say, I sent away for his schedule. As these things happen, I received his itinerary for the previous year and a flyer announcing his first firewalking instructors' training, upcoming in May. While the flyer listed as a prerequisite that participants must already have walked on fire, I very definitely felt my calling and applied anyway. I was accepted.

Tolly Burkan and his wife Peggy Dylan wanted to teach us every aspect of successfully leading firewalks. Since their own approach had been to travel around from place to place doing the walks, our three-week training would consist primarily of ten public firewalks with a lot of traveling in between, so that we would get a taste of life on the road. Thus, although our group of ten students came together in Sacramento, our initial two days were spent journeying in a motorhome up to Seattle, where our first firewalk would be held. This two-day waiting period was actually quite helpful for me, for I was able to be with a group of people who had already walked on fire and to observe, not arrogantly but, I think, quite logically, that we were all pretty much the same. I was certainly not their spiritual or psychological inferior, and I could thus reasonably expect to do as well as they.

Alas, on the day of my first walk, most of my reason and logic abandoned me. As the morning wore on (firewalks always happen at night, which really means that they happen for an entire day!) my body felt uncharacteristically tense; there was a low level anxiety, a sort of creeping quiet desperation which took over and gripped me. I was not hungry and I did not feel like talking. I kept thinking of the thousands of people who had already done this; I kept looking at my fellow trainees and thinking how we were genetically the same, how they were not doing some complex meditation that I did not know about. My mind would be somewhat reassured, but my body grew tenser still. Midday we were shown a brief news clip of Tolly walking across a *very* hot-looking bed of coals, and my stomach lurched in protest. I felt as if I had just witnessed an accident victim sprawled bloody across the pavement, so desperately unhappy was my body with what it had seen. I continued to fast and I talked even less. In a notebook I wrote, "I feel like I'm in an airplane, about to parachute into enemy territory."

I was at this point twisted by a combination of fears. The first and simplest was that I would severely injure myself. The second was that I would be too frightened to walk, a horrendous thought given the time, expense, and self-esteem I had committed to becoming an instructor. The third, combining the first two, was that I would walk, fail painfully, and limp home a crippled and embarrassed wreck. As evening approached, I found my mind less and less able to issue up reassurance, and more and more focused on my fears. And my body grew tenser still.

Finally, the workshop began. There were some fifty or so people, mostly looking as if they had just been told they had four hours to live. Tolly had quite a showman's style. Working the crowd, he first terrified us with what could go wrong, and then exploded the tension with his wonderful sense of humor. After an hour or so, we went outside and together constructed a very large pile of wood, kindling, and newspaper. Then we circled about it, holding hands, while Tolly doused it with a gallon of kerosene and set it aflame. In moments, we were blasted with such heat that everyone took two steps away from the fire's scattering sparks and billowing smoke. This was definitely not a summer-camp fire, nor even a homecoming bonfire. It was an inferno, and if it was designed to frighten, it surely succeeded.

Back inside we went, and for the next two hours Tolly prepared us for walking. What I remember best is agreeing with most of what he was saying, while at the same time feeling very concerned that I was not really hearing anything new. I was clearly waiting for some powerful technique or super meditation that would change me from 'one who burns' into 'one who doesn't burn' but as time passed I felt distinctly unchanged and increasingly vulnerable. Things gradually took on a rather surreal air. It felt as if we were all doing drugs together or, again, as if we were all in a plane behind enemy lines, lost in our separate thoughts, contemplating doom, barely breathing.

Finally, the time came. We returned to the fire, which had calmed somewhat into a large pile of glowing embers and smoldering hunks of wood. We held hands, chanting softly as Tolly took a heavy metal rake and carefully spread the coals into a path some twelve-feet long and six-feet wide. With each pass of the rake, sparks flew off in every direction and what little breath we were taking was filled with smoke. The heat was still so intense that people were moving away from, rather than toward, the fire, its red-orange glow pulsing, menacing, yet oddly inviting. My mind finally emptied and quieted, I was lost in the singing and transfixed by the fire. My body was trembling out of control, as if it were somehow freezing on this warm spring evening.

I could feel through their hands that those on either side of me were shaking also.

Tolly laid down the rake, stepped up to the fiery path, and, with just the briefest pause, walked quickly across the coals. I registered that he took six steps and that he seemed okay, when suddenly another person walked across, and then another. I noticed my head shaking, side to side, as I watched feet sinking down into glowing, red, hot coals. People continued walking, one after another, and our singing steadily picked up, becoming more excited, more vibrant. My mind was blank and making no decisions, while my feet, seemingly of their own accord, carried me slowly toward the top of the path. My trembling increased and I sang even louder. I noticed that I was standing next to a man who had struck me earlier in the evening as something of a jerk. When he suddenly walked across, my mind cried out "If he can do it, I can do it too!" Moments later I moved — seven quick steps — I had walked on fire!!

I was overwhelmed with joy and found myself wanting to applaud each succeeding walker. The energy between us continued to rise, higher and higher, becoming more and more excited. It was all so beautifully stunning — the fire, the circle, the singing, the stars, the moon — and the wonderful feeling of grass beneath my happy, happy feet. At last a strong shout of joy exploded through the group. There was some hugging, a rush of laughter, and then slowly we all filtered back inside.

The funeral parlor had transformed into a circus! A tangible wave of relief rippled through a room filled with happy chatter and excited giggles. We took some time for sharing our experiences, and miracle stories abounded. I became aware of a spot on my left foot which was feeling a little hot, just a little painful. I looked around and sensed that some other walkers were hurting too, including a fellow trainee who would turn out to be very badly blistered. I also noticed that the majority of people were feeling no pain whatsoever.

Later, as I called home to assure my wife and friends that I had survived it, feet intact, I began to feel a little let down. Obviously it had been a long, exhausting day. Somehow I had expected it to be more difficult; it just seemed too easy. I mean, if anyone could do this, then . .

My second walk came two nights later at the same location. I collected the release forms that night as people entered the room, and felt myself tense slightly as a pretty young woman arrived, moving very slowly on a pair of crutches. Her name was Kathy.[3] I would only find out later that she was a social worker for handicapped rights, that she worked in her spare time on a suicide hot-line, and that she had a bumper sticker shouting 'Expect A Miracle!,' but I could tell the moment I saw her that she was a determined and self-sufficient woman who was working hard to overcome *all* of the limitations in her life.

As I watched her throughout the evening, it became very apparent to me that Kathy was there to walk on fire. So I was rather apprehensive when, just before going out to the fire, her husband asked if people with cerebral palsy should firewalk and Tolly recommended against it. Somehow I think we all knew that Kathy did not take kindly to, nor listen to, people telling her what she could not do.

For myself, this second walk was very much the same as the first, though slightly colored with the memory of pain. I felt the same tension throughout my body and the body of the group. The fire was just as hot, and the path Tolly raked out seemed longer, if anything. My mind was every bit as incredulous when the walking began, and there was the same sense of shifting to a magical, otherworldly reality. I did manage, however, to be one of the first walkers, and thus felt double elation as I reached the other side, unburned.

At some point Kathy started moving toward the fire, walking on her crutches really, her legs and feet stiffly dragging behind. The electrical tension in the circle magnified tenfold. Ever so slowly she moved, shuffling into and through the fire, so slowly that at times she seemed to be standing still, up to her ankles in glowing embers. Each step was a major victory, first carrying her into the heart of the fire, and then slowly carrying her out toward safety. At the very end of the path she stopped, suddenly, and in the next moment she started screaming.

She was carried immediately from the fire and into the house, and later to a hospital, both feet severely burned, the skin already blistering and peeling. Somehow the firewalk continued, as one person was crazy enough to step forward in the midst of the terror and start the flow of walkers again. The mood afterwards was very subdued, however, as we had little energy for celebration given what we had witnessed. I remember being torn. On the one hand I felt like I was through with firewalking, and wanted never to be part of such a tragedy again. At the same time, I kept trying to believe that things do happen for good reason and that Kathy's experience would become an important contribution to my understanding of the firewalk.

Kathy would later say that she had been doing fine, feeling neither pain nor the slightest heat, all of the way to that final step. Then she looked down, and the image of her feet buried in burning embers was overwhelming, causing her to think she was doing the impossible and to hear her lifelong admonishments: You can't! You're unable to! You mustn't! At this point she began to burn. She asked that we not feel sorry for her nor responsible for her actions, and she demonstrated her personal power by healing in a fraction of the time that her doctors had predicted. She was truly grateful for the whole experience and stressed that she had in fact walked on fire very successfully for all but one step.

There was a newspaper reporter present that night who was timing the walkers with a stopwatch. He said the average walker took between a second and a half to two seconds to get across the coals and that Kathy had been on them for a full seven seconds before she screamed. So she had indeed firewalked the equivalent of some fifty feet (a current Guinness world record) without burning, and without even lifting her feet out of the fire. Through her extraordinary courage, Kathy had demonstrated what I would come to see as the two most important lessons of the firewalk: yes, we are capable of walking through extreme heat without burning; and yes, the fire is hot, we can get burned, and whether we burn or not depends more on our state of mind than on how we walk.

I would experience many other 'firsts' during the remainder of my training. One night I had my first 'cold' walk: I walked through the coals, and not only did I not feel any heat, I actually felt cold, as if I were walking through snow. An incredible sensation! The next night I had my first real burn, a screeching pain that sent me to bed with my foot wrapped in a cold, wet towel, very seriously debating the value of continued firewalking.

I also parachuted out of my first airplane, sat through my first Indian sweat lodge (another ancient and very potent ritual), and rappelled down my first rock face, as Tolly and Peggy found different ways to lead us through the lessons of the firewalk. And, most importantly to me, one night I chose to walk first — to offer the final words to the group, to prepare the coals, and then to initiate and model the experience by going first. That night went so well I felt confident that I could create firewalks on my own. I was ready, and excited, to go home and get started.

————————

It began raining early in the morning of Memorial Day that year, and the rain kept up through most of the day. My wife Penny and I were living with two friends in a very suburban neighborhood in Concord, just west of Boston. The plan was to have the firewalk right there on our very suburban front lawn. We called the local fire department and told them we were having a holiday cookout with an Hawaiian luau-style wood fire. I began to see that a rainy night could be a plus, as it would keep our neighbors indoors, and I went to the supermarket and bought a case of charcoal lighter, hoping that would be enough to keep the fire going.

For the rest of the day we all just sat around the house, shut in by the rain, and quietly freaked out. Someone would stare into a book for ten minutes without registering a word. Or someone would put water on to boil and then stand empty-headed before the tea cabinet trying to remember why. There was a lot of pacing, of moving from one room to another with no discernable purpose. And there was some courageous gallows humor, which sometimes worked a giggling release and other times only served to deepen the gloom.

Our good friend Jonathon just happened to show up that afternoon, in town for the holiday and wondering what we were doing. Jonathon is an engineer and possibly the most logical, rational, linear, left-brain I have ever known. When I told him our plans for the evening, he was at first very excited, for he only heard the part about my demonstrating the walk. As I slowly made it clear to him that everyone might walk on fire, his eyes bugged out and it looked as if the rest of his body would like to do the same thing. I asked if he would like to be the firetender, staying outside and keeping the fire going for us while we were inside preparing to walk. He gladly said yes, happy to be able to take part and witness the walk without feeling compelled to do something so utterly inconceivable.

Evening finally arrived, as did my friends. Once again I found myself sitting in a roomful of people waiting to have a root canal without anesthesia. The big difference was that this time there was no one present (myself included) who really knew that it was all going to work out. It is a basic truism that fear feeds on fear. If you are looking to your old friend for reassurance and instead see fear in his eyes, you will tend to feel frightened, which he will spot in your eyes, further frightening him, which further frightens you, which further frightens him, which further frightens you . . . and so on.

By this time I had come to understand two basic facts about people that are almost always operative at the start of a firewalk. The first is that we are very disinclined to intentionally move in the direction of pain, unless we have clear social approval, as, for instance, in the case of athletes or dancers. While we might understand and even applaud the marathon runner's contorted features and occasional shin splints, to intentionally step on a fire and then suffer injury is considered quite stupid by our cultural standards. The second fact is that our relationship to fire is governed by the deepest, most cellular, most instinctive level of our beings: virtually every life-form on this planet knows better than to move in the direction of fire, so again, a modern-day, well-educated human being would have to be pretty foolish to even consider such a practice, and doubly foolish to suffer pain as a result.

Yet my friends and I must have had our reasons, strong enough to carry us forward in the presence of our doubts and fears, for there we were. Despite a rather clumsy and halting presentation on my part, the evening progressed and our group's moment with the fire approached. I told them to take a little break while I went outside to see how the fire was doing in the rain. I found Jonathon keeping his lonely vigil, umbrella overhead, and I took a rake and poked very clinically through the fire, attempting to determine whether we had enough coals to do the walk. I was suddenly hit with the heat (the fire had done very well in the rain), with the fire's electric, glowing, orange burst of energy, and my stomach seized up with the outlandishness and

undeniable danger of what we were about to do. I took a deep
breath, put on a happy face, and went slowly back inside,
attempting to emanate all-knowing reassurance. My friends
later said that I was white with terror.

And so, we proceeded out to the fire. It was now raining
very lightly, a soft and cooling presence, and a wonderful blessing
and balance for our undertaking. We formed a circle, holding
hands, except for Jonathon, who stood dry and sensible beneath
his umbrella. The singing began, as I took the rake and began
spreading the coals: *all this earth is sacred, every step we take,
all this life is sacred, every step we take* . . . . As the fiery carpet
was first laid before them, there was a tangible group gasp.
Nothing I had said could have prepared them for the intensity
of the heat, for the explosion of sparks and smoke, for the
solid red-orange sheet of pulsing embers. Minds boggled, bodies
trembled, and our singing grew louder, viscerally driven.

I stood before the coals, my entire life summed up in the
exquisitely profound thought: "Either it works, or it doesn't,
here goes . . ." I walked across, no problem! I was then stunned
to see one friend following immediately after, and then another,
and another. Whereas the walks during my training had progressed
very slowly, half of our group had walked in the first thirty
seconds! I was not sure whether this was a result of their extreme
desire to walk on fire, or their extreme desire to be finished
with walking on fire, but they were all very happy, and in the
space of a minute we had shifted from unthinking terror to
exhilarating joy.

I looked over to Penny, who had not yet walked and who
was visibly shaking. I had had a dream just before returning
home in which Penny had stepped forward and burst into flames.
I was hoping that wouldn't happen, as I do love her quite a bit.
Also, any future firewalking that I was going to do would have
to rest on her support. For her part, she had always steadfastly
maintained that firewalking was not her sort of thing at all, and
that if her husband hadn't had the temerity to land one in her
own front yard she might have forever remained among the
blissfully uninitiated. But there it was, and walk she did, smiling
brightly all the way into my waiting arms.

We had by then reached the magical shift that most firewalks
achieve: the fire had become friendly and inviting, the singing

inspired, and the group intensely bonded, with a strong sense that anything was possible. As if to affirm it all and top it with a final encore, Jonathon stepped up to the fire, umbrella still raised, and strolled across the coals with wonderful aplomb, the perfect ending to an unforgettable dance. We were well on our way to an adventure that, years later, continues to provide a wealth of such moments.

two

THE CO-CREATIVE PROCESS

The intelligence capable of orchestrating the diversity of all the cells in the human body is equally capable of orchestrating the diversity of the human family.[1]

To view the universe anew is to change in feeling and being. Just as there is no mind without body, no spirit without matter, there is no cognition without affect, no observation without personal change, no unmoved mover.[2]

The universe begins to look more like a great thought than a great machine.[3]

It does indeed seem possible that we alive today could witness the beginnings of the emergence of a high-synergy society, a healthy social superorganism. If so, we could be among the most privileged generations ever to have lived.[4]

The question people so often ask is why.

Why stand barefoot before a path of glowing, red-hot embers and choose to step forward? Why run the risk of serious pain and injury for a few seemingly impossible steps? Why dance and sing with strangers around a fire in the dark; why take part in an ancient and primitive rite of passage; why even ponder such a strange and unlikely activity?

I have found there are as many answers to the question 'why' as there are questers to ask it, that each potential firewalker must ultimately discover his or her own answer before stepping forward. And, I feel that one universal answer to the question 'why' lies in the very nature of fire itself.

The discovery of fire by human beings, and the relationship we have developed with it as we have learned to harness its power and turn it towards purposeful good, is without question one of the major contributions to the successful evolution of our

13

species. Fire has made it possible for most of the people of this planet to live in climates that would otherwise be too cold. It has given to our diets a vast array of foods that, without cooking, would be unpalatable and of very different nutritive value. It has enabled us to work creatively with metals, opening an entire industry which began with the forging of the simplest tools and has steadily progressed to the fabrication of the minutest microchips. And it has been the power source and driving force of the industrial and postindustrial ages, the life-blood of our automobiles and airplanes, our cities and factories, our most complex surgical operations, our rockets to the moon.

Even in warmer tropical climates where fire has not been necessary for heating, cooking, the development of tools, or the fuel of industry and transportation, people have known that their lives were made possible by that great fire in the sky, the sun, and have treated their earthbound fires as offshoots, or little brothers, of that greater fire. Though the choreography has differed from one time and place to another, there has never been a developing culture which has not developed and followed certain rituals involving fire. Such fire rituals are intrinsic to human culture, for it is universally recognized that fire is an essential element for life on this planet, to be treated at most times with love, reverence, and thanksgiving, at other times with adoration and idolatry, and at all times and all places with the utmost of respect. Thus it can be said, as it so often is, that the discovery of fire was one of the most important moments in the history of humanity.

Whenever I think about the discovery of fire, I imagine a brave and curious human being coming upon a blaze in the forest or on the plain, quite attracted to the fire's warmth, to its beauty, to its dancing, flowing quality so similar to that other wonderful stuff, water. Such a person would quite naturally reach out to touch this bright, new substance, and thus discover — ouch! — that fire is hot and fire burns. The discovery of fire undoubtedly involved the simultaneous uncovering of this very basic natural law, this simple and painfully obvious truth that *fire burns.*

Slowly, over time, early men and women learned to use this basic fact about fire — that it burns — and to turn it towards their purposeful good. They learned to heat their homes, to

cook their food, and to melt and forge important tools and
implements. Slowly they learned to control fire, to harness its
burning energy and use it, although a constant throughout the
learning process was the painful lesson that if they were not
very, very careful, then fire would all too easily burn out of
control, turning from life-improver to life-destroyer. This has
always been fire's basic message, its essential nature: it will
burn, possibly for good, possibly for ill, but always and without
doubt, it will burn. And, outside of the firewalking experience
itself, this basic fact about fire has been confirmed over and
over and over again, by all people in all times and all places.
Without exception and beyond doubt, the law has always been:
fire burns.

As individuals born into this world, we generally receive our
indoctrination into the nature of fire within our first couple of
years. We touch the hot stove, the burning candle, the lit cigarette,
and we personally discover fire — Ouch!, that's hot, this stuff
called fire burns. As we grow, we learn to use fire in a thousand
and one helpful ways, and, inevitably, we pick up our share of
accidental burns. And throughout our lives, again, outside of
the firewalking experience, we never encounter anything but
confirmation upon confirmation of the basic, unalterable fact
that *fire burns.*

Therein lies one major answer to the question, Why walk
on fire? Each time a person successfully walks on fire, each time
a person brings bare, tender flesh into contact with the extreme
heat of glowing embers, and does not burn, then he or she
demonstrates that it is possible to reverse, or suspend, or at
the very least modify, this most concrete and unquestionable
of natural laws. The fact that fire burns, juxtaposed with the
fact that firewalking can be successful, suggests that human
beings might be able to play a more direct role in the formation
of physical reality and its governing laws than is ordinarily
thought possible. Furthermore, in opening to that possibility, it
is rather difficult not to then wonder if there are other 'certain'
laws which are in fact flexible or mutable, and if there are other
unsuspected human resources which we might learn to bring forth.

This is the draw of the firewalk, its beauty, its lessons, its
awesome power: that we as human beings are connected to and
play a role in the creative processes of our world. People walk

on fire as a way of graphically demonstrating that they are active participants in the creation of reality, as a way of experiencing that in fact reality can be shifted, altered, changed, and created anew, and that the human spirit can and does play a causative role in such change and re-creation.

This does not mean simply that we create change through our deeds and actions, but that, in fact, *we contribute to the ongoing creation of reality through the special medium of human consciousness.* It means that our thoughts, feelings, words, and deeds matter; that our attitudes, our beliefs, our aspirations, and our dreams matter; that our essential human consciousness matters — *makes material;* that our inner worlds are influential in the manifestation of external reality. A firewalker approaching the fire is saying, "How I think matters, how I feel matters, the belief I am holding matters, the desire I am dreaming matters." The firewalker realizes that the next few steps in her life will unfold according to who she is as an individual, and according to her own unique way of being in the world; that the fire will burn, or not, depending largely upon her own personal responses to her world, and her own personal state of consciousness.

This, of course, is a radical departure from the scientific, deterministic viewpoint that oversees most of Western culture. Since the days of Galileo and Newton, we have grown to believe in a universe that is ordered, structured, and governed by natural laws, the workings of which can be observed, understood, and manipulated by intelligent humans, but which ultimately exist previous to and apart from the human experience. Such a viewpoint draws a very firm line between the objective world, which is external to and independent of human consciousness, and the subjective world, which is made up of a person's thoughts and feelings. It argues that the formation of the objective is in no way touched by the subjective, and that a person's internal states have no causative effect upon external reality. Indeed, our medical science is only very recently, and with the greatest reluctance, beginning to give up its steadfast denial that a person' s thoughts and feelings can have a causative effect upon his or her own body. It is still generally considered quite irrational to say that a person's thoughts and feelings can have any effect whatsoever upon the external world.

This way of looking at the world, limited mostly to the past few hundred years of Western civilization, has enabled us to chart with precision the movement of planets, stars, and galaxies, to know exactly when the sun will rise and set each day, to understand the workings of levers and wheels and pumps and gears. It enables us to drop a steel ball from two miles up and predict to the millisecond when it will touch Earth. It enables all of the miracles of modern transportation, communication, and computation. It enables us to understand the atomic and subatomic structure of matter and to use that understanding to unleash extraordinary energies. All of this and so much more has grown from a worldview which insists upon a firm separation between the internal world of human beings and the external world in which they move, a worldview which makes a great deal of sense, a worldview which is proven again and again by the very gifts and wonders which it enables. To argue against this point of view, to say that human thoughts and feelings have a creative impact upon the formation of reality, would seem to open a door into chaos and confusion, and to refute the clockwork universe that science is offering and so amply demonstrating.

The worldview which I am suggesting does not deny any of the veracity nor the validity of science. Rather, it says that science has perfectly described the world which it has perceived thus far, *and* that there is much yet to see and describe for which we will need to broaden our most basic understandings. For instance, we can safely say that at the time of Isaac Newton all of the laws of quantum physics were every bit as true as they are today. Quantum physics does not deny Newtonian mechanics; it encompasses it and then goes beyond. It was the successful evolution of the Newtonian worldview which would eventually enable the insights and applications of quantum mechanics. And it is the successful evolution of quantum mechanics which is now opening the doors to a new science, one which will successfully blend the subjective and objective universes, and one which will describe the role human beings can play in the ongoing creation of reality.

Physicists were the first scientists to sense this shift to a new science when, contrary to all of their training, the dividing wall between the objective observer and the externally observed began to break down, along with many of the other basic assumptions of classical physics. Starting with Einstein's Theory of Relativity in 1905, the tidy clockwork world of Newton and Descartes, with its separately defined objects and its clear cause and effect relationships, slowly unraveled until Einstein himself declared: "It was as if the ground had been pulled out from under one, with no foundation to be seen anywhere, upon which one could have built."[5] Though there were many different discoveries and revelations contributing to this shift toward a quantum worldview, there was probably none so thoroughly unsettling to the scientific world than the suggestion that total objectivity — the very backbone of scientific investigation and experimentation — was fundamentally impossible.

The real difficulty with this and similar aspects of the quantum worldview is that they seem to run in total opposition to common sense, leading many to think that while quantum mechanics may accurately describe subatomic reality, it has no relevance to 'normal' reality. For many of us, the natural laws of classical science still obviously describe the whole picture in our normal day-to-day reality. However, as a wealth of literature[6] in the past decade has made clear, there have always been people, and at times entire cultures, for whom the quantum worldview has made perfect sense. Mystics and shamans, Taoist priests and Sufi dervishes, yoga masters and Indian healers — for such people the insights and revelations of quantum physics are neither surprising nor alarming. Indeed, it is what they have been telling us all along! And while they may not have developed the technologies of Newtonian science, their lives have been far more ecologically grounded and environmentally sane. There is nothing in the quantum worldview which must ultimately run counter to common sense, though the senses common to late twentieth-century Western humanity are clearly suffering from such a wide range of imbalances and aberrations that it will require a major leap in understanding to embrace this 'new' reality.

In their *Manual for Co-Creators of the Quantum Leap*, futurists Barbara Marx Hubbard and Ken Carey outline some of the steps toward this new worldview. They assert that "quantum transformations are traditional. Nature proceeds by long periods of incremental change marked by radical discontinuities, such as the leap from non-life to life, or single cells to animals, or animals to humans. Therefore we expect a quantum change to occur from humans to the next stage."[7] They feel that the key to this leap, a leap which they and many others say is happening now, during the final years of the twentieth century, is the evolution of the human race to a level of consciousness through which it will be able to actively participate in the ongoing creation of reality. They speak of the co-creative human; one who is aware of and aligned with the intention of creation; one who is consciously cooperating with the designing intelligence; one who awakens to and makes manifest the next stage of evolution.

This is a slightly different 'evolution' than the one that science has been teaching us about for the past hundred years. To the scientist, evolution is a very logical, and ultimately predictable, unfolding of circumstances set into motion billions of years ago. There was, it is thought, a 'big bang,' out of which all of the matter and energy of the universe came into being. From that moment forward, things have evolved, one thing leading quite naturally and linearly to the next, various chemicals interacting with various other chemicals. Some water here, a few lightning flashes there, and stars evolved, planets evolved, our very special planet Earth evolved, our very special earthen atmosphere evolved, non-life evolved into life, life evolved with Darwinian logic, apes evolved into *Homo sapiens*, and so on. There is no actual creative intelligence required for this scenario, except perhaps at the time of the big bang. After that, He, She, or It sat back and rested, apparently content to just watch the show. The death, or at least retirement, of God is critical to this way of thinking, for the allowance of an *ongoing* creative intelligence, an intelligence which could still be actively participating in the creation of reality, would seem to deny or confound the scientist's desire to perceive and understand an orderly universe. After all, if Somebody is still fiddling with the basic nature of things, then everything we learned today might be different tomorrow. At this point, most scientific minds begin to boggle.

The evolutionary perspective which Hubbard and Carey describe assumes an ongoing creative process, a divine presence, the will and hand of God, which has been organizing and directing the unfolding of our world and all worlds from the very beginning of space and time. There probably was a big bang ("And the Lord said, 'Let there be light!' "), and all that has followed has been the slow and gradual movement, or evolution, of the Divine into more and more complex forms with greater and greater capacities for self-consciousness. The evolutionary perspective assumes this divine intention: to become a world as gloriously complex as Terra Firma, and to become a race of creatures capable of consciously knowing — of knowing that they know, that they are gods embodied, and that it is their destiny to become active participants in the ongoing creation of reality. "Our awareness that God or the designing intelligence of the universe is expressing as us is the 'open sesame' of the next stage of evolution."[8]

We must not shy away from this profound leap simply because our past experience seems to counsel against it. True, the mass of humanity has thus far demonstrated neither the power, nor morality, nor even the inclination of gods embodied. Evolution means change; *we are changing.* Let's not be caterpillars arguing against the possibility of flight.

It is easy for us to understand that a child, while unable to perform or even imagine the procreative acts of an adult, certainly carries those acts in potential. Given time and proper nourishment, the child will grow, and one day, magically, astonishingly, the child will change. It will have reached its new stage of growth, and a whole new set of rules and possibilities will apply. Humanity has been such a growing child and now, with all of the fear and excitement of emerging sexuality to a budding adolescent, the world is changing about us and within us as we are called to actively play in the greatest sex of all, the very creation of reality. As George Leonard has written, "But this new species *will* evolve . . . . What was once impalpable now summons us to dismantle the walls between ourselves and our sisters and brothers, to dissolve the distinctions between flesh and spirit, to transcend the present limits of time and matter, to find, at last, not wealth or power but the ecstasy (so long forgotten) of commonplace, unconditional being. *For the atom's soul is nothing but energy. Spirit blazes in the dullest clay. The life of every woman or man — the heart of it — is pure and holy joy.*"[9]

Enormous though the task may be, we are not without help. There have always been those individuals, rare for the most part, who have fully understood this evolving life of 'pure and holy joy' and have been able to practically demonstrate their active participation in the ongoing creation of reality. Humanity has easily recognized these individuals, proclaiming them as Christ and Buddha, or as masters and saints. Barbara Marx Hubbard has referred to such people as 'evolutionary mutants,' those who demonstrate the next stage of human evolution through such practices as healing, telepathy, manifestation, prophesy, etc. They have lived their lives as beacons, as fingers pointing toward the future, invariably echoing the words of Jesus: *All that I do, you shall do, and more.* They have left a wealth of guidance for the evolving human, maps for the evolutionary journey, teachings which may have eluded us in the past (like teaching sex education to a three-year old) but which begin to make perfect sense during this age of transformation.

One very old 'evolutionary mutant' that we in the West have just recently been introduced to, and are just beginning to listen to, is the firewalk. The practice of firewalking has existed for thousands of years in dozens of different cultures as a powerful teaching for the evolving human. It has served first as a very graphic demonstration of what is possible, and as a clear and usually unforgettable model of humans interacting with their world in a more evolved manner. Many have found that the simple act of viewing a firewalk, or even a video of a firewalk, has greatly expanded their vision of human potential. The firewalk has further served as a very practical course of instruction for those who would consciously pursue and support their unfolding growth. Each journey across the fire offers an immediate lesson in the essential connection of mind, body and environment.

There often seems to be a firm and solid wall separating our ordinary, pre-evolutionary world from the extraordinary world of evolving humanity. The life of each evolutionary mutant has served to soften this wall, causing breakthroughs, opening windows, and making cracks that the rest of us might peek through, catching glimpses, fleeting visions, of our future possibilities. The firewalk has been a dance through these cracks, an actual experience of stepping over the border between the two worlds and, if only for brief seconds, a breathing in of the special vibratory quality of a long promised land.

I believe that the firewalk has arrived *here*, in the very heart of scientific culture, and *now*, at the onset of a monumental evolutionary leap, because it can ultimately serve as a bridge between the two worlds, greatly reducing the stress and danger of the leap. Firewalkers agree with most of the findings and conclusions of the Newtonian worldview: that we live in an orderly universe, and that there are natural laws governing our world which cause things to be the way they are. In addition, firewalkers suggest that there is a creative process which intends the orderliness, a creative process which intends the laws of nature, an *ongoing* creative process which underlies and is the source of all of reality, causing all things to be the way they are. *We, as conscious human beings, are a vital part of that process.* God is alive and well, humans are just beginning to fully *realize* this, and walking on fire is a preview of coming attractions.

A major message of the firewalk and a major theme of this book is that there is an ongoing creative process — which I will be calling the 'co-creative process' — which determines the way the world is, the very fabric of reality and the laws which govern it, and each of us, to the extent that we consciously embrace our potential, is a vital and integral part of that process. This means that reality is not just the mechanical and linear unfolding of prior natural law, but that it is continuously influenced and created anew by the combined input (co-creative) of all of the conscious life on this planet.

The data from the firewalk is quite clear: the difference between the person who walks across a bed of coals without the slightest sensation of heat or pain, and the person who takes one step and is immediately and seriously burned, is not the texture of the skin, the speed of the walking, the heat of the coals, the amount of moisture on the feet, or any other external consideration. Such considerations certainly contribute to the experience but, ultimately, the difference between success and failure during a firewalk is the individual walker's internal process, or present-time state of consciousness — the sum total of his or her thoughts, feelings, attitudes, beliefs, and expectations. The firewalk is a way of graphically demonstrating that our external world is continuously influenced by our internal world, that our thoughts and feelings have creative power, that we are intimately involved in the co-creation of reality, and that we are, indeed, ultimately responsible for the unfolding, evolutionary process of life on Earth.

It is, of course, not necessary that we walk on fire in order to experience our role in the co-creative process. It is only necessary that we be willing to take a very large step into that possibility — the possibility that each of us has a very definite creative impact upon this world. Such a step will almost always be frightening, as we are stepping into a very unknown realm with truly immense responsibilities. Still, it is a step which must be taken.

And it can so easily lead into dancing.

three

AN ANCIENT
EXPERIMENT

*We stood in a ring of clasped hands around the coals, which
were by now glowing a beautiful yellow-white color. Though I
knew by their color that they were at their hottest temperature,
they seemed gentle and soothing to me, almost mesmerizing, I
felt as if we were made of the same stuff. I broke the circle
and stepped up onto the bed. Across my face I felt the dancing
flicker of a burning log, which had not yet relinquished itself to
coal. Fixing my sight on a spot at the other end, I began to pull
myself towards it. I felt like a wind gently lifting and falling as I
moved along the continuum, and, after a timeless moment, I
stepped off onto the other side. Exhilaration and ecstatic joy
swept through my being, I had to fight my body to keep from
jumping into the air — but it was someone else's turn. To my
surprise, Megan stepped to the edge. I remember how my breath
and heart became stilled. I watched her young grace as she
glided across with a sureness that brought tears to my eyes. She
circled around to stand next to me and in a very strong, knowing
voice said, "Mom, I'll never have to die of cancer. Maybe I'll
never die at all!"*

*The depth and swiftness of her assimilation of the firewalking
exercise took my breath away. People began to move more
swiftly to the coals, and I felt an exhilarated energy-pattern
begin to form itself. Teo suddenly grasped my hand and pulled
me to the fire. We stepped up together and began our walk.
About two-thirds of the way across, she whimpered, "Mom,
it's getting hot." I answered, "You can do it, Teo, you can, you
can," and we reached the end and jumped into the pool of water
awaiting us. It was too much for me; I was so elated, I let out
a little yell. Everyone was experiencing the same exuberance,
and people began to join each other in twos and walk across
the fire.*

Even though a few people sustained some blisters, we all

25

shared such a feeling of empowerment . . . It was a feeling of belonging to something good and joyous: a force of light.[1]

A good starting point for understanding the firewalk is an appreciation of the fact that it is one of the oldest and most widely spread rituals that our planet has ever known. Contrary to the tone and suggestion of most of the publicity surrounding American firewalking over the past few years, the firewalk is not something which was thought up in the hot tubs of Esalen, and is really much more than the latest 'hot' workshop to come out of California. Indeed, my own research has turned up no fewer than 25 places around the world where the firewalk has been happening quite independently of its current popularity in the United States and at least one culture where, according to the natives' oral history, they have been firewalking since the very beginning of time.

The Kung people, bushmen of the Kalahari desert in Africa, are just such a culture. The Kung have been living in a single, relatively small portion of the Kalahari desert for thousands of years, their ancestry stretching back to prehistoric times. Since they live nomadically within such a forbidding environment, they have very little in the way of material goods, and have compensated by developing an extremely rich and sophisticated tradition of ritual and ceremony.

The most important of the Kung rituals is the firedance. Occurring three or four times a month, the firedance is a truly ecstatic healing ritual. When the need for healing within the community is felt, a fire is started and the dance begins. The dancers are the acknowledged healers of the tribe, those with the strongest healing energy. The rest of the people sit in circles, making music and singing special healing songs.

For hour after hour, the healers will dance around the fire, ever faster, the intensity building. They dance so hard and so long that they wear a groove, and then a circular ditch into the earth. Finally, after many hours, a moment arrives when the dancers' healing energy becomes so strong that their dancing around the fire becomes a dancing into the fire. One dancer steps into and through the flames, while others stoop to pick coals up in their hands and rub them into their chests, showering coals about their heads and dancing ever more ecstatically, ever more feverishly. At some point a climax is reached and the dancers gradually slow, collapsing into a state of trance, prayer, reverence, and awe. At this point they pour healing energy out to the members of the members of the community which need it most.[2,3]

In the Greek village of Ayia Eleni, the firewalk is a yearly ritual, climaxing a spring festival in honor of Saint Constantine and Saint Helen. A handful of men and women, members of a quite unorthodox Christian sect called the Anastenarides (the preliminaries include the sacrifice of a lamb), prepare for the walk with hours of trance-inducing music and dancing. Finally, feeling possessed with Saint Constantine's healing and protective powers, and holding sacred icons in their hands (Saint Constantine is said to have walked into a burning church to save its icons from the fire), they walk barefoot into and through the coals, again and again, dancing and swirling, until the fire is danced out and only gray ash remains. Though the orthodox church would prefer that it were otherwise, this is such a regular part of Greek life that it is included in tourist brochures.[4]

In Japan, the firewalk is a very common practice at certain Shinto Buddhist temples. Here again, the firewalk is primarily a religious experience, though the Japanese approach is much more formal. The head priests of the temple conduct the event, with very specific ritual and ceremony marking each step of the way as the fire is built, lit, and prepared for walking. There is also much singing and chanting and playing of sacred instruments as the priests gather themselves around the fire. The coals are raked into a twenty-foot path, packed down smooth and evenly, and then the head priest, in flowing robes, stands before the coals, offers a prayer, and walks sedately across. He is followed by the other priests, one at a time, who walk in order of their rank within the temple. At this point all of the onlookers, visitors, and members of the village, old and young alike, are free to join in and walk across. Many, many do.[5]

Similar stories and descriptions crop up in places all over the world. In those countries which have had a Buddhist influence (India, China, Tibet, Nepal, Sri Lanka, Brazil) the firewalk tends to follow the Japanese model. The walkway is usually a straight path, anywhere from twelve to thirty feet long, and raked fairly smooth. The walk itself is a simple one, from one end of the path to the other. The priests are definitely in charge of the event, which is most often open to anybody who cares to follow.

For other cultures, such as the Kung and the Anastenarides, the experience is more a wild and ecstatic firedance than a firewalk. There are reports of Christian sects in both Spain and Bulgaria, offshoots of the Anastenarides, which also do firedancing, though in connection with different saints. In Bali, firedancing is a coming-of-age ritual for seven-year-old girls, learned in their formative years by watching the dancing of their elders. Hawaiian Kahunas (spiritual leaders) are said to dance on lava flows as a demonstration of their power, and throughout Fiji, people walk and/or dance on heated stones. In these places the ability to walk or dance upon fire tends to be viewed as a special trait or power of the individual, a sign that he or she is uniquely possessed, and the actual firewalk does not tend to include the community at large.

In addition to firewalking and firedancing, there are also many examples around the world of firehandling. Egyptian and Algerian dervishes swallow burning coals, a practice reported in Sumatra as well. Algerian fakirs will bring their flesh into contact with red, hot iron. Within the Christian fundamentalist movement of the southern United States, firehandling is often considered to be a sign of spiritual possession, akin to speaking in tongues. Within the shamanic tradition around the world, various demonstrations of the shaman's 'power over fire' are rather common.[6]

As common and widely spread as the firewalking experience is (I will henceforth use the term 'firewalk' to refer to the whole field of 'human flesh meets extreme heat' experiences), there has been to date very little serious scientific investigation of the phenomenom. Most of the examples of firewalking around the world that I have been able to gather are basically anecdotes, the subjective reports of often untrained observers. If examined more closely, some of these examples would probably turn out to be either intentional shams and circus stunts, or sensational occurrences which in fact have perfectly reasonable explanations. However, there remain enough reports from reliable witnesses (Buckminster Fuller, Joseph Chilton Pierce, Dr. Andrew Weil, Norman Cousins, Dr. Carl Simonton, National Geographic, and The British Medical Association, to name a few) that only the most stubborn skeptic

could refuse to admit that firewalking is, in most instances, a
graphic demonstration of non-ordinary reality.[7]

Setting aside for the moment what is actually happening at
a firewalk and what is actually proven or not proven, we can
quite safely say that firewalking is one of Earth's oldest and
most widely spread rituals. There are few practices which so
consistently show up in such a wide range of different cultures.
In addition, the many varying styles and manners of firewalking
that have developed suggest strongly that it is a practice which
was discovered independently in different times and places, as
if the firewalk were intrinsic to human nature, something that
we were just bound to do. For all its bizarre and sensational
aspects, it is simultaneously a very common human experience,
or at least very common to the human experience.

The one unifying thread that is found throughout this investigation of the firewalk is that it arises primarily as a religious
experience: people walk on fire in connection to, and as a reflection
or expression of, the religious beliefs of their culture. As it is
with the Greeks, in so many places it is the climax of a religious
holiday, a way to fervently celebrate a special moment in the
yearly cycle. Or, as in the case of the Balinese, it may serve
as an initiation or rite of passage, a baptism by fire. Likewise,
when it comes to explaining how it can happen, virtually all
firewalkers relate it to the possession by or propitiation of specific
saints, gods, or powers within their own cultural religious context.
Thus, the firewalk comes to us essentially as a spiritual practice,
a ritual, almost as common to the people of our world as the
religious impulse itself. In fact, outside of what has been happening
in North America, the only purely secular reference to firewalking
that I have ever come across is a comment by Pliny the Elder
that certain Romans were exempted from paying taxes if they
demonstrated the ability to walk on hot coals without burning.

While the rising tide of modern science would eventually
push it out of the Western world, the firewalk seems to have
had a place in early Judeo-Christian culture. There is the biblical
story of Shadrach, Meshach, and Abed-nego, who prove that
they are divinely connected when they are tossed into the fiery
furnace by Nebuchadnezzar and do not burn. Two further biblical
references to firewalking are Proverbs 6:28: 'Can one go upon
hot coals, and his feet not be burned'; and Isaiah 43:2: 'When

thou walkest through the fire, thou shalt not be burned.' There was also a Florentine monk who was canonized as Saint Igneus because of his ability to walk through fire unharmed, giving firewalkers everywhere their very own patron Saint.

A second thread which is woven throughout the world's firewalking experience is the possibility of failure. That is, everywhere that we encounter people walking on fire, we also hear warnings of the danger involved, and very explicit tales of the worst that could happen. Virtually *every* reference to firewalking that I have uncovered includes such stories. The reports of firewalking failures cover a spectrum from minor blisters to third-degree burns to fatal injury. Experienced 'master' firewalkers tell of times when they were very badly burned as a result of failing to first reach the proper state of consciousness. An Iowa State College professor described a Ceylonese firewalk which he witnessed in 1957 in which twelve of the eighty walkers were injured, with one dying. In many places, such as Singapore, where the firewalk is the climax of a week-long Hindu celebration, a few bad injuries out of hundreds of participants are considered a given and necessary part of the experience. Even the Kung, who have impressed me as the world's firewalking elite, explain that the non-dancers must be ready at all times to prevent the dancers from going too far, and getting burned as a result.

The point is this: yes, this is an experience of going beyond normally accepted limits, but no, this is not an experience of there being no limits at all. The firewalker is stepping into a world in which the day-to-day laws of fire and flesh, the laws with which food is cooked and homes are heated and accidents are painfully paid for, have been temporarily suspended, while new laws have been created in their place. People get burned at firewalks when they fail to recognize those new laws, and when they fail to properly negotiate the existing limits of the situation. Firewalkers do not stop fire from burning. Rather, they temporarily redefine its relationship to human beings so that a certain amount of contact is possible. When they overstep the newly defined limitations, they get burned.

It is for this reason that I call the firewalk 'an ancient experiment.' It is a ritual, a ceremony, a religious celebration, and the possibility of being burned gives it an added dimension — that of immediate and objective feedback as to the effectiveness of the practice, a very graphic feedback which is generally not part of the religious experience. (Except for the shamans, mystics, high priests, seers, and psychics, all of whom achieve a high level in their culture's religious hierarchy precisely because of their ability to manifest the world of religion in rather concrete ways.) When we participate in most religious rituals, or when we pray, sing psalms, light special candles, pass holy cups, or partake of blessed substances, we must ultimately provide the meaning of such experiences ourselves, on a subjective level. Very seldom in such instances do we expect or receive objective confirmation that the ritual has been successful. In fact, the essence of most religious practice is faith: that we participate fully without need for objective proof.

In calling the firewalk an experiment, I am suggesting that it is a practice which extends beyond its obvious religious nature to include a measure of very basic scientific investigation. Firewalkers the world over step forward onto hot coals in order to test their beliefs concerning the creative process. It is a way of exploring their culture's definition of deity (the Creator), the nature of their personal relationship with said deity, and the extent to which they can consciously mediate change within that relationship. The firewalker has accepted some hypothesis which promises that if certain specific preparations are observed, then it will be possible to walk on the fire without burning. After the walk, the firewalker has some very immediate and not at all ambiguous data to consider — pain or no pain, burn or no burn, injury or no injury — which lead in turn to a confirmation of the original hypothesis, or to a need to develop a new one.

For instance, if you were an Anastenaride, you would believe in a world created by the Christian God and governed to some extent by the living presence of saints. Further, you would believe that if you properly engaged the spirits of Saint Constantine and Saint Helen, through a day-long ritual culminating in total abandonment to trance-inducing ecstatic dance, then you might be possessed by the powerful healing presence of Saint Constantine and enabled to dance on a bed of hot coals for an hour without burning. And, if you then followed that formula, year after year after year, attaining the same basic results, you would have proven, to your satisfaction, some very basic laws about the nature of your world. The fact that you could walk without burning would tell you that miracles are possible, and to some extent within the creative reach of human beings. The fact that dancers sometimes get burned (one Anastenaride speaks of being so badly burned — a sign to him of imperfect faith — that he vowed, and deeply regretted, that he would never dance on the fire again) would tell you that it is not a process to be taken lightly, that there is always more to be learned, and that there are limitations, possibly, even to the powers of Saints.

I realize that some scientific minds are turning over in their gravity at the thought of equating such primitive heathenism with science. For too many people, the very idea of reconciling religious truth with scientific truth, and denying or compromising neither of them, is impossible by definition, or at least very difficult in practice. To be sure, if the firewalk is science at all, it breaks too many rules to be the science of the Western world. The actual field of study has a large number of changing and hard to manage variables; there is an absolute absence of any recorded data; the 'scientists' involved are active participants in the experiment; and, a cardinal sin, the participants are using their own bodies as the means of measurement. No, it is most certainly not the science of Galileo and Newton, perhaps not even the science of "Sesame Street"!

Still, for most of the world's firewalkers, the firewalk is very clearly a method for testing their beliefs about the nature of reality, and very definitely a way to gather good, hard data upon which to base future actions. It is a specific procedure, repeated in 'laboratories' around the world for thousands of years, which has given people a better understanding of the creative processes which govern nature, and of humanity's role within those processes. It is indeed an ancient experiment, and the fact that it has now made its way into late-twentieth-century America suggests that it is possibly in the process of becoming a modern-day experiment as well.

———————————

The experiment came to the United States through the efforts of a man named Tolly Burkan. Tolly is a Californian who has been involved in the human potential movement since the late sixties. In 1976, he was shown how to firewalk by a friend who said she learned it from a Tibetan monk. Tolly was already an accomplished group leader and eventually came to see the potential of adding the firewalk to his teaching. So, in 1978 he designed a weekend workshop that included firewalking, and started offering it in California. In 1982, with the encouragement and assistance of his wife and partner, Peggy Dylan, Tolly created a format that was four hours long and open to the general public, and started leading firewalks on a regular basis throughout the United States and in parts of Europe. Since then, Tolly has led well over ten thousand people through the firewalk while amassing, through a lot of trial and error (there was no one to show him how to do any of this!), a wealth of first-hand experience.[8]

By 1983, there were other people starting to lead firewalks also, the first (and most notable) being a man named Tony Robbins. Tony learned the practice by attending several of Tolly's workshops and carefully watching what Tolly was doing until he felt confident that he could do likewise. He has gone on to become the P.T. Barnum of firewalking, staging five-hundred-person events in Manhattan and landing in most of the major media, including a live walk on "The Merv Griffin Show," and a listing in Guinness for the world's longest recorded firewalk (38 feet).

Throughout 1984, there was a proliferation of people leading firewalks as Tolly began training instructors in earnest (I participated in his first instructors' training in May of 1984) and as others developed the skill on their own, a la Tony Robbins. That autumn, it seemed as if the firewalk was happening everywhere. It was covered in *Newsweek, Time, Life, Look, Rolling Stone, People* and, via UPI and AP, virtually every newspaper in the country. Tolly was on "Donahue" and "All Things Considered" and Tony was on "The Merv Griffin Show." During one very short stretch of time, I did three TV appearances, six radio talkshows, and was covered in ten different newspapers. And in January of 1985, I did a firewalk in a parking lot in the middle of Manhattan which showed up on all three New York late news programs, the Independent Network News, and in *New York* magazine. A conservative estimate at that point in time would have put the number of people in America, Europe, and Australia who had been led through the coals by any one of several dozen instructors at about one hundred thousand.

Alas, by the spring of 1985 the firewalk's day in the public eye was pretty much at an end. Partly this was due to the media's reluctance to cover such a story more than once, or (with few exceptions) to cover it with anything more than "That's Incredible!" sensationalism. Partly it was due to the inevitably weird and culty appearance of a group of people standing around a fire in the dark, holding hands and chanting songs, and the public's basic distrust of such things. And partly it was due to the fact that only a handful of instructors were still leading firewalks.

The various individuals who have led firewalks in this country over the past few years are only very loosely associated, if at all. There is no firewalker's guild, no newsletter, and we have yet to hold a firewalker's convention. Nor is there an umbrella organization or central individual who is aware of and in touch with all, or even most, of what is going on in the world of fire-walking. This makes it difficult to say with any certainty who has done and/or continues to do firewalks, how many instructors there are altogether, how many people have participated in firewalks, etc. Thus, whatever I do have to say about the American firewalking movement is for the most part based upon my own experience and the experiences of a few instructors with whom I am in close contact, in combination with an assortment of rumors and anecdotes that I have picked up along the way.

The main reason that within such a short period of time there remained very few people still leading firewalks is that sooner or later just about everyone gets burned. In fact, I know of no one who has firewalked more than ten times without getting at least one nasty burn. For some instructors, their first bad burn is enough to convince them that this is not really their line of work after all. For others, it is the first firewalk that they lead in which half the group gets burned. There seems to be no getting around the possibility of burning (believe me, I've tried!), so unless one finds a way of putting it into a healthy perspective, leading firewalks becomes harder and harder to do. This is why there are only a dozen or so people who have continued to lead firewalks for any appreciable length of time.

Of course, if burns were the main event, we all would have quit a long time ago. Firewalkers are not a bunch of S & M freaks who have hit upon an exotic new way to abuse the body. For most people, most of the time, firewalking is a painless experience with a wealth of positive ramifications. And, anyone who firewalks often must eventually reach a philosophical understanding of the occasional burns, seeing them as part of the learning process, and accepting them as very specific and data-rich feedback in the ongoing experiment.

Thus, while there are not hundreds of firewalk leaders roaming the land, there are twenty or so who, like myself, have continued to teach, mostly in a low-key, private, word-of-mouth manner. A few are very spiritual in their approach and would probably object to my describing the firewalk as a scientific experiment and to any suggestion that they are in fact participants within it. There are two or three others who take a totally secular approach, trying to distance themselves as much as possible from any religious or mystical associations. The rest, like myself, fall somewhere in the middle. To the extent that we are experiencing and reveling in our connection to the creative forces of our world, I would say that we are all practicing religion. And to the extent that we are exploring and testing our ability to consciously manipulate those forces, I would likewise say that we are scientists of sorts, following in a long tradition of red-hot footsteps.

Since the technique of virtually all American firewalking instructors is descended from Tolly Burkan's experience, the actual logistics of a firewalk do not change too much from one instructor to the next. On the other hand, we are all, as instructors, continuing to develop our own approaches as we go along, making gradual changes in accordance with our personal experiences. This means that eventually there may be a wide variety of different styles of firewalking in this country. Thus, the description of my own firewalks will be a good presentation of what firewalks look like. However, another instructor, or even myself in another year or so, could describe things quite differently.

Penny and I always do our firewalks at night because in daylight (or stage lighting, or camera flashes) the coals appear gray instead of glowing red. This does not mean that they are any less hot, it just means that the participants do not visually experience the heat. It is similar to putting the high beams of a car on in daylight — the full energy of the light is there, but there is no visual sensation of it. I do not feel that it would be any less effective or safe to do firewalks in such light. Tolly has led walks in Scandinavia during the season of constant light, and I once did a firewalk that was totally lit up in the process of filming it. However, this very much changes the emotional and psychological impact of the experience. That is, in order to fully 'get' whatever one is going to get from walking on fire, it is helpful, if not necessary, to vividly and viscerally experience the fire.

I use hard wood because it burns hotter and does not turn to ash as easily as soft wood. When measured, the coals have ranged in temperatures from 1000-1500°F. The fire is allowed to burn for at least two hours, which I have found to be the minimum amount of time required to get a large enough bed of coals for the walk. About seventy or so pieces of wood are usually burned, again, because I have found that this amount gives us just enough coals for the walk. However, I have tried to keep my walks limited to twenty to thirty participants. Other instructors, who sometimes firewalk with fifty to several hundred participants, quite naturally have to burn larger fires for longer periods of time.

While the fire is burning outside, I lead the group through a lecture/workshop which is basically an abbreviated, live presentation of this book. My goals each time are to get people as comfortable as possible with the idea of firewalking, to facilitate a sense of closeness and bonding within the group, to help clarify each individual's personal reasons for wanting to walk on fire, and to provide a broader context for the experience so that it can have a positive, ongoing impact in other areas of the participants' lives.

When the fire is ready for us, and we for it, we go outside and hold hands, forming a circle around the brightly glowing coals. I rake the coals into a path about eight feet long by four feet wide, which allows for about four steps for the average walker (though it has been crossed in one very large step on occasion!). I have found that this is long enough for most people to feel the validity of what they are doing (if they are going to at all) and that it is just the right length to fit aesthetically within a circle of twenty or so people. I very lightly tamp the coals down with a shovel, trying to make the path as smooth and even as possible so that there are no hills or valleys to negotiate as we are walking.

Ultimately, my goal as I have prepared firewalking paths

over the past few years has been to make each path as much
alike as possible. I strive each time to use the same type of
wood, the same amount of wood, to burn it for the same length
of time, to rake it into a path of the same dimensions, and to set
up the same basic environmental circumstances. This enables me
to view any data that a walk provides, such as burns, or people
walking extremely slowly, and to feel confident that the results
I am looking at are due to the individual's subjective reality, or
the combined creative energies of the group, rather than some
changing variable in the fire itself. Thus, in my own case, I have
been the first person to cross a path of hot coals over a hundred
times, and I have gotten a nasty burn on nine of those walks.
Because I know that I have been stepping forward onto a path
that has been the same each time, I also know that the times
I have been burned have somehow been caused by something
other than the fire; by some subtler, non-physical factors, such
as mental and/or emotional preparedness.

Once I have the path prepared to my liking, I step up to the
fire, pause for a few breaths, and then walk across. Those in the
group who wish to walk then do so; usually about 90 percent of
a group walks. There is no pressure put on people to walk; in fact,
I encourage participants to listen to their own inner guidance
and I create a very positive context for those who choose not to
walk. Once it gets going, a lot of people who were sure all night
that they would not walk find themselves drawn to the fire. For
most people, the walk entails three or four rather straightforward
steps from one end of the path of coals to the other. Sometimes,
depending on the group involved, the firewalk evolves into
a firedance.

With some groups, the whole evening feels very somber and
serious; the fear and the sense of danger never quite subside,
and the walking tends to be very tentative. Other groups slowly
shift to a light and playful feeling, and the walking turns to
dancing. During such nights, partners often walk hand in hand,
and parents carry their children across. Children sometimes
choose to walk on their own. My youngest firewalker to date
was six. People have done cartwheels through the fire, and have
walked across on their hands. Some people have walked backwards,
others have walked very slowly, others have stood still, and still
others have reached down to pick up coals. I have watched one

person sit down in the coals, and another lie completely flat on them, his hair included! And I have watched lots and lots of dancing.

Sometimes we dance until the coals are out, a path of black ash. Other nights there is a long lull in the walking and a shared sense of completion in the group. However the firewalk ends, there is always a strong burst of elation throughout the circle, with much shouting and clapping, hugging and celebrating. Eventually, we all go back indoors and take some time to share about the experience and to look toward how we can carry its meaning back into our lives. The energy in the room is always very high, and the sharing is very excited and inspired, with a powerful sense of 'the possible human' running through the group. Even for those who chose not to walk there is usually a strong feeling of having participated in something very special, and of having made a very important personal choice, rather than being swept along by the group.

The feedback which Penny and I later receive tells us that for many people the firewalk is an unforgettable experience, one which continues to impact their lives long after the actual event A common response is: "After walking on fire I found it easy (or at least easier) to confront my boss, to face my illness, to overcome my other fears, to risk being more intimate, etc." For so many people the firewalk serves as a graphic demonstration, a living model, of a very different way of walking through this world. That half hour around the coals, walking on fire and watching others do the same, becomes an undeniable example of what is possible for human beings, and a potent seed for further breakthroughs and transformations.

To be sure, there are those who do not share in this enthusiasm, those who are unimpressed after walking on fire, those who do not accept the premises nor celebrate the results. In this modern version of an ancient experiment, their well-reasoned arguments are certainly grist for the mill, very definitely data which must be considered. To the extent that we are studying human beings in relationship to the creative processes of their world, the responses of each and every person involved will inform us and serve to deepen our understanding. I believe that firewalking has persisted through time and space to arrive here and now in the center of Western thought because the vast majority of people who have observed or participated in a firewalk have come away with a strong sense that something out of the ordinary and very special happens there, and that the firewalk presents an important teaching to our world. Our challenge is to approach it with minds wide open, neither fearing its implications nor presuming our own conclusions, so that we may truly learn whatever there is to learn, and so that we may broaden our understanding of ourselves and of the creative processes of our world.

four

THE SKEPTICAL MIND

When we are certain that a phenomenon such as firewalking does not happen, we are really saying: "My basic knowledge of how the universe works is so complete and so accurate that the cosmos holds no more surprises for me. I know all the real truths and the details will all fit them."

How sad . . . If only experience and life would not keep teaching us how little we know.[1]

Sit down before fact like a little child, and be prepared to give up every preconceived notion, follow humbly wherever and to whatever abyss Nature leads, or you shall learn nothing.[2]

Doubt is not ultimately transcended through beliefs. Doubt is a state of mind that is fundamentally without content. It is an expression of the contraction of the being. It is not cured with positive beliefs that are the opposite of doubt. It is cured by the release of this contraction so that there is a continuity between consciousness and forms and relations, an unobstructed continuity between the being and Reality altogether.[3]

The first barrier which most people encounter on their way to the firewalk is something which I call the skeptical mind. The skeptical mind is that part of us which tends to doubt and distrust certain things, especially things which we have never experienced before, such as firewalking. It is a 'show-me' attitude, which assumes that something is false until proven true, a predisposition of disbelief toward anything which would stretch us even slightly beyond our current convictions about the nature of things. Persisted in, it becomes a mentally, emotionally, and physically ingrained habit, a fixed posture of skepticism, from which it is impossible to even entertain notions such as firewalking, much less to participate in and truly learn from such realities.

The skeptical mind is a total way of being in the world

which is endemic to our culture, a highly valued trait within our scientific, medical, legal, media, business, and educational communities. All of us carry some degree of the skeptical edge in our lives, though for some it is much sharper than for others. It is a deeply rooted pattern of psycho-physical response, taught to us at an early age, and supported by virtually all of our cultural institutions.

Above all, the skeptical mind is viewed as absolutely essential to our survival in these modern times. This is a dog-eat-dog world after all, filled with harsh truths and hard realities, filled to the brim with shams and charlatans, rip-offs and scams, so many fictions masquerading as fact. Our survival depends upon our ability to separate the snake oil from the real thing, to discern the true from the false. Thus, we talk of healthy skepticism, of street-smarts, of hard-bitten cynicism, and of cold, relentless logic, all terms which suggest strength and intelligence to us. Asked to define the opposite of skepticism, we will usually come up with words such as naivety, romanticism, idealism, and innocence, all suggestive of weakness and stupidity.

In fact, the word skepticism means doubt, distrust, and disbelief, and its true opposites are faith, trust, and openness. The more we approach the circumstances of our lives with the attitudes of doubt, distrust, and disbelief, the more fully committed we become, mentally, emotionally, and physically, to the skeptical mind and the resulting posture of skepticism. The more fully we have adopted a posture of skepticism, the more difficult it becomes to approach anything in life with the attitude and posture of open faith and trust. This is especially true for new things, strange things, foreign things, unheard of things, 'too good to be true' things, and 'impossible' things. Eventually, a deeply ingrained posture of skepticism operates like a set of blinders which will effectively screen from one's awareness anything 'out of the ordinary.' It is then no longer a matter of doubting and distrusting such possibilities — the skeptical mind simply will not see them to begin with.

I must stress at this point that in using the term 'the skeptical mind' I am not implying that the mind is by nature skeptical. Quite to the contrary, I believe that the human mind is essentially open, trusting, and believing and that skepticism is a trait which most minds learn which then develops into an overall way of being in the world, a posture of skepticism, very much to the mind's detriment. Ultimately, skepticism is nothing but a bad habit, necessary in the way that bad habits are always necessary, but ultimately of no redeeming value to the human species.

To those who might argue that skepticism is vital to good science, I would answer that the very best scientists are children. During their first seven years, children are endlessly exploring, touching, tasting, and smelling life; testing, trying out, and learning, learning, learning, absorbing vast quantities of data. Their brains expand in great bursts of cellular growth, their eyes and ears wide open and accepting of everything. They steadily expand their understanding of the world, figuring out gravity and nourishment and human relationship, a breakthrough every hour, a Nobel prize worth of discovery every day — and they do it all, this prodigious learning, without the slightest trace of skepticism, without the slightest need for doubt, distrust, or disbelief. Rather, it is precisely the child's wide-eyed innocence and absolute believing which makes such learning possible.

Likewise, to those who would argue that a good, healthy dose of skepticism is necessary protection in this cruel-hearted world, helping us to 'wise up' and 'know better,' keeping us from buying all of the various Brooklyn Bridges that life offers, I would point out that it is informed intelligence that keeps us from such follies, not skepticism. It is quite possible to be wide-open and trusting of all that comes one's way and to still say no to those things which sound false or misleading. In fact, experienced con artists claim that the best marks are those who appear to be rigidly skeptical, as it is simply a matter of using their prejudices against them. A skeptical mind is invariably a closed mind, is invariably a crippled mind. Truly, skepticism is neither essential to the learning process nor essential to the intelligent negotiation of life, and is ultimately a serious hindrance to both. This has not, however, prevented the skeptical mind from becoming one of the most highly valued and firmly rooted traits of Western culture.

It has been through such a deeply rooted posture of skepticism that the Western world has always viewed the firewalk. To date there have been only a few scientific investigations of the firewalk, and what little literature there is on the subject is for the most part anecdotal in nature. There have been a small number of

Western institutions that have gone off to various parts of the world to report on the subject, and they have always confirmed that it is in fact happening. Many such reports have included a theoretical explanation of the event, while on other occasions the investigators have admitted to being stymied by what they witnessed. Yet, despite the widely known and highly provocative nature of the firewalk, very little serious scientific investigation of the phenomenom has ever been pursued.

This is especially ironic since the scientific community has for so many years dismissed out of hand most, if not all, paranormal phenomena, such as the firewalk, for being anecdotal, unverifiable, and experimentally unrepeatable. Since the early 1980s there have been a number of firewalkers such as myself traveling about, in full public view, and essentially performing the same experiment over and over and over again, with the same basic results, while enthusiastically inviting full scientific scrutiny. Yet, as I say, the scientific community has for the most part been unwilling to approach the firewalk, unwilling to study it, and unwilling to learn from the data it presents.

Quite to the contrary, there has always been a rather studious avoidance of such a study. As Dr. Andrew Weil points out: "Hardly any physiologists or medical scientists have studied the phenomenon, and those who have written about it have mostly tried to make it appear unremarkable. Their aim is to defuse the challenge it poses to the materialistic conception of the human organism."[4] Up until a few years ago the Western world, entrenched within its posture of skepticism, was content to simply say, "It's impossible; it's a trick, a sham; it can't be happening" and to let it go at that, enough said, no need for any further thought, just another instance of phenomenal flotsam from the uncivilized world. Over the years, however, the reports from well-respected observers have slowly gathered, saying that it is indeed happening, that the coals are very hot, the feet uncalloused and untreated, and that real people are really walking without burning. These reports, coupled with the recent well-publicized firewalking in the United States, have made it impossible for the skeptics to simply deny the experience any longer. Yet this has not led, as one might have thought, to an eager rush to understand how it could be happening, but instead to the next defense of the skeptical mind: that of explaining it away.

'Explain-aways' begin to arise when the skeptical mind is finally willing to admit that firewalkers are in fact doing what they have always been claiming to do, that the coals are hot, and that the walking happens — for the most part without burning. Having acceded that much, the skeptical mind is usually not at all willing to then allow that this happens for the reasons that the firewalkers give: that it is a demonstration of some new evolutionary capacity of humankind, or of mind over matter, or of possession by God, or of connection to the spirit of the fire, or of any other such 'exotic' explanation. No, indeed not. At this point the skeptical mind says: "Enough is enough. While firewalking may be fact, there must surely be, must surely be, some perfectly reasonable and totally physical explanation." That is, "Yes it is happening, but it is only something which looks difficult and really isn't, like an optical illusion, and here is an explanation. We've explained it away, and now back to serious matters." Unfortunately, as Dr. Weil puts it, the real appeal of all 'explain-aways' is that they avoid "any reference to the mind or the power of consciousness to modify physical reality."[5]

I do not mean to suggest that science is some great and nasty monolith which has unfairly spurned the poor firewalk these many years. Rather, I am saying that science, in so thoroughly committing itself to the necessity of the posture of skepticism, has by definition greatly limited its field of enquiry and what is permitted to count as 'good science.' It has developed a knack for quickly explaining away any data which manage to slip through the perimeters of the current scientific paradigms. Harking back to Einstein's comment, "It was as if the earth was pulled out from under one," we can certainly understand the scientist's reluctance to allow human consciousness into the creative machinery of life; it does make for rather messy data!

The reigning 'explain-away' for years has been that firewalking is a demonstration of something called the Leidenfrost effect. The Leidenfrost effect, named after the German scientist who first studied it, is what happens when you sprinkle water onto a very hot skillet, and, instead of immediately evaporating, it retains its shape and bounces around on the skillet for a few moments. This occurs when the heat is at just the right temperature to evaporate the bottom layer of the drop of water. The vapor then, in effect, becomes an insulating layer for the rest of the drop, protecting it from the heat. The bottom layer of water will continuously evaporate, while the rest of the drop above continues to feed water into it, until eventually the whole drop disappears. Extrapolating, rather extravagantly I think, from that piece of data, skeptics have reasoned that what happens at a firewalk is that participants get so nervous beforehand that their feet sweat and that, a la Leidenfrost, they are protected from the heat of the coals by a thin layer of insulating sweat.

Lately, a different 'explain-away' has been getting a lot of press. This argument draws a distinction between temperature and heat energy, pointing out that while two objects may be heated to the same temperature, they will contain different amounts of heat energy depending upon their differing masses, and that it is heat energy which causes burning, not temperature. As an example, imagine reaching into a hot oven to retrieve a baking pan. Though the air inside the oven and the baking pan are both heated to the same temperature, your hand will not be burned by the air because it is of such little mass that it holds very little heat energy. The pan, however, has a much higher mass, contains much more heat energy, and will burn you if you do not protect your hand. This theory continues by saying that burning embers contain very little mass in relation to the mass of human feet and thus cannot contain enough heat energy to do any damage.

A major refutation of these, and any other 'explain-aways' that the skeptical mind might come up with, comes from burn specialists. Those who have worked in hospital burn units for any appreciable length of time have invariably treated victims of similar fires, i.e., those who have stepped accidently on campfires or upon stray barbeque coals, or have come into brief contact with fireplace logs. Such specialists are generally quite explicit about what ought to happen when a person steps on a fire of the sort that firewalkers use: instantaneous second- and/or third-degree burning. This is expert testimony, coming from years of direct experience with different types of fire and its effect upon the human body. As I say, most of the doctors that I have spoken with have been quite clear that something extraordinary is happening at a firewalk.

I say 'most of the doctors' because I have known of a few burn specialists who have landed in the skeptic's camp, arguing that it is impossible to get badly burned at a firewalk. However, even the most sophisticated of arguments against the possibility of being burned by hot coals tends to break down when you talk to someone who has actually been burned, and has suffered greatly, from such an experience. I have had six campfire burn victims show up at my firewalks, each having once been very badly burned by a campfire. All of them successfully firewalked, and all were totally certain that the fire which had burned them earlier in life was much cooler, and their contact with it much shorter in duration. One was so impressed by his experience that he is now leading firewalks himself. Still, this is at best anecdotal evidence.

The main problem with any explanation of why 'you really can't get burned at a firewalk' is that people do in fact get burned at firewalks! As mentioned in the previous chapter, I have not come across a single reference to firewalking *anywhere* that did not include some warning about the possibility of being burned. In other parts of the world, there are reports of people who have been crippled or fatally injured while firewalking. While, to the best of my knowledge, no one has ever been so seriously burned in the United States, it is not at all uncommon for people to experience burning pain and to develop blisters as a result of firewalking. I could safely say that all continuing firewalkers eventually get a nasty burn, and that at the end of any given firewalk there are at least a couple of walkers who are feeling pain. These are generally pretty benign affairs: a few sharply stinging spots on the bottoms of the feet, lasting for an hour or two, and then lingering as blisters on the sole of the foot for a few days, or at most a hobbled week or so. I know of several people who have gone to hospital emergency rooms in great pain after firewalking, including three who were diagnosed by the receiving doctor as having severe second-degree burns, and of one man who spent a month on crutches after one of my firewalks. I have personally had a few rather long, painful nights myself, my foot in a bucket of cold water, when I wished very much that it was impossible to get burned at a firewalk!

But people do get burned, all the time. And while burns and blisters are a somewhat unpleasant aspect of firewalking that I often wish would go away, they do at the same time very clearly serve to validate the process. Having watched thousands of people go through the firewalk, and having followed up with many who were burned, and many more who were not, all that I have seen has led me to the very firm conclusion that burns are somehow caused from inside the person, rather than by the fire. Each time I lead a firewalk I use the same amount of the same kind of wood, and I burn it for the same length of time, raking it into a path of the same dimensions, meticulously preparing it in the same way. And yet, from firewalk to firewalk, from experiment to experiment, sometimes there are burns, and sometimes there are not. The fire has burned as a constant, unchanging stimulus. The only changing factor has been the psycho-emotional state of the individual walkers.

Even more compelling is the testimony of experienced walkers, such as myself. To have walked on fire a dozen or more times, to have had the experience on some nights of being able to do just about anything with the fire — dancing, slow dancing, standing still, laughing through it all and feeling no heat whatsoever — and then to stand in front of another fire and hear a voice inside screaming "not tonight!" and sure enough, with the first step forward, to experience a burst of heat and a piercing pain: having gone through this more than a few times, and swapped notes with others who have done likewise, I am firmly convinced that the primary cause of burning at a firewalk is the consciousness of the individual walker, in combination with the collective consciousness of the entire group involved.

The testimony of burn specialists, combined with the continuing experience of thousands and thousands of firewalkers, would seem to present a good case for the basic premise of firewalking: that a fire which would ordinarily burn does not, and that human consciousness is a primary causative factor for this phenomenon. Yet, even with such evidence, most skeptics, firmly committed as they are to a posture of doubt, distrust, and disbelief, will continue to generate 'explain-aways.' I have watched the minds of some people, just minutes after firewalking, start sending up the disclaimers: "That fire didn't seem so hot," "It was only a few steps," "It was only a few seconds," "We walked so fast," "If everyone did it that must prove you can't get burned." This no longer surprises me, for it has been my experience that most if not all of us will have to wrestle through such moments of

skepticism, such dark nights of the soul, while our minds scramble
to invalidate the simple miracle of the firewalk.

Indeed, I find it difficult to even write the word 'miracle,'
much less announce that I will be performing one with twenty
other people next Friday night at 10 pm! Presumptuous, to say
the least, with an unhealthy dose of hubris. And yet, looking
the word 'miracle' up in the dictionary, I find it defined as "an
event in the physical world that surpasses all known human
or natural powers and is ascribed to a divine source." Which
is exactly what a firewalk is.

Let's divide this definition into three parts. First, a firewalk
is certainly an event in the physical world. These are real feet
stepping onto real fire without really burning. It is most definitely
not a case of mass hypnosis or shared hallucination or any
such thing.

Second, it is an event which surpasses all known human or
natural powers. The emphasis here is on the word 'known,'
meaning that while firewalking is beyond our current understanding
of human or natural powers, it is by no means unknowable.
Very often the vehemence and, at times, the outright anger with
which skeptics view events like firewalking stems from the mistaken
belief that such paranormal phenomena discount the laws of
nature, or that they deny the fact that we do live in an orderly
universe which can be systematically studied and understood.
The firewalk can seem like a very large slap in the face to those
whose lives are devoted to such study, both contradicting and
threatening their life works, that they will typically react by
arguing vigorously against its possibility.

But firewalking is not, by any means or manner of reckoning,
a refutation of the laws of physics or a denial that there is an
underlying order to this universe which can be systematically
understood. It is merely a firm reminder that there are still large
gaps in our knowledge, that our minds must remain relentlessly
open to new learnings, and that our understanding must be
expected and permitted to grow. Simply consider the lessons that
Copernicus, Galileo, Columbus, and Einstein brought to the
world: each introduced radical new concepts that were contradictory
to the known laws of nature in their time; each met with hostile
skepticism; and each, ultimately, ushered in a fresh new wave of
understanding which encompassed and went beyond all that was

known before. In like manner, the firewalk is a teaching which goes against our current understanding and which promises to deliver several important insights into the workings of the world. It only remains for us to have the courage and the willingness to truly look, listen, and learn.

The third part of the definition of a miracle is that it is an event which is ascribed to a divine source. Looking further through the dictionary, we find that 'divine' is defined as 'God-like,' and 'God' is defined as 'the creator.' Given the basic premise of the firewalk, as introduced in Chapter 2 — that there is an ongoing co-creative process, or divine intelligence, which determines the way that the world is, the very fabric of reality, and the laws which govern it; that each of us is a vital and integral part of that process; and that all human beings are potentially co-creators of this world — then it follows that the firewalk may indeed be ascribed to a divine source, which is ourselves!

Harumph and pshaw, yikes and arrgh, the textbook skeptic reels away from this suggestion that we are divine, literally feels revulsion towards such a notion, turns red in the face, grits teeth and clenches fists, screams of pantheism and paganism, of witchcraft and heresy; or chuckles wryly at such misinformed romanticism, lightly dismissing the very idea as naive, primitive, and sadly innocent.

We have now arrived at the root of the skeptical mind, at the very source of all the skepticism that the world has ever known and experienced. For behind all of the doubting, all of the distrusting, and all of the disbelieving of the posture of skepticism, lies this essential doubt, this essential distrust, this essential disbelief in ourselves as co-creators, in our connection to the primary creative forces of this world. *The basic denial of our true divine nature becomes a denial of all of life.* The basic stance of skepticism taken toward our own true role as co-creators becomes an ingrained habit of skepticism which colors every other aspect of our lives.

Simply consider this: if our basic premise is correct — that we contribute to the creation of reality through our thoughts and feelings — and we disagree, saying that our thoughts do not have creative impact and that our feelings do not have creative impact, then it will follow, quite ironically, that our thoughts and feelings will not have creative power and we will be quite

right in proclaiming our lack of divinity. This is the original
self-fulfilling prophecy (actually it is a self-frustrating prophecy),
the catch-22 of all catch-22s. The more fervently we argue against
our co-creative powers, the more surely we empower that reality.
The more clever and complete our proof that we are not divine
by nature, the more evidence we will be able to find to support
our lack of divinity. As Richard Bach puts it so concisely in
Illusions: "Argue for your limitations and sure enough, they're
yours."[6] To which we might add: "The more clever and determined
your argument, the more limited you will be." And then a corollary:
"Argue for your greatness and that too shall be yours."

Of course, it is quite true that as we look out at the world
we see very little evidence of such greatness, very little evidence
of humankind's divine nature, very little evidence that human
beings somehow contribute to the creation of the external world
through the movement of their internal processes. We must
constantly remember that arguing from past cases has little
relevance during evolutionary leaps. Caterpillars cannot conceive
of flying; apes cannot conceive of conceiving. Like a child-king,
humanity has long lived with the promise of power while being
too young, too immature, too unevolved, to truly fulfill that
promise. We have had our many masters, our Christs and Buddhas,
the evolutionary mutants, living examples of our true nature,
breathing reminders of our ultimate potential, always demonstrating
the possible while saying, "You can do this too." That we have
as yet failed to realize our full potential can be an indictment of
humanity or a promise for the future. I am inclined toward the
latter view and feel that the firewalk's present-day arrival in the
land of skepticism suggests that we may be ready at last to fully
embrace our true nature.

Every firewalker is saying about himself or herself: There is
an ongoing, co-creative process which determines the very fabric
of reality and the laws which govern it and I, as a conscious
human being, am an integral part of that process; there is a
divine, creative energy pulsing through all of this universe and I,
as a conscious, evolutionary human, am the living embodiment
of that divine energy. As we, individually and collectively, begin
to truly have faith (which equals belief without proof, the very
opposite of skepticism) in this possibility; as we truly honor our
own divinity; as we truly believe in the creative impact that we

have upon our world; as we take full responsibility for our vital roles as co-creators; as we finally and completely lift the veils of skepticism and doubt to behold the magical child, the wondrous, ancient, and eternal soul, the higher self, the holy one, the Godhead, the Christ, as we look upon ourselves and say, "Yes, amen, I am that I AM, so be it!"; then, by reflection, we have also affirmed this for our entire world. We can then experience a co-creative energy which is flowing through each of us, through all people, linking all of humanity together as one, and deeply and profoundly connecting us to the living consciousness of this planet.

Thus is our age-old prophecy and dream of heaven on Earth, of one peaceful world, made manifest. One who experiences that all of life is divinely connected finds it impossible to ever knowingly harm another; finds oneself, indeed, compelled toward a life of good and harmonious thoughts, words, and deeds. It is the transformation of our entire planet, and it begins with each of us looking inside and saying, "Yes, I am divine, I am co-creator of this world; my every conscious moment *matters*, deeply, fully, profoundly."

The skeptical mind will point to the world as it is, saying, "Read the papers, watch the six o'clock news, observe the hope-lessness, the helplessness, the despair, the confusion, the stupid depravity of our race, Where is the divine, where are these promised Gods, what is this foolishness!?" This is like the scientist removing a fish from water to study it upon a laboratory table for several hours until it is proven that fish can't exist because the damn thing died! Likewise, in allowing and strongly investing in a deeply-ingrained and profoundly rooted atmosphere of skeptical doubt, distrust, and disbelief, we have created an environment which is poisonous to the human spirit, which is openly hostile to our divine nature, and which works totally against the realization of our greatest dreams and most inspired possibilities. Indeed, the term 'healthy skepticism' is an outright lie, and could not be further from the truth, for skepticism always poisons, always attacks, always belittles, always defeats. All skepticism is by nature and definition unhealthy, for it begins with the denial of the essential human spirit, a denial which tragically prevents that spirit from coming forth in the world. Far from protecting, such chronic skepticism stifles and suffocates the body, narrows the vision, depresses the mind, inhibits relationship, and argues feverishly, and oh so cleverly, against the very possibility of embodied spirit, against the very precious possibility that we are each co-creators of this life.

Still, it must be conceded that all of these words are bound to fall like so much water on the rock-hard logic of the skeptical mind. We will probably never manage to completely convince the skeptical mind of the essential goodness of humanity, nor of its essential divine nature, nor of its vast reservoirs of untapped creative potential. The forever self-defeating nature of the skeptical mind is such that it cannot see beyond the created limitations of its own presumptions. Thus, we could do happy cartwheels through the hottest of fires (and have), laughing all the while, and the skeptical mind will immediately explain it all away, without considering for even the briefest moment that it might be true, that there might be a very new and different way of looking at the world. And, if we were then to point out the explicitly suicidal nature of such arguments, the skeptical mind would only dig in deeper still, threatened and offended and ever more determined to put an end to such nonsense. "Argue for your limitations and they're yours," warned a reluctant messiah. Sadly, the skeptic argues on, bound and determined to be dead right.

There is the story of a monkey who saw a caged bird and reached through the bars of the cage to grab it, thinking of dinner. Once having grasped the bird, however, his hand became too large to remove through the narrow bars. Though freedom lay in simply releasing the bird, the monkey just could not let go of something which had once seemed so important, and thus eventually died, still clinging to the bird.

Let us not also perish while clinging to a vision of ourselves which is negative, limiting, and stuck in the past. Our greatest teachers have told us that entering into the new world will require the easy innocence and open faith of a child. The evolutionary leap and the leap of faith are one and the same: a courageous leap beyond the narrow bars of skepticism and into a new world of abiding trust and unshakable belief in the divine nature of humankind. It is a leap which each of us must take individually, deeply affirming our divine purpose, acknowledging responsibility for our role as conscious participants in the evolutionary process, and accepting and gladly exercising our ability to positively impact our world. Slowly but surely an atmosphere of openness, faith, trust, and belief will be created, an atmosphere which will affirm, nurture, and support the very best that we could become, the very best of all possible worlds.

five

THE POWER OF INTENTION

I regard as will the sum of psychic energy which is disposable to consciousness. According to this conception, the process of will would be an energetic process that is released by conscious motivation.[1]

One of the principle causes of today's disorders is the lack of love on the part of those who have will and the lack of will in those who are good and loving. This points unmistakably to the urgent need for the integration, the unification, of love and will.[2]

The enhanced will, made over to the interests of the Transcendent, receives new worlds to conquer, new strengths to match its exalted destiny. But the heart too here enters on a new order, begins to live upon high levels of joy; that is, the sea of delight, the stream of divine influences.[3]

You can get it if you really want it.[4]

The only strong scientific data that we have on the act of walking on fire comes not from the world's many firewalkers (given the lack of any serious studies), but from the experience of all of those people who have ever unsuccessfully walked on hot coals. These are the accidental burn victims: people who have stepped on campfires or stray barbeque coals, or who come into contact with fireplace embers; those who show up severely burned at hospital emergency rooms. As mentioned in the previous chapter, I have spoken with several such burn victims, as well as doctors who have treated burn victims, and their combined testimony has been fairly conclusive: when human flesh comes into contact with glowing, red, hot coals such as those at a firewalk, the result will be instantaneous second- and/or third-degree burning, with a great deal of pain.

These accidental, unsuccessful, and badly burned 'firewalkers' form a sort of control group for the firewalking experiment. They are the only people to step on hot coals outside of the special environment which is created for a firewalk, and without any of the specific preparations which are common to firewalking. To gain an understanding of how firewalking can work, just how it is that human flesh can come into contact with such extreme heat and not burn, it should help to look at both successful firewalkers and accidental burn victims, contrasting their experiences and ascertaining what the former were doing that the latter were not.

I have made a fairly extensive study of firewalking as it happens around the world, and as it is being done by several people in America, and what strikes me the most is that everyone does it differently. Everyone tends to offer different explanations and to stress different factors as being critical to the experience, and many times these explanations and critical factors are not only different but totally contradictory. One person says you should relax, look down at the fire, and merge with coals. Another says you should tense your body, look up in the air, and think about cool moss. One group says it is a practice for very advanced, long-studied adepts, while another says that anyone can do it if they want to. One says you must abstain from sex, another says you must never eat meat, another says you must believe in Saint Constantine, another says you must be totally free from fear, and still another says you must feel your fear and use it in a positive way.

Sifting through the varied experiences of firewalkers all over the world, and contrasting these with the experiences of burn victims, I have found that there are two specific and very definite psycho-emotional factors which always seem to be present for any successful firewalker, but which are not there for those who are badly burned. They are: *a clear intention to walk on the fire,* and *a firm belief in the body's safety.* I have yet to find any successful firewalker, from any country, background, religion, tradition, rationale, belief system, philosophy, or motivation, who had not satisfactorily fulfilled these two requirements before walking. (Including several skeptics who have firewalked in an attempt to debunk the whole thing.) It is equally apparent that when people are badly burned by fire, including those at firewalks, they are lacking, to some degree, in one or both of these two factors.

Remember that the basic premise of the firewalk, and of this book, is that we are able to modify the creative processes of our world through the movement of our thoughts and feelings; that the state of our internal, subjective, psycho-emotional environment has a causative impact upon our external, objective, physical environment (including our bodies). Two very important keys to our internal world, and thus to our effectiveness as co-creators, are the clarity of our personal intention in a situation, and the quality of our personal beliefs.

First, the power of intention: our intention in a given situation is the measure of our will, our wanting, our preference, and our desire, regarding the outcome. On the mental level, it is the thought: "What I want is this." On the emotional level, it is a thrust of feeling, an urging, a yearning, a compelling toward or away from something. For different situations in our lives, our intentions will cover the spectrum from a sharply-focused, overriding, and thoroughly visceral intention — "I must have it now. I will settle for nothing less!" — to a vague, unexamined, and somewhat depressed intention — "Ah, I really don't care." To intend, to experience personal will, is the very root of what it is to be human. Even those who would advocate a life without goals or desires are at the same time advocating the fulfillment of a specific intention. For each and every situation of our lives' unfolding, there will always be some intention, some goal, some desire, some degree of personal will. As Otto Rank has written, "The human being experiences his individuality in terms of his will, and this means that his personal existence is identical with his capacity to express his will in the world."[5]

For all too many of the situations of our lives, we will actually have more intention, more desire, more wanting than is necessary or healthy. We generally think it quite obvious that everyone wants or clearly intends the good things in life: to be healthy, happy, and wise, and to have fulfilling relationships, wonderful families, good jobs, and lots of money. The truth is, our intentions are rarely so crystal clear and unconflicted. We may want a good, high-paying job while also wanting to avoid heavy responsibilities, maintain a lot of free time and not take risks. We may want to be healthy while also wanting to smoke, drink, and lead a stress-filled life. We may want a perfect marriage while also wanting to avoid feeling tied down, experience the special excitement of being with someone for the first time, and resist the need for personal changes. In each of these examples we may typically find ourselves wanting or intending all of the described and conflicting outcomes with equal sincerity and fervor! Indeed, the usual state of affairs is that we have a million and one different wants and intentions, all aiming in different directions, and many in direct conflict with one another.

This is true of most people who come to a firewalk, for while they certainly may want the experience of walking on fire, they may also want to avoid being the only one who does not do it, or they may want to get their money's worth, or want to be able to tell people what they have done, or want to prove something to themselves, or want to avoid pain at all costs, or want to avoid taking any risks, or want to go along with the crowd, or want to not go along with the crowd, or want to just satisfy their curiosity, or want to disprove whatever the workshop leader is saying, or any combination of these motivations and many others. Therefore, as they step toward the fire, instead of having one clear and undivided intention such as "I want to walk on fire," what most people have are a mishmash of different intentions, and separate, all too often conflicting, wants and desires.

It is likely that many of these intentions align with the basic intention to walk on fire. For example, "wanting to prove one's courage" is quite consistent with the intention to walk on fire. On the other hand, there are other possible intentions which are in direct opposition to this, such as "wanting to avoid pain," or "wanting to not take any risks." One who is strongly holding either, or both, of those two intentions will feel strongly conflicted if also holding the intention to walk on fire. And still other intentions, while being essentially in agreement with the intention to walk on fire, will nonetheless overshadow it in importance and priority. For instance, wanting to be part of the group energy is certainly in alignment with wanting to walk on fire. But if you have given your intention to be part of the group a priority over all of your other wants (a good definition of peer pressure), then you may not notice that you have lost your intention to actually walk on fire, and will thus be increasing your likelihood of getting burned

We might say that *each and every intention that we have gives birth to a stream of creative energies moving toward the fulfillment of that intention.* The intention to walk on fire sends a stream of energy flowing from the person who has the intention to the other side of the fire. The intention to avoid pain at all costs sends a stream of energy flowing *away* from the fire. The person who stands before a bed of coals while harboring each of these intentions will experience inner conflict, a divided will, and his or her creative process will likewise be conflicted, divided, and diminished.

The only intention that a person must have before a firewalk is the clear intention to participate in the act of successful firewalking. Obvious though this may sound, it is not necessarily an easy thing to arrive at. From the point in time that fire first burned each of us, from that time early in our lives when we each received our personal initiation into the nature of fire, from that time forward we, along with reasonable and sane people everywhere, have spent our lives with one and only one clear and unchanging intention regarding the element fire: *do not touch.* Oh, we may play with passing our finger quickly through a candle's flame, but on the whole, and especially when dealing with a large fire such as that at a firewalk, we never want to touch it. We never sit around the fireplace and decide that what we would like to do is stick our feet into it. Nor, while making our morning coffee, do we ever get the idea that what we would like to do next is place our hands upon the bright red, electric burner. Rather, our intention, our will, our preference, our desire regarding the element fire is always very clear and unchanging: treat it safely at a distance and be very, very careful with it; come only close enough to be warmed and to use its energy; and never, ever touch it, for it burns.

Thus, the person who steps accidently on a campfire or stray barbeque coal does so in violation of a deeply-held intention to not touch fire. If we could somehow freeze time in the moment just before such a person's foot touches the coals and ask him, "Do you want to step on fire?" the answer would always be, "No, not at all, there is nothing I would rather do less!" A moment later, when his foot actually touches the fire, he is invariably burned, and we say that he has had a bad, bad accident.

The dictionary defines an accident as an unintentional

occurrence, something which occurs against the intention of the person involved. When a person accidently (without intention) steps on a fire and is badly burned, in the moment that his foot makes contact with the fire he is in direct and very intense conflict with a lifelong intention not to touch fire. *That conflict is the burn.* That is, it is the person's improper intention for the reality in which he is currently moving which ultimately causes the burn.

Conversely, all successful firewalkers, whatever their background, belief system, or philosophy, whatever reasons they have for firewalking, whatever preparations they consider to be important (including skeptical debunkers who do not prepare at all), have in one way or another arrived at a clear intention to in fact walk upon the fire. A successful firewalker has managed to reverse a lifelong intention to not touch fire, has somehow managed to change a deeply ingrained cellular instinct which counsels human beings and virtually all other life forms to stay away from fire, and has created instead a new intention: "I want to walk on fire." Thus, in the moment that the firewalker's foot touches the coals there is no conflict between his actions and his intentions, and consequently no accident — the fire does not burn.

What I am saying is that if we truly and clearly want to walk on fire, then our personal creative processes may somehow alter reality to permit the experience (I discuss more on the actual mechanisms in Chapter 7). If we truly and clearly do not want to walk on fire then we are creating a reality in which touching fire will most often lead to serious injury. This is the power and importance of clear intention: to participate consciously and actively in the co-creative process of this world, to contribute to the formation of reality through the strength and force of our personal will.

My experience around the firewalk has given me great respect for the power of intention. Looking through the rest of my life, I have come to see that anytime I step forward into action that is in conflict with my intention, or anytime I do something which I really do not want to do, then I am in all likelihood going to get burned. When we step forward onto fire without intention to do so, the feedback is instantaneous and undeniable. We immediately know that we have done something we really did not want to do. In other situations of our lives, the results are the same, if not always as dramatic: when we take actions which are in conflict with our strongest intentions, we will get burned, always.

If you work at a job you really do not want to do, you are getting burned all the time. If you stay in a relationship you really do not want to be in, you are getting burned all the time. The 'burn' may very well be subtle, unapparent, and easily overlooked. The 'burn' may be a strain, or just another little problem, in your relationship with a person in the situation. The 'burn' may be a stress, a tension, or a minor little contraction or pain somewhere in your body. The 'burn' may be a reluctance to truly do well, a precursor to failure. The 'burn' may be a sluggishness or sloppiness in your actions, just a small degree of unconsciousness which will greatly increase your chances of accidents and mistakes. One way or another, the fact remains the same: go against your will and you will pay the price. Overriding your will in a situation never fails to create inner conflict, splitting your creative energies, diminishing your power, and curtailing your ability to intelligently respond. Stepping forward when you really do not want to is the ultimate act of disempowerment. It always weakens, always wounds, always renders you less than you are capable of being.

On the other hand, if you keep your actions in close alignment with your strongest intentions, do what you want and want what you do, and you feel inwardly united, your energies become focused and you are fully empowered to the very best of your capabilities. When your intention is simply clear, when you harbor no doubts about where you are going and what you are wanting, when your will is sharp, focused, and one-pointed, then you are acting at the upper limits of your potential. Indeed, if it can be done, you will do it. This then is the promise of intention: when your intention is clear and undivided in a situation, and you are willing to step forward in alignment with that intention, then you are living at full strength and at the upper limits of your creative possibilities, and if you can succeed in a situation, you will.

The power of intention is not a new idea, by any means. Doctors and healers throughout time and in many places have spoken of the will to live, that illusive and unmeasurable factor which, after all the pills and potions have been administered, ultimately makes the difference between a person's living or dying. As Dr. Larry Dossey succinctly puts it, "The patient with the will to live frequently outlives his prognosis. He doesn't die on time."[6] People who have wanted, above all else, to live — "I Want To Live!" — have managed to recover from the world's most incurable of diseases. People who feel conflict at the thought of living on, whose wills are not so clear, who want to live but ... , so often succumb, despite the best of prognosis and treatment. Though doctors struggle with this factor, given its unquantifiable and hard-to-control nature ("Is the will to live evidence of an effect of consciousness on the physical world?"[7]), they recognize it nonetheless and know that a patient has a much better chance of surviving when he has compelling reasons to survive, when his will to live is strong, and when the power of his personal intention is clear and unconflicted.

There is a co-creative process, causing all of the things of this world to be the way that they are, and causing our bodies to manifest as health or sickness. Each of us contributes to the co-creative process, and contributes especially to the health and sickness of our own bodies. Intention is a very large part of our individual creative contribution. Faced with a life-threatening illness, it is the person who creates a strong, unwavering intention to live on, more fully than ever before, who stimulates and mobilizes the body's healing energies, allowing the full miracle of healing to occur.

There is the little engine that could, the boy with his finger in the dike, Ulysses, John Galt, Helen Keller, Horatio Alger, the American Revolution, The Right Stuff, a list that could go on and on without end. Throughout our world, the stories, songs, myths, and tales that have inspired us so much, that carry so very much meaning to people everywhere, are those which document, bear witness to, and remind us of the unlimited and unstoppable power of the human will. This is a song which we never grow tired of hearing, a song exhorting us to go on reaching for the stars, for if we want them urgently enough then they shall surely be ours.

The firewalk, in a very neat and elegant manner, elevates the power of intention from the realm of anecdote and poetry, and supports it with good, hard data. When a person walks on fire with no intention whatsoever of doing so, and thus with a lifelong intention of not touching fire, then he gets badly burned. When a person walks on fire with a clear and unconflicted intention to do so, then he does not get burned. When a person walks on fire with vague or mixed intentions, then he will usually receive a mixed experience: mostly not burning, but getting a painful blister or two.

The skeptic's viewpoint regarding the power of intention is that certainly if we have a strong, clear intention, then we will tend to work harder at something and persist at it longer, thereby increasing our chances of succeeding. The firewalker's experience takes this a bit further, suggesting that our thoughts and feelings can have a creative impact upon external reality, and then demonstrating the power of a strong and clear intention to sharply focus our thoughts and feelings, and thus our full co-creative abilities. The firewalk very explicitly shows us that anytime we hold a clear and unwavering intention, then all of our creative energies are mobilized toward that outcome, and a host of latent and inherent possibilities may be called into play.

I am *not* saying that because we can walk on fire we can therefore do anything else we may want to do. That is an obviously simplistic and easily disproven statement. What I am saying is that when we have a clear intention, and are willing to act in alignment with that intention, then our creative energies are aligned, we are empowered to the greatest of our potential, and if we can succeed in that situation, we will. We still have to make intelligent choices. Whether we are successful or not depends upon whether our intention and our actions are in harmony with our world; that is, is our intention reasonable for the environment in which we are currently living?

Children want lots and lots of things which they never receive. Prisoners want their freedom, failing businessmen want things to get better, the vast majority of athletes want to finish first and yet do not, and unrequited love is the oldest story in the world. In addition, of course, the will to live, powerful though it may be, has been fighting a losing battle against death since the beginning of time. (Conversely, there are those elderly patients who have prayed in vain to be relieved of the burden of their bodies.) The fact of the matter is that if we could somehow measure it, we would find a vast sea of the world's wanting and intending to have gone unanswered and unfulfilled.

Thus, the firewalk is by no means a claim that we are unlimited beings who can do absolutely anything we want. Rather, it is a demonstration that humans participate to some degree in the creation of the limits of this world, and thus can exercise some measure of control upon manifest reality. It remains for us to discover the full extent of our co-creative powers, to continually test our limitations, uncovering more of our possibilities while learning to accept the non-negotiable demands of our world. In the words of Lawrence LeShan, "Reality is only partly our invention; it is also partly our discovery. Our task is to discover how much and in what area which is which; and then to determine how much new freedom this gives us and what we can do with it."[8]

I often tell my groups that though they successfully walked on fire that night, if they should go to a barbeque the next day, have a few beers, and proceed to stick their feet into the barbeque pit, then they would in all likelihood get burned. Nor can a successful firewalker necessarily expect to be able to stick a hand into a woodstove or grind a lit cigarette into a palm. Though I feel certain that all of those acts are in fact possible I have also found that success in any situation depends upon the intention of the person involved *in relationship* to the unique set of circumstances surrounding the person. Thus, clear though our intention may be, our surrounding environment (including other people/intenders) is often more powerfully focused in a different direction. (This is one reason why paranormal phenomena so often fail under laboratory conditions.)

An example from my own life may illustrate this point. Penny and I lead two-day workshops that begin on a Friday night with a firewalk. At the time of this incident, I had been firewalking for a year and a half, and had developed a lot of ease and certainty in my walking. That night I walked several times, each time slower than the time before, finally stopping and standing still in the coals for a few long seconds, at ease, quite calm, no problem, not even the slightest burn.

The next night of the workshop, we were leading the group through a sweat lodge, another very powerful ritual. The sweat lodge requires heating several stones in a wood fire for a few hours and then transferring them into a small tent, where the group gathers to have a very intense, sauna-like experience. While in the process of carrying a hot stone on a shovel from the wood fire to the tent, I accidently stepped, barefooted, on a single stray coal. I immediately became aware of the heat, a burning sensation, and I dropped the stone in very definite pain. The pain stayed with me for a while and lingered as a small blister for a few days.

What struck all of us who were present so deeply was the incredible contrast between my experience of the two different fires. One night I was standing still in a bed of glowing embers, smiling calmly. The next night I was grimacing in pain from a brief contact with a single coal.

It is quite apparent that a major factor in this experience was my personal intention. The first night I knew exactly what I was doing, where I was going, why I was doing it, etc. My intention was clear, very focused, and contained not a trace of conflict, confusion, or doubt. The second night my intention was to carry a hot stone from the fire to the lodge, to do it as quickly as possible, and then to lead the group through a wonderful experience that had nothing at all to do with firewalking. Thus, when I stepped on the coal I did so without intention, accidently, and my body reacted with a nasty little burn.

Equally important was the fact that on the first night, my surrounding environment was totally engineered and intended toward the act of firewalking. Everything that we had done together had led up to and was supportive of the intention to walk on fire. As I stood in the middle of the coals my friends laughed and sang, happily celebrating my actions, eager to join in the play. On the second night, the environment and the group were intended in a very different direction, and when I recoiled from the burning coal, people gasped, and there was a sense of alarm and worrying whether or not I was okay.

Thus it is critical that we have a clear intention before we act, and it is just as critical that our intention be in alignment with the world surrounding us. At a firewalk, we completely engineer the environment toward the purpose of firewalking. The selection of the sight, the laying and burning of the wood, the two, three, or more hours of preparation, the logistics of the actual walk, all serve to literally build human intention into the environment so that when a person steps toward the coals with an intention to walk upon them, the surrounding environment is totally supportive of his actions. A firewalk is a place where it is reasonable to hold the intention: "I want to walk on fire." A barbeque or a campfire is not a good place to want to walk on fire because it is intended toward an entirely different purpose, and one would need a very strong and clear personal will to succeed under such conditions.

The world will always impose definite and specific limitations upon us. Whether a certain limitation, such as 'fire burns,' can be altered in a certain situation or not, depends upon the unique qualities of both the individual involved and the surrounding environment. A powerfully clear intention does not guarantee success. But it does guarantee that one's greatest strengths and furthest reaching capabilities will be called into play.

There are, then, two aspects to the power of intention. The first is that we take responsibility for the formation and holding of our desires, that we focus our thoughts and feelings toward clear, creative intention. The second is that we have the sensitivity and awareness to know what is true of our world in any given moment, that we learn the difference between stretching toward a new and exciting possibility, and walking stupidly into a brick wall.

Just how much power is there to a clear and focused intention? My experience with the firewalk has led me to believe that, when it is very important to us, we may well be able to walk through any of life's brick walls. There may ultimately be no limits to the power of the human will, no limits to our ever-unfolding potential. I have also come to appreciate how important it is that we structure and educate our world to be open and supportive of our evolutionary possibilities, that we ouselves, in effect, become a surrounding environment which is totally intended toward the nurturing of a brave, new humanity, a world resounding with "Yes!" for all that we will.

six

WALKING ON
PLACEBOS

I will go a step further with my will, not only act with it, but believe as well; believe in my individual reality and creative power.[1]

"Reality" is what we take to be true. What we take to be true is what we believe. What we believe is based upon our perceptions. What we perceive depends upon what we look for. What we look for depends upon what we think. What we think depends upon what we perceive. What we perceive determines what we believe. What we believe determines what we take to be true. What we take to be true is our reality.[2]

Man is not disturbed by things, but by his opinion of things.[3]

In 1975, Harvard-educated Dr. Herbert Benson published *The Relaxation Response,*[4] a simple book which has made a major contribution to the unfolding understanding of the human body/mind. To write the book, Benson undertook a scientific investigation of Transcendental Meditation (TM). His goals were first to establish if there were in fact any physical benefits to be gained from meditation, as the TM practitioners claimed, and second, if so, to see if such meditation could be stripped of its religious underpinnings and presented and successfully practiced within a purely scientific framework.

Benson succeeded on both counts. First, he gathered and has continued to gather an impressive body of data which demonstrates quite conclusively that the mind does in fact have a very definite impact upon the body, and that through the simple practice of meditation a person can effectively generate a number of positive bodily responses such as relief from headaches, lower blood pressure, lower cholesterol levels, relief from angina pains, and the alleviation of many of the symptoms of excess anxiety. (The full list of possible benefits continues to grow.) Benson thus showed that a large percentage of the illnesses and diseases that plague modern people are in fact mind/body problems which can be successfully treated by the individual herself, through a mostly mental practice, and without resorting to drugs or surgery.

Benson then went on to demonstrate that such benefits could be attained through a purely scientific meditational practice, without a need for any of the specific religious and esoteric belief systems which had, until his work, always surrounded the act of meditation. He called the practice the Relaxation Response. It simply requires that a person settle into a comfortable position, with eyes closed, while passively focusing on a single mental device (he used, for example, the word 'one'), for fifteen to twenty minutes, twice a day. This easily learned and practiced discipline, engaged in over a period of time, has been shown to encourage a vast array of positive healing responses, proving that the mind plays a very critical role in the sickness and health of the body.

Nine years later, Dr. Benson came out with a second book, *Beyond The Relaxation Response,*[5] which, as the title implies, took his understanding of the practice and power of meditation a good bit further. For this book he drew on his continuing clinical experience with the Relaxation Response and added to it his findings from a study of certain Tibetan Buddhist monks of the Indian Himalayas. These monks practice a form of meditation called *gTum-mo* Yoga, which involves being able, through meditation, to raise the body's temperature by several degrees, generating a very tangible increase in radiant heat. It is reported that the very adept at this practice are able to sit naked, on a cold winter's night in the mountains, and generate so much heat that they melt the snow around them.

In 1981, Benson and a small research group went to the Himalayas to study this practice. After observing several practitioners with an array of scientific instrumentation, they found that, indeed, such monks were able, through the power of their minds, to raise their body temperatures, at will, regardless of their surrounding environments. His experience with the Tibetans gave Benson further data on the role of the mind in our bodily processes, and led him to add a new element to the Relaxation Response — that which he calls the Faith Factor.

The Faith Factor is the individual's deeply-held personal beliefs about reality. In adding the Faith Factor to the Relaxation Response, Benson is saying that, as effective as the Relaxation Response is, it is even further enhanced when it engages the individual's personal belief systems. Specifically, this involves using as a focal device a word or phrase that has special psycho-emotional significance to the individual meditator, such as 'Jesus Christ' for Christians, or 'Shalom' for the Jewish, or 'Allah' for Moslems. Benson is careful to point out that he is not recommending any specific religion or belief system. Rather, he is saying that what matters is that the individual meditator be personally connected, through her personal belief system, to the word or phrase that she uses during meditation.

The point that Benson is driving toward is that our beliefs about reality matter, that, indeed, our personal beliefs about reality have a great deal to do with how we experience the world. In Benson's own words, "If you truly believe in your personal philosophy or religious faith — if you are committed, mind and soul, to your world view — you may well be capable of achieving remarkable feats of mind and body that many only speculate about."[6]

This brings us to the second factor which, along with clear intention, I have found essential to all successful firewalkers: *a firm belief in the body's safety*. This is the Faith Factor applied to firewalking. As an individual approaches the coals, her personal belief system will be a strong contributor to her overall experience. Her personal beliefs about reality, and about fire and flesh, will contribute largely to the experience which she creates.

Our personal belief systems are made up of the thoughts, notions, and ideas which we feel to be true of our world at any given moment in time. Our beliefs are the primary assumptions which we are making about our world: what it is, why it is, how it works, what its limitations are, and what its possibilities are. They also include the assumptions we make about our own place in the world: who we are, why we are, how we work, what our limitations are, and what our possibilities are. Our belief systems, whether examined or not, totally define our world, setting its parameters, influencing its directions, and selecting its possible range of experience.

Our beliefs are derived directly from our ongoing, day-to-day, sensory contact with the world. They are representations of reality, our own personal interpretations of the world, drawn from our own personal experiences of the world. It is by no means necessary that our beliefs be true, or even testable. For indeed, our beliefs are comprised much more of emotional force than of logical reasoning. We feel our beliefs much more than we think them. They are of the heart much more than of the mind. When we believe in something, we are feeling confidence in it without any need for proof. We have had an experience of the world, from which we have drawn a conclusion, an interpretation, a representation — we have formed a belief — and we simply know that we are right. We have faith in it. We believe it.

The newborn infant arrives without a personal belief system. (We might just as accurately say that she believes in everything.) As her days unfold, she has specific personal experiences of the world from which she derives specific personal beliefs about the world. Experiencing pain after touching a lit candle, she will hence forth believe that fire burns. Hurting her head when she bumps into a wall, she will believe that solid objects present impenetrable barriers. Playing outside on a rainy day, she will believe that water makes you wet. Seeing that her parents take care of all of the needs in her world, she will believe them to be omnipotent and all-knowing.

In addition to those beliefs derived from her direct contact with physical reality, she will also develop a wealth of beliefs through contact with her family and her surrounding culture. Thus, she may believe that sugar gives you cavities, and spinach makes you strong, and a good girl always eats everything on her plate. Or she may believe in Santa Claus, the Easter Bunny and the Tooth Fairy. Or she may believe that Russians are evil, that Blacks are lazy, that Italians are gangsters, and that boys are all after one thing. Or she may believe in Jesus Christ, or Allah, or Buddha, or the Tao, or the Pope, or the President, or flying saucers, or bigfoot, or cooties. The list is truly endless, and the only thing that we can say for certain is that she will believe.

As she grows older and wiser, many of her beliefs will be discarded, old toys that no longer serve. She will know one day that Santa Claus does not exist, that the stork does not bring babies, that the moon is not made of green cheese and, whether gladly or sadly, she will let such beliefs go. Other beliefs will grow stronger with the test of time, as they are tempered in the cauldron of her daily experience. Still other beliefs, such as 'fire burns,' will go forever unexamined and unquestioned, seemingly obvious to all, the basic assumptions upon which her personal vision of reality is based.

If she happened to be born into the Western world sometime during the past few hundred years, then it is possible that she will find herself driven to vigorously ridding herself of any and all false beliefs; that she will in fact come to distrust the very notion of believing in something, and that she will consider it very important to supplant all of her beliefs with hard, solid proof. For, to a very large degree, the onward march of scientific culture has been a determined march against human belief systems. Much of this war against belief has been of great service to humanity, since so many of the superstitions and old wives' tales that the world has known have been of such obvious detriment to our race. It is of great benefit to all people that we no longer labor under the false beliefs that the world is flat, that the Earth is the center of the solar system, or that the plague is caused by an angry god. It is of even greater benefit that we continue to discover scientific facts and to find practical applications for such facts.

However, we make a very big mistake when we begin to think of beliefs as the opposite of factual knowledge, as if the path to truly informed intelligence necessitates the sacrifice of all believing. Facts are simply a different way of knowing than beliefs. And while it is true that facts will quite often invalidate and supplant certain beliefs, it is equally true that all of the factual knowledge in the world can be found to rest upon specific untestable assumptions, and that even the 'hardest' of sciences ultimately are rooted in belief. Indeed, the question is not really whether or not it is good to have belief systems — they are an intrinsic part of human nature, as necessary to our daily life as the air we breathe. The question is what role our belief systems play in our lives, and how we get the most out of them.

In many ways, our beliefs are like the software in a computer. They are by no means the absolute truth, and they can definitely be changed at will. Yet for as long as we are holding onto them, they run the show. For starters, our beliefs, to a very large degree, determine the way in which we will perceive the world. We will tend to miss, overlook, screen out, or ignore any data which does not agree with our preconceived notions about reality. The person who believes strongly in position A will be open to and thus will find an abundance of evidence to support that position. The person who believes strongly in position B will likewise find an abundance of evidence to support that position. And yes, both will be able to statistically 'prove' their positions with good, hard numbers!

There is, then, a very circular nature to our use of belief systems. We begin our lives with an eyes-wide-open and totally unbiased experience of the world, from which we derive or form specific beliefs about reality. We then perceive the world, experience it, see it, hear it, taste it, touch it, and sense it, through the beliefs that we are holding, which leads us to perceive further evidence to support our beliefs, which further validates those beliefs, which leads us to perceive further evidence, and so on. This is why people tend to become more and more conservative as they age, growing ever more set in their ways, as the freshly-chosen beliefs of youth gradually harden through years of self-confirming experience.

This circular, self-confirming process of belief systems can be both a very serious problem and a vital source of personal creative power. The real danger of beliefs is that obviously they can bring us to a vision of reality which is totally divorced from the truth. Thus, when a ship sails out beyond the horizon one day and fails to return, the belief is born that the world is flat, and for the next several hundred years an entire culture is penned-in and limited, its actions dictated by a single mistaken notion. Our beliefs can so easily be false and misleading, and when so they always limit us to some extent. This is why science (along with certain spiritual traditions) has campaigned so rigorously against beliefs. They are often a yoke of ignorance and limitation beneath which humanity must struggle on its path toward greatness.

However, beliefs are definitely a two-edged sword, and though they may well limit us, they can just as easily free us toward our vast creative potentials. It is not that believing per se is ignorant and limiting. Rather, it is that we tend to choose, hold, and operate through such ignorant and limiting beliefs. The challenge is not to give up believing, for believing is essential to our nature. *The real challenge is to choose, hold, and operate through intelligent, uplifting, and fully empowering beliefs.*

A good example of the positive creative power of beliefs has been demonstrated by something which the medical world calls the placebo effect. A placebo (from the Latin *to please*) is a substance such as a sugar pill, which has no specific medicinal ingredients and yet, when administered to a patient, results in a definite improvement in the patient's condition. In a typical study of the placebo effect, we might take a roomful of people all suffering from extreme migraine headaches, and to half the room we would give the best known cure for migraines. To the other half of the room we would give a sugar pill, while leading them to believe that they were receiving an effective medicine for their problem. In study after study such as this, the placebo has registered a surprisingly high rate of success, and in some studies has done even better than the medicinally proven drug.

The active ingredient in the placebo is the patient's own belief that what she is doing will help her. That is, a person with a physical ailment may be given a placebo and experience real physical improvement if she deeply believes that she is receiving the best of treatment. Studies have indicated that the placebo effect is probably operating to some extent in all medicines and treatments, and with all doctors and healing systems, because the patient must always have some beliefs about her situation and the steps that she is taking to remedy it. Those beliefs will always help, or hinder, her healing process. To say it very simply: if the patient believes strongly in her medicine, or believes strongly in her therapeutic program, or believes strongly in her doctor, or believes strongly in her own inner healing resources, then she is holding positive creative beliefs and increasing her chances for recovery. If, on the other hand, she instead believes, as it might say in the newspaper, that 75 percent of all cases such as hers are terminal, then she is using the power of believing to limit her healing potential.

While the medical world has long been aware of the placebo effect, most doctors and researchers have done everything they can to discount it, avoid it, and generally outlaw it. Research procedures, such as double-blind studies, have been designed to minimize the effects of both the patient's and the doctor's beliefs, with the goal being to prove the effects of 'real' medicines.

In so doing, there is the implication that the placebo effect is not really healing people, or if it is, that they were not really sick in the first place. This despite the fact that the placebo effect has been shown to be operating effectively in such a wide variety of cases that we should be embracing it as the miracle cure of all miracle cures! Rather than devising studies which will lessen the impact of the placebo effect, we should be studying it in depth to discover just how far it can go and how we might use it better.

The problem is that we are a culture, and especially a medical culture, which is based upon a firm belief in physical causation. The placebo effect, on the other hand, indicates to us that the mind very clearly has creative impact, at least as far as an individual's body goes. As Andrew Weil has pointed out, the very term 'placebo effect' is inaccurate and misleading, for it places emphasis on the placebo and the 'effect' that it has somehow 'caused.' He suggests that we think instead in terms of the 'placebo response,' which would indicate the healing capabilities of an individual who has, for reasons that seem rooted in mind, responded to the placebo in a health-inducing way. This is still a difficult pill for conventional medicine to swallow.

Thus, while a medical researcher will be quite pleased to discover that compound X eliminates virus Z, she will not be nearly as excited if you show her that 'the patient's firm belief in the inner healer' has eliminated virus Z. In the first case, we have a clear-cut and easily quantifiable case of physical cause and effect: the patient takes this pill, this frequently, and in these amounts, and the virus disappears within this time period. In the second instance we have a case that is not at all clear-cut and probably unquantifiable in which the patient's mental state has a positive impact upon the body. This is good for the patient, but if we cannot duplicate it exactly for the next person, then what is the point?

The point is that there is a steadily mounting body of evidence which says that the individual's personal belief system may be the most potent medicine that we will ever know. The point is that, as Benson puts it, "If you truly believe ... you may well be capable of achieving remarkable feats of mind and body that many only speculate about." The point is that, as my ongoing experience with the firewalk has demonstrated, if you have a firm belief in your body's safety, then you may stand in the midst of a glowing, red, hot path of burning embers and feel wonder instead of heat, and be healed instead of burned.

Strong belief works in tandem with, and is the perfect compliment to, clear intention. Our intention in a situation serves as the mental component and focus of our creative energies. It is mostly thought, and the clearer it is, the more power it generates. Our belief in a situation operates more at the level of our emotions, releasing and channeling the creative force of our feeling energies toward the fulfillment of our intention. When our intention is very clear (I want to!) and we believe very strongly in our prospects (I feel certain that I can!) then our creative energies are aligned and we are moving toward the realization of our goals at full strength.

As they do with their intentions, people typically arrive at a firewalk filled with conflicting and opposing beliefs. On the one hand, they may have heard about the firewalk from friends who have successfully walked, or they may have come across it in the media. They will therefore have some good evidence to support the belief that they can walk on fire. On the other hand, having been burned a number of times before in their lives, as we all have, and usually by far less threatening fires, they will have a strong and hard-to-ignore body of data to support the belief that if they dare to participate in a firewalk, they may very well get burned again. Because beliefs are derived from sensory experience — because they grow directly out of our daily contact with the world — some degree of conflict in our beliefs is virtually inevitable, given that the evidence surrounding the firewalk continues to be confusing and contradictory.

To some extent I may sway a group toward a belief in the possibility of firewalking during my presentation. But the real argument for the believability of firewalking occurs when the actual walking begins. What happens then is that I walk through the coals, quite simply and obviously without burning. In that moment it does not matter if people cannot understand it, and it does not matter if all of their previous experience has taught them that fire must burn. The simple fact is that they are seeing it being done, and because beliefs are derived from sensory experience, because *seeing is believing* (as are hearing, touching, tasting, and smelling), each person now knows that he or she can do it too. As the walk progresses, it becomes easier and easier for each person who participates because the experiential body of data within the group which supports the possibility of safe firewalking continues to grow.

Thus the second essential ingredient for successful firewalking — a firm belief in the body's safety — is simply met by one's attendance at a firewalk. It is virtually impossible to disbelieve in the safety of firewalking when one has witnessed other people doing it successfully. All that is required (in addition to a clear intention on the part of each individual participant) is that somebody go first, opening the door to a whole new belief. It is generally not my own walk which shifts the belief of the rest of the group. Knowing that I firewalk both professionally and frequently, most people will witness my walk without believing that they can do it too, just as they can witness an adept or expert at any other activity without feeling empowered to do likewise. When they see another participant walk, however, especially someone they know has never done it before, someone they feel is just like themselves, then their belief shifts dramatically.

There is another recurring phenomenon at firewalks which demonstrates the creative power of our beliefs. It is not at all uncommon for people (especially experienced walkers, who have firewalked five or more times) to report that when they first walked through the coals, they felt that they had in fact badly burned their feet, and that there was a tremendous feeling of pain. Nevertheless, they continued standing in the circle, singing, seeing other people overjoyed with the act of walking. Perhaps they even walked once or twice again themselves. By the time we all gathered back in the room, much to their surprise, their feet showed no sign of even the slightest of burns.

I have been through this experience several times myself and am convinced that it is the atmosphere of the firewalk, the singing, the joy, the excitement, the belief that we are doing something grand and wonderful, which serves to generate the placebo response, allowing people who have actually injured themselves to be healed. I am also convinced that if we were to grab a person at such a time, pull them aside, and shine a bright light on a foot to see what the problem is, that we would in all likelihood discover a serious problem in need of hospital treatment. Because we simply allow the firewalk to continue, the full sensory report of the environment is in support of the beliefs that this is a healing experience, that all of us are okay, that we have done the right thing, and that we have good reason to feel joy. If we were to pull a person aside, it would be similar to many clinical and hospital situations; the full sensory report of the environment would tend to support the belief that something is wrong, and that something must be done quickly to remedy that wrong.

I realize that I am committing what is, to some, the cardinal sin of offering subjective experience as evidence. Indeed, given the nature of the firewalk, I cannot yet conceive of a way to objectively test many of my hypotheses. Removing people from the atmosphere of the firewalk for even a moment to see what is happening on the soles of their feet, or asking people to walk on coals in clinical and easily controlled laboratory situations, would be to remove them from the very sensory data which helps to create their experiences. The firewalk is a vivid demonstration of something which physicists have been suggesting for some time: that total and absolute objectivity is just not possible; that the mere act of observing an experiment changes it; that the way that an experiment is designed absolutely conditions its outcome; that, in the simplest of terms, human consciousness is inextricably involved in the creation of this world. The firewalk is an argument for the fact that through the thoroughly subjective forces of personal will and personal belief, tangible changes in the objective world can be made. More to the point, the firewalk is an argument for the fact that the distinction drawn between subjective reality and objective reality is essentially false, that the two realities are in fact merged, and that personal will and personal belief occur and have their impact in the area where these two realities come together.

As mentioned at the beginning of Chapter 5, it is these two factors — the individual's intention for the situation (personal will) and the individual's belief system (personal belief) — which must in one way or another be satisfactorily engaged to allow for successful firewalking. That is, all successful firewalkers will have some degree of intention to actually walk on the fire and some degree of belief that their bodies will be safe as they do so. Conversely, accidental burn victims, as well as those who get badly burned at firewalks, will come in contact with the fire while holding an overriding intention not to touch fire and/or an overriding belief that fire must burn.

As an example, there have been a number of scientists who have firewalked in the past few years with the purpose of debunking the whole thing (*The Skeptical Inquirer*, Fall 1985.) Typically they have been quite skeptical and disbelieving as they approached the firewalk, and have not done any of the special preparations that specific firewalking instructors have deemed as important. Then, having successfully walked, they claimed to have disproven firewalking by demonstrating that it is simply impossible to get burned, and that no special and exotic powers of human consciousness are involved in it.

In fact, it was such reports that enabled me to become clear on exactly how the individual's consciousness is involved. In contrasting the firewalking debunker's experience with the accidental burn victim's experience, the factors of intention and belief come through loud and clear. The skeptic who approached a path of glowing, red, hot embers, determined to set the record straight by walking on them, had definitely decided to walk on the fire, and had definitely created a specific and clear intention to bring fleshy feet into contact with hot coals. The skeptic who approached a path of glowing, red, hot embers had also created, through a belief in the Leidenfrost effect, the low mass of the wood coals, and/or the observance of other people walking on fire, a firm belief that his or her body would be safe. Rather than debunking firewalking, such experiences have offered some of the strongest and most precise confirmations of the theories that I am presenting here, simply because they have so strictly eliminated any other possible factors. All that remains is for skeptics and other firewalkers, having reached the opposite side of the fiery path, to look back and truly appreciate just what *they* have done.

seven

THE BODY
ELECTRIC

The taboo against subtle phenomenal existence originated in conventional religion, which anciently taught that practitioners should not associate with negative spirits. With the development of scientism, a new taboo has replaced the religious one, based on the doctrine that material existence is the limit of life and there is no such thing as a subtle world or a subtle dimension of existence. This doctrine is a misconception — a lie — yet because of these taboos, millions of human beings have gone on for centuries presuming that subtle phenomena do not exist.[1]

Energy is the only life, and is from the Body; and Reason is the bound or outward circumference of Energy.[2]

Phenomena which seem extraordinary or paranormal *have been observed by people throughout the ages, and have been documented in so many cultures that the occurrence of these events can hardly be questioned. However, the techniques and beliefs which foster these talents and empower individuals to perform extraordinary feats are as varied as the cultures from which they arise. Yet one common thread runs among them — some concept of a force or energy that transcends the mundane understanding of the human body.[3]*

When I was twenty years old, I discovered I had a love and affinity for giving massage. The woman who I would be in relationship with for the next several years had a complimentary love and affinity for receiving massage, so, from that perspective at least, we were the ideal couple. I had never taken any lessons or read any books about massage, nor did I have any previous experience with it. Instead, doing it was a gradual learning process of intuitively exploring and experimenting, and being guided along the way by the feedback my friend would give me.

For the first year or so, my experience of giving a massage

was straightforward and easy to understand. I would reach out with my hands and contact a variety of physical states — tightly knotted muscles, stiff joints, taut skin, cold extremities — which I somehow knew to be less than optimal. Then, through gentle physical manipulations, I would coax the body toward a different set of conditions which I recognized to be healthy and beneficial — loose muscles, flexible joints, relaxed skin, and warm extremities. It was all very simple, and very logical to my way of thinking, my friend quite enjoyed it, and with time and practice my skill steadily improved.

Then some strange things began to happen. When I would place my hands on certain areas of her body, I would feel sensations of very intense heat. This heat was like nothing I had ever encountered before. It tended to move around, appearing in different places during different sessions, and it was definitely not the same sort of heat that I was accustomed to feeling around tight muscles or inflamed joints. As I continued to massage, I gradually noticed a variety of other strange new sensations in addition to the heat. At one place I would feel a very gentle tingling sensation, like the pins and needles of a limb which has fallen asleep. At another place I would feel a very intense buzzing, almost as if I had placed my fingers in an electric socket. Pressing very deeply into certain other areas, I would experience a very sharp sensation, as if I had pressed down onto the point of a needle. Finally, whenever I was massaging, I began to notice warm currents of *something* flowing through my arms and hands, and my friend began to notice similar warm currents of *something* flowing through different parts of her body.

To me, this experience of *something* within the body, *something* which I could feel flowing through my body and *something* which I could reach out to touch in another body, was very real, very tangible, and very substantial. There was no question at all that it might have been simply imagined or 'all in my head.' There was an undeniably physical quality to the various sensations and, as I explored them further, I found that they could be quite reliable guides in the process of giving a massage, that my hands would be drawn to work in certain ways with no conscious feedback from my friend. As my experience grew, so did my conviction that this *something*, which I thought of simply as *energy,* was critically important to the body's health. Yet, as far as I knew, the medical culture and physical education I grew up with was either unaware of this energy or choosing to ignore it.

I was eventually led to a study of traditional Chinese medicine and the ancient practice of acupuncture. There I encountered a philosophy and healing science which had been aware of, and systematically working with, this *energy* for over three thousand years. The Chinese call it *chi* (or *Qi*), and they consider it to be a very subtle bio-energy which circulates throughout the body, filling every cell, governing every organ, and fully regulating all of the body's processes. They have charted the major currents, or meridians, of this flowing *chi,* which they claim serve as an organizing matrix for the physical body. They further claim that if there is a blockage of *chi* flow in a meridian, it will eventually cause a corresponding problem in a part of the body. Likewise, when confronted with a physical illness or disease, they look first to the meridian system, then find the blockage and release it, thus mending the organizing matrix and allowing the physical body to heal. Through the study of acupuncture, it became clear to me that what I had been experiencing during massage were various degrees of *chi* blockage, and gentle ways to improve its circulation.

The Chinese, I went on to discover, are not the only culture to be working with this vital energy. A survey of the world's healing systems shows us that, in fact, awareness of an essential bio-energy and development of a practical means for working with such energy is very widely spread. Throughout India, the energy is called *prana;* in Hawaii and many Indonesian countries it is called *mana;* the Japanese call it *ki;* in different parts of Africa it is called *num, nye,* or *voodoo;* Sufis call it *baraka;* the Iroquois call it *orenda;* and it is *yesod* to Jewish cabalists and *the Holy Spirit* to Christian ecstatics. The belief in an essential spiritual energy which concretizes as matter, and is the source of illness and healing in the human body, is basic to all Native American cultures, and to all of the world's shamanic traditions. Indeed, outside of the modern Western world, one is hard pressed to find any culture which does *not* postulate the existence of such energy.

Not that the idea of an essential biological energy is a stranger to Western thought. Hippocrates himself wrote of a 'soul substance' which flowed throughout the body and which was the body's natural healing force. Later, Paracelsus would speak of a 'vital force,' Galvani (an early discoverer of electricity) of 'life-force,' Mesmer of 'animal magnetism,' vonReichenbach of 'odyle' or 'odic force,' Blondlot of 'N rays,' Boirac of 'nerve radio-activity,' Jung of 'psychic energy,' Burr of 'Life-fields,' Reich of 'orgone,' and contemporary Russian scientists of 'bioplasma.' Indeed, this *energy something* has been a sort of Holy Grail throughout the evolution of Western medicine, sought after by many but never quite pinned down in a satisfactory way.

A real difficulty is that while this energy may be easily observed, experienced, and to some degree utilized, it seems impossible to fully comprehend it in the manner to which Western thought is accustomed. In the words of electrical engineer and energy researcher Laurence Beynam: "There is an energy in living organisms that is weak and unpredictable, but it can be refracted, polarized, focused and combined with other energies. It sometimes has effects similar to magnetism, electricity, heat and luminous radiation, but it is none of these. Attempts to control and employ the energy have met with little success; investigators have not yet defined the laws governing its operation."[4] Thus, instead of one clear path of knowledge beginning with early experiences of energy, slowly gathering data, building insight upon insight, and culminating in an all-embracing and clearly communicated energy science, what we have instead is an Oriental bazaar of notions and potions, a thousand and one weird and different names for this *something*, along with a thousand and one different (and often weird) 'discoverers' of it, each with their own unique, and all too often contradictory, energy systems. Is it any wonder that mainstream science has chosen to ignore it altogether?

Guy Murchie, in his remarkable *Seven Mysteries of Life*, characterizes this long-running debate between the mechanists — those who believe that everything, including life itself, can be explained ultimately in terms of the interactions between molecules — and the vitalists — those who believe in abstract forces such as bio-energy which somehow bring life to everything, saying: "It is not an easy issue for . . . if vitalism challenges man's reason, mechanism disturbs his soul. And the resolution of this conflict is intimately bound up with the mystery of the whole universe."[5] This goes right to the heart of our difficulties with understanding energy, for if we can allow that there will always be a strong current of mystery flowing through this life of ours, if we can allow that there will always be the unknown, the source of breathless awe and wonder, then I would suggest that energy resides deep within the mystery, is enfolded deep within the unknown, and is the very currency of so much of our wonder. Thus, while I will venture to say much in this chapter and the remainder of the book about energy and how it works, let it be understood that there is much about it which I do not, and possibly cannot, fully understand.

To begin with, there is the whole problem of what to call it. The Chinese *Tao Te Ching*, one of the most important books of Chinese culture, opens with the comment: "The Tao that can be named is not the real Tao." This explains the thousand and one different names for energy as humans try nonetheless, because truly we must, to substantiate and systematize the unknown. For myself, I began with calling it 'the energy' and have at other times tried 'chi,' 'prana,' 'the living-energy,' 'the life-force,' 'bio-energy,' 'subtle energy' and 'the vital life essence.' No name has ever felt wholly accurate, or wholly descriptive, or proper in every usage. My sense now is that, just as matter can only accurately be described as a sometimes particle/sometimes wave, depending on how we look at it, so this energy is both a substantive stuff *and* an abstract process. To the extent that science proceeds in a mechanistic fashion, searching for the ultimate billiard ball that sets all the others in motion, it has glimpsed this energy as substantive stuff. To the extent that science is unwilling to deal with abstract forces, it has missed it altogether. And to the extent that human nature is unable to hold both states as being simultaneously true, then the mystery will abide. To put it another way, this energy is both noun and verb. The only accurate name for it would have to allow that it is an abstract force, like gravity, knowable only through its effects, while at the same time allowing that it is concrete substance, capable of being gathered, stored, measured, directed, etc. Since our language does not yet provide such words, we will have to do the best we can. I will mostly refer to it simply as energy, trusting the reader to understand that I am referring to subtle energy fields and currents peculiar to living organisms.

In the early twentieth century, instruments began to be
developed which were sensitive enough to objectively measure
energy. Since that time a large body of data has been generated,
on many different fronts, which points to the electromagnetic
energy fields and energy currents which are an essential part
of all living systems. To be sure, much of this research has been
controversial. In some cases such as Kirlian photography, which
is purported to be a way of photographing the fields of energy
surrounding living forms, critics have argued that the technology
involved is causing certain effects, and that what we are seeing
in a Kirlian photograph is merely an effect of the Kirlian technique
itself. (Personally, I have been very impressed by the Kirlian
evidence.) In many other cases, such as Reich's 'orgone boxes,'
the experiments have had too much personal input from the
experimenters to suit most scientists. Indeed, like the energy it
would study, there is a subtle, not quite substantial, and all
too subjective nature to much of the science of such energy.

Still, beginning in the 1930s with H.S. Burr's[6] seminal work
at Yale, there has been a gradual accumulation of 'hard' data to
support the hypothesis of subtle energy fields which govern the
human body. Burr set up a series of ingenious experiments, later
repeated by other researchers, which demonstrated that all living
organisms are surrounded and encompassed by their own energy
fields, which he called Life-fields (L-fields). He showed that
changes in the electrical potential of the L-field would lead to
changes in the health of the organism. By leaving some trees on
the Yale campus hooked up to his L-field detectors for decades,
he was able to demonstrate that the L-field is affected by changes
in environmental electromagnetic fields caused by such things as
the phases of the moon, sunspot activity, and thunderstorms. He
found he could detect a specific field of energy in a frog's egg,
and that the nervous system would later develop precisely within
that field, suggesting that the L-field was the organizing matrix
for the body. In his work with humans, he was able to chart
and predict the ovulation cycles of women, to locate internal
scar tissue, and to diagnose *potential* physical ailments, all through
the reading of the individual's L-field. It was this latter finding,
leading to his very vocal insistance that the L-field is *primary*
to the physical, that would eventually have Burr vilified for
'wishful vitalism.'

Burr's work has been carried forward by his student and colleague, Leonard Ravitz. Ravitz has focused especially on the human dimension, beginning with a solid demonstration that the human L-field is very affected by the lunar cycle, reaching a peak of activity at the full moon. Through work with hypnotic subjects, he demonstrated that the L-field is directly related to changes in a person's mental and emotional states. "Both emotional activity and stimuli of any sort involve mobilization of electrical energy, as indicated on the galvanometer, hence, both emotions and stimuli evoke the same energy. Emotions can be equated with energy."[7] Most intriguingly, and a sure step to the rites of vilification, Ravitz showed that the L-field as a whole disappears *before* physical death.

Another very strong contribution to our understanding of energy has been made by Robert O. Becker, M.D. (*The Body Electric*, 1985). Beginning with a desire to better understand why bones sometimes refuse to heal properly, Dr. Becker's search would eventually lead him from the regeneration capacity in lower organisms to the realization that that capacity is supported by the existence and strength of electromagnetic energy currents. It is now known that for all life-forms, including human beings, there is a 'current of injury' — a stream of electrons — flowing from the wound beginning at the moment of injury, and that as the injury heals, changes in the current can be detected and measured. Becker has since found that electrical stimulation can promote healing (though he worries over unknown possible long-term effects) and that exposure to strong electromagnetic fields can depress the human immune system. He considers it beyond dispute that there is an electrical dimension to the human organism, that it is very primary to the body's functioning and its healing process, and that future medicine will be based upon understanding and learning to manipulate bio-electricity.

Yet another body of 'bio-electric' data is being generated by the Chinese, who have invited the West to come study *chi* as it is demonstrated through the practice of acupuncture and by Chinese *chi kung* (manipulation of vital energy) masters. One such Western researcher is Dr. David Eisenberg, a Harvard Medical fellow who has spent several years in China, studying their medical practices and tracking down demonstrations of *chi kung*. Several of his experiences are shared in *Encounters With*

Qi[8] and he is so obviously skeptical throughout his many encounters that his observations strongly suggest the reality of *chi kung*. Like the Tibetan monks studied by Benson (in fact, Benson accompanied Eisenberg during part of his studies), Chinese *chi kung* masters learn to generate extra quantities of energy and channel it toward physical demonstrations, including the moving of objects at a distance. They also claim that *chi kung* is the explanation for many psychic phenomena, such as telepathy and clairvoyance. Though Dr. Eisenberg feels that he saw no 'proof' of *chi*, he was clearly impressed enough to write his book and give it the title that he did. He feels strongly that it would be well worth our while to accept China's invitation and vigorously investigate the claims of *chi kung* masters.

There is already, here in the West, strong evidence for the existence of energy fields which radiate through and beyond the human body, as well as evidence that they can be measured, and that a person's internal condition can be gauged from such measurements. There is already evidence that interpersonal communication at a distance, and the movement of external objects, is possible through these energy fields. There is already evidence that the bio-energy field is strongly affected by the flow of emotions and by our mental processes. There is already evidence that an organism's energy is adversely effected by many environmental influences, including common electrical currents found in any home. There is already evidence that this energy is a vital part of the healing process. There is a great deal of evidence that the energy field somehow functions as an organizing matrix in the bodies of people, animals, and plants. Yet, as impressive as the research is[9] and as important to the working of the body as energy undoubtedly is, it is still not a part of any Western anatomy books, and systems and concepts of 'energy medicine' are still looked upon rather condescendingly by most doctors and medical researchers.

Some of this reluctance to accept the concept of a basic, vital bio-energy stems precisely from the fact that it has had such a long and experimentally unfulfilling past. Like the boy who cried wolf until nobody would listen, far too many have enthusiastically exclaimed about this special vital force without holding definitive proof or conclusive results. Also, having its roots in antiquity leads many skeptics to the conclusion that it

is an antiquated concept. Nor does it help that it is central to
the healing systems of shamans, witch doctors, medicine people,
and most if not all non-technological cultures. Finally, alas, it is
quite true that it has often been a favored notion for quacks of
all kinds. (Which has resulted in some very sincere and serious-
minded people being branded and persecuted as quacks, for
instance Anton Mesmer and Wilhelm Reich.)

An even larger problem has been that most of the evidence
for such energy (and, until the last fifty years, all of the evidence)
has been subjectively attained. Since Western science is firmly
rooted in the demands of total objectivity — that any evidence
be derived from external sources and independent of human
thoughts and feelings — and since for the past three hundred
years Western medicine has been derived solely from such science,
there quite simply is very little *acceptable* evidence of such
energy. There is only a lot of hearsay and speculation, some
interesting stories and amusing anecdotes, but certainly no good
hard data, and most certainly nothing which could be expected
to advance the cause of medicine. Thus a wealth of experience
such as my own, that of acupuncturists, *chi kung* masters, yogic
adepts, accomplished faith healers, shamans the world over,
clairvoyants, sensitives, psychics, dowsers, and those with auric
vision, is all pooh-poohed as poor science and placed on the shelf
with Bigfoot and UFO's. Medical science closes its eyes to what
may well be *the single most important fact about the body.*

This is not meant as a criticism of science per se, nor do
I wish in any way to diminish or devalue the extraordinary
accomplishments of modern medicine. What I do wish to suggest,
very strongly, is that a full and comprehensive understanding of
this basic bio-energy is simply not possible within the confines
and demands of total objectivity. Furthermore, I would suggest
the human body is the very best instrument for studying this
vital energy, that the individual human being, through thoroughly
subjective processes, is the very best means for exploring, evaluating
and, to whatever degree it is possible, quantifying such energy.
This is not to say that research laboratories, technological devices,
and objectively obtained data will not be important in our
searching, but that we must pay attention to and be willing to
learn from the first-hand reports of those who have personally

explored energy in its various movements and manifestations through the mediums of their own bodies.

Bad science, indeed! But is it really? Science is basically any area of knowledge which deals with a body of facts which have been systematically derived and organized, and which show the operation of general laws. At the heart of all science is the scientific method, the method of research in which a problem is identified, relevant data is gathered, an hypothesis is formulated, and the hypothesis is empirically tested. Testing something empirically means verifying it through experiment or experience. So science does not, by definition, rule out the veracity of subjectively attained data, nor the idea that through such information one may reach a truer understanding of the world. It is only in the Western world during the past three hundred years of the Cartesian-industrial-technological scientific revolution that the idea of total objectivity has taken such hold, and that the notion of a clear and distinct separation between the objective scientific observer and 'the world out there' has been so firmly insisted upon. While that viewpoint has yielded some very practical and spectacular results, it is not a totally accurate description of reality nor the only way to do 'good science.'

As already mentioned, this has been apparent in the world of quantum physics for some time now. Physicists have gradually been coming to grips with the fact that total objectivity is a myth, that it is impossible to truly remove the observer and his subjective processes from the world that he is observing, and that, in fact, the very act and manner of observing the world changes it in some way. The world described by quantum mechanics is not at all the predictable, clockwork, precise world of Newton and Descartes. Rather, it is world shot full of human thought and human values, a world in which the observer and the observed turn out to be two faces of a single organism, inextricably linked and connected, each forever affecting the other.

Many will say that, while this may all be well and true for the special atomic world being studied by quantum physicists, it is not at all relevant for the day-to-day physical reality being studied by the other sciences, and that in our daily, common-sense world, total objectivity is possible and its benefits obvious. Such critics will deride any attempts to formulate a 'quantum biology,' an approach to the body which embraces and utilizes the concepts of quantum physics. In so doing, they simply ignore the well-documented works of scientists such as Benson, Burr, Ravitz, and Becker, in addition to well-documented phenomena such as spontaneous remission of illness, faith healing, acupuncture, biofeedback, hypnosis, and the placebo response, all events which point to the powerfully causative effects of the individual's subjective processes. Thus, instead of studying and learning to apply the obviously potent placebo response, medical researchers go to great lengths to control it out of the picture; instead of really investigating and attempting to sort out what actually happens in the many, many cases of people recovering inexplicably from catastrophic illnesses, we find these cases all lumped together under the rubric of 'spontaneous remission,' and that's that! Like the scientists lambasted by Einstein for drilling only where the drilling is easy, too many doctors and researchers tend to steer away from any data which is hard to measure, not readily applicable, or difficult to deal with on personal terms.

As stated above, until we free ourselves of the confines and demands of total objectivity, we may never even experience the existence of the body's basic bio-energy, much less come to understand it and work with it. If we fail to understand this energy, then we will perforce fail to understand a great many phenomena which are rooted in energy. As, for instance, the practice of firewalking.

In previous chapters, I have described the two factors which I feel are always present in successful firewalkers: a clear intention to actually walk on the fire, and a firm belief in the body's safety. While these factors may explain the psycho-emotional cause of successful firewalking, they do not answer the more compelling question of why exactly the flesh does not burn. I believe that the body's vital energy is the agent of protection during a firewalk. The state or condition of the body's vital energy system is determined by the individual's consciousness (intention and belief), and the energy then mediates between the feet and the coals to prevent burning. That is: the human body is infused with and surrounded by a substantive energy field, and it is within the capacity of that energy field, under certain conditions, to protect the body from otherwise harmful circumstances and to empower the body in extraordinary behaviors.

I have been led to this explanation of the firewalk by several different experiences. The first was my own long history with energy. Fifteen years of personally exploring this energy, within my own body and the bodies of my clients, plus all that I have been able to learn from so many other 'energy-explorers,' has left me no doubt that, where the human body is concerned, virtually anything is possible and energy is the source. I have seen convincing evidence for both instantaneous healing and spontaneous remission from 'incurable' illnesses. I have witnessed accomplished martial artists perform feats of strength which simply cannot be explained in terms of muscle size. The efficacy of the ancient science of acupuncture has been demonstrated to me time and time again. In all of these and in so many other phenomena that I am aware of, the evidence points to the existence of a bio-electric energy field and the vast possibilities that it enables. So the notion that energy could empower a person to walk safely through hot coals came quite easily to me.

There are also the personal reports from firewalkers around the world. The Kalahari Kung speak of *num*, which they define simply as 'the healing energy,' and say that when your *num* is 'boiling over' (at full strength), then the fire cannot hurt you. In Greece, the firedancers say that you must first be filled with the spirit of Saint Constantine, and go on to describe this state, much as the Kung do, as a warm current which flows through the body. Similar reports of being filled with, or possessed by, spirit come from many other firewalking cultures, and while the name for the spirit changes, the actual descriptions of how it feels are very much the same. I have spoken with dozens and dozens of firewalkers in America, and I often hear the same descriptions of warm, tingling currents flowing within the body, or descriptions of the body surrounded by brilliant radiant light. Thus, I have found that most firewalkers, regardless of their cultural background, tend to describe the physical sensations of the experience in very similar terms. I have further noticed that those descriptions are the same as the descriptions by people of the living bio-energy in all of the other energy phenomena that I have studied, including my own experience as described at the beginning of this chapter.

Another telling piece of evidence for the existence of energy is that even hair does not necessarily burn during a firewalk. Though I have seen firewalkers stand still in coals up to their ankles, I have found that the hair along the lower legs and on top of the toes is usually not even slightly singed. One man actually lay down in the coals, the back of his head sinking into the heat, and upon later inspection I found that his hair was unaffected. While I have yet to witness it, there are reports of firewalkers from other cultures who actually shower live coals upon their heads, again without the slightest burning of hair. Knowing the ease with which hair burns, there obviously must be some very potent form of protection in such instances. Given that hair is essentially dead matter, it is hard to imagine that the protection is somehow coming from chemical changes within the body (as some firewalkers have theorized). Rather, the notion of a protective energy field surrounding the body, including the hair, is quite compelling.

It appears that clothing is likewise immune to burning during a firewalk. Again, there are reports from other cultures of people who trail linen robes through the fire without any burning. I have witnessed two different people go rather slowly through the coals on crutches, without causing the slightest damage to the rubber tips of the crutches. I know of several instances when a person has forgotten to remove a band-aid from the sole of his or her foot, only to discover later that it was totally unaffected by the fire. And, I have watched (and filmed) one person actually sit in the coals for several long seconds, again without even slightly singeing the fabric of his pants. Thus, as with hair but even more so, we are led to think in terms of an aura of protection which encompasses the body and anything else within its immediate range. And again, *energy* fits very well as an explanation.

To begin to understand how energy could actually protect the body, its hair, and its clothing from extreme temperature, or perform the many other wonders for which it is accredited, we should certainly look first to those who have had the most experience with it. However, before doing so it is important to realize that the various maps of this energy, and the systems for working with it that have been devised by so many different cultures and 'energy explorers,' will invariably have their differences. It must be kept in mind that the map is not the territory, and that the very best of attempts to systematically represent energy will of necessity be influenced by the subjective processes (i.e.

intentions and beliefs) of the individuals involved, and thus will tend to differ from other such representations.

For instance, the Taoist tradition of China and the Yogic tradition of India are two of the most ancient approaches to the body and its energy known to our world, each the end result of thousands of years of ongoing research, each representing the accumulated experience of thousands and thousands of individual energy explorers, and each a very concise and well-developed system, with complex mappings of the energy and effective means for working with it. One might expect that, with so much combined wisdom, the two systems would have arrived at pretty much the same place, with similar, if not identical, descriptions of this world of energy. In fact, there are some very distinct differences between the two systems in their ways of mapping the energy and in their approaches toward working with it. The thoroughly objective scientist who believes that there is a thoroughly objective reality 'out there' which may eventually be fully delineated by a thoroughly objective observer will frown skeptically at these variations in systems, seeing them as proof that all this bio-energy stuff is only so much imagination and not really physical at all. To such scientists, the notion of two thorough investigations of the same phenomenon coming up with two different representations is adequate proof that one or both of the investigators must be wrong.

My own hypothesis is this. There is a very subtle bio-energy which radiates throughout the human body, filling every cell, governing each organ, regulating all of the body's processes, and surrounding the body as a protective aura, or energy field. Under certain circumstances, this energy has the capacity to empower the body in extraordinary ways, such as firewalking, miraculous healing, or sitting naked in the snow and generating heat. This energy is very much connected to and interactive with the individual's conscious and unconscious processes, and thus will tend to reflect the unique consciousness of each individual, and of individual cultures. The very nature of this energy is such that it will only be understood by a science which has eliminated the separation between subjective and objective realities — a science which fully honors and expects the co-creative input of each individual human being, rather than trying to factor that input out, or ignore it altogether.

Our study of energy begins with the understanding that we will invariably encounter many different maps along the way, and that our work initially is to search among the different systems for any common truths or unifying threads that might be found. My own search has turned up two such truths upon which virtually all approaches to energy agree. The first is that energy is the connecting link between the body and the mind. The second is that energy serves as the organizing matrix or controlling intelligence for the physical body.

Energy is the connecting link between the body and the mind. Leaving aside the whole notion of bio-energy for a moment, this can be a difficult statement for many people to accept, simply because the very idea that the body and mind are connected is highly suspect, if not downright ludicrous, especially in Western culture. There has a been a long history in the West of well-reasoned thought that carefully separates mind from body, spirit from matter, mankind from nature, organic from inorganic, living from non-living. This separation finds its roots in the very beginning of Judeo-Christian culture, in *Genesis*, when God created man by breathing life into a lump of clay. It reached its culmination thousands of years later when Descartes offered his famous pronouncement, "I think, therefore I am."

The underlying philosophy of Descartes' statement is that we humans are essentially living, thinking, non-material beings who come into, inhabit, and enliven the basically dead, material stuff of the body. The mind and the body are understood to be two totally different things, irreducibly separate, which join together very tenuously for a short time to allow the miracle of human life. The mind, sparkling with a will for eternal life, is the good guy in the unfolding drama, while the body, so very imperfect and doomed eventually to fail and die, is a necessary evil. The rest of the world is unthinking, nonspiritual matter, an exquisite clockwork mechanism set into motion eons ago by a benevolent God to serve as a playground/workshop for us humans.

This idea that the mind is separate from the body, that the spiritual is separate from the material, is easily one of the single most important thoughts of the past three hundred years, for without it most of the scientific-industrial revolution would not have been possible. It is rare, for instance, to find a culture which believes strongly that the mind and the body are of one essence and connected, and which is also able to develop the practice of autopsy, a vital contribution to the progess of Western medicine. For such cultures, like the Chinese, Egyptians, and Hindus, each of whom developed highly-sophisticated medical practices, a 'dead' body must be treated with all of the respect and reverence of a 'living' body. (The very notion that we might learn more from the study of a dead body than from the reports of a living energy-explorer is incomprehensible to such cultures.) Likewise, it would be impossible for a culture which experiences the living spiritual energy in all things, such as the American Indian culture, to bulldoze, dynamite, pave, mine, dam, and pollute the Earth the way that industrial man has done, and continues to do. Thus, much of the vast progress and the many technological wonders of our current age would never have been possible without there first being a culture which believed strongly in the idea that mind and body, spirit and matter, man and nature, are irreducibly separate.

It is a very powerful idea. If only it had the added advantage of being true! Yet, as is becoming increasingly clear to such disciplines as quantum physics, holistic medicine, neuro-immunology, and ecology, and as many native cultures have experientially known all along, the dividing lines between body and mind, spirit and matter, and man and nature have always been false and misleading. By all means, such divisions can appeal sometimes to our common sense, and are useful for the development of certain lifestyles, but in the final analysis we humans are connected mind and body, and are ultimately connected to each other and to the Earth itself. The medium of that connection, which makes us whole beings and connects us to the rest of our world, is energy.

During my years of exploring energy, I have made one basic observation over and over again. Whenever I meet a person who has had a direct personal experience of energy, he or she will invariably profess to a belief that the mind and the body are connected as one. Whenever I find a person arguing strongly for the separation of mind and body, it is invariably the case that such a person has seldom if ever experienced energy. That is, the belief that the mind and body are separate is not compatible with an experience of energy, while the belief that they are connected is. To say it another way, since energy is the medium of connection between the body and the mind, to argue vigorously for the separation of mind and body is to argue energy out of experiential existence. To vigorously argue against the existence of energy is to create and experience that the mind and body are divided and separate.

Remember the skeptical mind and the blinders that it can impose upon a person's perception and experience of reality. Over the past few hundred years, the West has developed a firmly entrenched posture of skepticism toward any notions of bio-energy or the whole body/mind, and will point to its extraordinary scientific achievements, all attained without the slightest accommodation to such theories, as proof that these notions are all so much 'wishful vitalism' and uninformed imagination. In so doing, Western people have lost the fundamental experience of wholeness — the common source which connects all of life — and have lost all sense of, and capacity for, living harmoniously with the world. We may very well turn out to be dead right about the separation of mind and body as our divided nature blows the world to pieces!

On the other hand, to adopt an attitude which says that mind and body are of one common source, essentially connected, the two sides of a single coin, is to open to the living energy which is the common source, the medium of connection, the very coin itself. Likewise, the more strongly one believes in the reality of an all-pervasive energy, the more experientially apparent it becomes that the mind and body are connected as one, that the human family is connected as one, that all life upon this planet (and rocks are alive!) is fundamentally connected as one. This all-connecting oneness is the essence of what Aldous Huxley called 'The Perennial Philosophy,' and for eons the rewards and benefits of this philosophy of wholeness have been obvious to all who have fully embraced it.

To understand how the mind and the body can be one whole entity and yet appear to be so very different and apart, we must first understand the phenomenon of vibration and the way that it affects our world. As an example, we know from studying nature that H_2O is a molecule formed by two hydrogen atoms interacting in a specific manner with one oxygen atom, and that when the atoms of this molecule are caused to move at a certain rate of vibration, they manifest as what we call water. We further know that if the atoms are caused to move at a much faster rate of vibration, they will manifest as steam, and that if they are caused to move at a much slower rate of vibration, they will manifest as ice. Thus, one basic stuff, H_2O, can manifest as three different states, with qualities ranging from the bare substantialness of steam to the rock-hard concreteness of ice, depending entirely upon the rate of molecular vibration of that stuff.

I believe that energy is the basic 'stuff' of the human being. At its quickest rate of vibration, it manifests as the mind, the light and ethereal and apparently non-physical realm of thoughts and ideas, of dreams and imagination. At its slowest rate of vibration it manifests as the dense, structured, and, it would seem, purely material realm of the physical body. But the two realms are never really totally distinct and separate. Rather, the body contains within it the seeds of the mind, just as the mind contains within it the tracks of the body. The mind and the body are of one single essence, two ends of single spectrum of vibration, with energy as the single thread running through the whole, the living-medium which, according to its differing rates of vibration, is manifesting here as mind, here as body, and here as everything which lies between and beyond.

Having experienced that the mind and the body are essentially whole, with energy as the medium of connection, virtually all energy explorers will agree that *energy acts as the organizing matrix for the physical body*. By this it is meant that within energy is contained the intelligence, the information, and the overall pattern from which the body is grown and maintained. Thus, at the beginning of an individual human life, at the primordial meeting of egg and sperm, there is also in attendance an individualized field or body of energy which carries all of the data the new embryo will need to form and develop along human lines. (Remember Burr's work with frog eggs. He found that he could detect different voltage gradients along different axes of the eggs, and that the frog's nervous system always grew along the strongest axis.) Throughout the life of the body, the energy field continues to operate as the organizing matrix or pattern, governing the body's processes and functions, its limits and its possibilities, its reasons for illness and its means of healing.

A skilled acupuncturist can detect and diagnose blockages of flow in a person's energy field (the *chi* meridians) long before any actual physical symptoms have begun to manifest, and then will work with the *chi* to prevent problems before they show up. Even when a problem physically presents itself, the acupuncturist's major focus is still to work with the energy behind the symptom, rather than the symptom itself. The underlying understanding of this and all energy healing systems is that energy is primary to the physical body, governing all of its workings, and that all sickness and health ultimately originate in energy and its operating principles.

This leads us to the mind. Just as energy has a causative impact upon the body, so, to some extent, does the mind have a causative impact upon energy. Some will say that the mind is totally at cause, that thought is totally creative, and that anything which we persist in thinking will become manifest in our bodies and within our world. Such people also tend to leap from "I walked on fire," to "I can do anything I want!" On the other extreme are those who say that thoughts have no impact at all upon the person's body, much less upon the external world; that it basically doesn't matter what one thinks.

My own experience has led me to believe that the mind certainly has a great deal of impact upon the energy fields which govern the human body and the world in which it moves. I stop a bit short of saying that the mind is totally creative, for there is too much direct evidence against the idea that if one thinks something, it will immediately happen. Yet, as I pointed out in Chapter 4, given that we are passing through great evolutionary changes, the moment we pronounce limitations upon the creative power of the mind, we may, through the power of our own pronouncements, be creating those very limitations. So I am rather careful about investing heavily in any such limitations, and am keeping my mind open to its furthest reaching possibilities.

It *is* clear to me that the mind and body are derived from the same energy source. As human beings we are fundamentally whole and connected, and the various parts of ourselves — the bones, blood, flesh, organs, thoughts, ideas, images, dreams, aspirations, intentions, beliefs, ever-flowing feelings, deep-running emotions, spirit, soul, highest self — are in fact just different reflections of one essential living reality. Through the connecting medium of energy, a change in one aspect of this whole system will automatically reflect as a change in every other aspect; this is the basic tenet of the holistic sciences. Since the mind is the part of our experience which we are most able to consciously change and control, it follows that the mind very definitely has a large measure of creative, causative impact upon the body.

To reiterate: mind and body are two extremes of one vibratory spectrum of energy. At different rates of vibration, this one common energy manifests as the different 'parts' of a human being. Communication between all of the parts is constant and instantaneous, and any change in one part will always be reflected through the medium of energy to influence a similar change throughout the whole. The mind is the part of the human experience which is most accessible to conscious control and thus a vital key to the formation, growth, and maintenance of the body, and to the ongoing creative process of the individual.

With such an undertanding, it is not surprising that placebos work, for a mind which strongly believes that things will get better is a body getting better. Likewise, in the face of the most gloomy of prognoses, the mind which forms a clear and unwavering intention to live on is a body living on. A mind which wants very much to walk on hot coals and firmly believes that it is safe to do so is a body walking through the fire without burning The work before us is to continue our exploration of this living energy world where body and mind merge and interact, where placebos work their magic and spontaneous remissions occur, where flesh, mind, and fire all come together to create burning or not-burning. We stand poised on the threshold of a quantum biology — a clear and practical science which understands and embraces the body's living bio-energy fields. The rewards of our study promise to extend beyond medicine to touch our whole world.

Ever since Einstein's $E=mc^2$ was so forcefully demonstrated above the city of Hiroshima, even us civilized folk have known that the material world is infused with energy, though we find it easier to think of the energy in hydrogen atoms and oil fields than of the living-energy in trees, animals, and human beings. We have learned that even the smallest speck of matter contains within it vast quantities of energy, and we have developed means for tapping that energy in great expansive bursts, both frightening and awesome in their implications. Ironically, we worry over our dwindling energy reserves and fight an endless variety of energy wars. Truly, we are dying of thirst in a sea of water.

It is time for us to look to the human form, to our own bodies, and to wonder just how much energy they represent, and how many megatons of vital force are carried within *each cell*. What are the means for tapping and releasing this vital bio-energy? How do we cause it to explode into creativity? What is the role of the mind, the breath, the heart, the spirit? As we develop the ways of human fusion, just how far will energy take us, and what new worlds will lie within our reach?

eight

THE CHALLENGE
OF LIFE

*'Adaptation energy' is a basic feature of life itself. The length
of the human lifespan appears to be primarily determined by the
amount of available adaptation energy. A better understanding
of it promises to show us how to improve recovery from any
kind of exhaustion and perhaps even to prolong life.[1]*

*In arguing for the salutary effects of danger, Dr. Sol Roy
Rosenthal . . . divides the sports world into two categories. There
are RE (risk exercise) sports such as skiing and skydiving, and
non-RE sports such as tennis and golf. Dr. Rosenthal notes that
the same amount of energy invested in the two kinds of sports
by the same person is likely to produce quite different results.
For example, tennis tends to exhaust, while skiing exhilarates.
Moreover, RE sports are likely to encourage a healthy attitude
toward winning and losing. While the enjoyment of non-RE sports
such as golf and volleyball often is tied up with winning, sports
involving risk are generally enjoyed for their own sakes . . .
"All forms of exercise are excellent," Dr. Rosenthal says, "but
risk exercise is essential."[2]*

*The alternative to fear is not some great answer that will
ultimately prevent our being chronically and mortally afraid,
which we all are, and which people are in general. Such knowledge
is not even possible. The alternative is to recognize fear as an
ordinary mechanism of the body beyond which we can, and
should, in any moment feel and breathe.[3]*

At some point during every firewalk I lead, I take the time
to go through the group, asking the participants to state as clearly
as they can just what brought them to the firewalk, and to share
what their intentions are in wanting to be part of such an experience. I have now listened to over two thousand people state
their intentions, and can say without any hesitation or uncertainty

that the main reason that people want to walk on fire is to help them in some way overcome their fears, or at least better understand them.

Probably the second most common purpose for wanting to walk on fire is the one I introduced in Chapter 2: the individual wants to vividly experience making a vital contribution to the co-creative process. Other common intentions people bring to the firewalk are: wanting to feel they are connected to the Earth, wanting to give their skeptical mind a strong jolt, or just wanting to satisfy their curiosity. But the most compelling reason, far and away, is fear. People come to the firewalk because the very idea of it frightens them, and they sense that if they can do this fearful thing, then perhaps they will have discovered a path through many of their other fears.

I suspect this is true for firewalkers everywhere. While different cultures certainly have different understandings of the firewalk, and different ways of describing its purpose, for the individual who is actually about to step forward onto the fire, there is almost always going to be some feeling of fear. This is true because all of humanity shares a very sane and healthy instinct which counsels not to touch fire. Overriding viscerally experienced instinct is always frightening. Furthermore, as mentioned previously, in every report of the firewalk I have ever encountered there has been some mention of the fact that people do sometimes get badly burned. In the face of possible serious injury and pain, the universal human response is to experience fear.

This is definitely true for myself. As I tell most of my groups, and to the chagrin of some listeners, although I have done this more than a hundred times, the fear has by no means gone away. Yes, it helps that I have done it so often, that I have seen so many others successfully do it, and that I have managed to understand the safety of the practice as well as I do. I have watched people stand still up to their ankles in the coals, pick coals up and mash them between their palms, do cartwheels, sit down, lie down, and I have done many of these things myself. However, I have also been badly burned on occasion, as have many others, and all that I have been through has left me no doubt that my success or failure at a firewalk is rooted in my own mind. To the extent that I do not absolutely know myself on a given night (and I never do), I am at some degree of risk.

Having been through the downside of that risk too often, I rarely get through a walk without encountering any fear at all. (And on the nights that I am not frightened for my own feet, I can still be frightened for others.) So fear is very much a part of the firewalking experience, and discovering a way to overcome or move through the fear is an essential step for firewalkers everywhere.

———————————————

I have found it helpful when dealing with fear to view it as a two-phase process. Thus, I will be referring first to *excitement* and then to *contraction*, two very different psycho-physical experiences which we tend to run together under the single heading of 'fear.'

The word 'excite' comes from the Latin *excitare*, meaning "to call forth, to summon, to put into motion or activity, to arouse." In physics it means "to raise (a nucleus, atom, etc.) to a higher energy state" and in physiology it means "to produce or increase a response." For our purposes I will define 'excitement' as *a generation and release of vital bio-energy which we experience anytime we perceive a threat or challenge to our well-being.* Something happens in our world which we, on some level, decide is threatening. It does not have to in fact be a threat, and many of the things which we fear are not. It is enough that we believe or perceive that we are threatened. The perception of a threat or challenge automatically causes a generation and release, an expansive rush, an *excitement*, of vital bio-energy, the same energy which I discussed in the previous chapter.

In addition to the expansion of energy within the body, excitement is usually accompanied by a number of physiological changes: the adrenal glands flood the body with adrenaline, the heartbeat quickens, respiration increases, the pupils dilate, all of the senses become sharper and more finely attuned, and every muscle in the body slightly contracts. All of this happens in the split second after we perceive a threat or challenge to our well-being, or ongoing survival, and all of it — the rush of energy and the bodily manifestations — prepares us for action, giving us what we will need to deal with the perceived threat or challenge.

Scientists often call this whole process the fight-or-flight response, in reference to the two major ways that we have historically dealt with the various threats and challenges of our world. If, for instance, one of our ancestors were walking down life's path when suddenly a saber-toothed tiger loomed ahead, huge and undeniably threatening, such a person would experience a strong surge of excitement, which would give her what she needed, hopefully, to either fight harder than she had ever fought before, or run faster than she had ever run before. If, years later, she were crossing the road and suddenly noticed a large truck speeding toward her, she would experience the very same surge of excitement — adrenaline pulsing through her body, her heart beating faster, her breath deeper, her senses sharply focused, and her muscles contracting — all in the single moment before she leapt out of the way of the truck. If she were given the news that an invading army were poised on the outskirts of her city, she would again experience all of the same bodily manifestations of excitement, empowering her in the next moment toward fighting hard or running fast.

Excitement is of obvious benefit and importance to us, for it is essential to our ongoing survival. In fact, throughout the entire spectrum of life, from the lowliest amoeba to humanity itself, we see this same program in each and every organism: *threaten or challenge the ongoing survival or well-being of the organism, and it will respond by generating and releasing extra energy to meet the threat through either fight or flight.* If we block a plant's access to the sun, it will, having no recourse to fight, immediately begin to generate energy to do its very best to move back into the light. If we change the salinity of a bacterium's culture, it will immediately begin to generate energy to do its very best to move to better water. These are basic automatic responses found at the most basic levels of life, automatic and immediate responses to any threats to the organism's survival, programmed responses which operate as survival mechanisms to support the continuation of the organism, the species, and life itself.

As organisms increase in complexity, so do their definitions of 'well-being,' or ongoing survival. In essence, an organism will generate the energy of excitement and the fight-or-flight response upon being presented with any threat or challenge to its individual bodily survival, or to anything which it experiences as necessary to its ongoing well-being. Thus, we find creatures fighting or flighting to protect their young, to protect their food source, to protect their territory, to protect the queen mother, to protect the hive, to protect the herd, or to protect their master. While the definitions of well-being may shift from species to species, and while the actual means of fighting and/or flighting are of infinite number and incredible cleverness, the principle always remains the same: threaten or challenge the ongoing survival or well-being of an organism and it will respond by generating and releasing vital energy to meet the threat or challenge, energy which will be spent to empower the organism in fight and/or flight.

This is so critical to our understanding of the firewalk that it bears repeating: when the ongoing survival of a living organism is in any way threatened, or when a living organism is challenged to either adapt to a changing situation or suffer unwanted consequences, it will respond by generating and releasing, by calling forth, summoning, stirring up, arousing — exciting — vital bio-energy to meet the threat or challenge. Life cannot and does not program for failure. To the contrary, while all living organisms must eventually die, they will generally continue to vigorously strive for ongoing survival right to the very end. (Though humans, and some other more evolved creatures, are capable of 'going gently into the night,' and of conceiving and committing suicide.) This striving for ongoing survival, this most basic law of living organisms, carries with it the mechanisms to generate the energy needed to optimize success.

In the human kingdom, we find that at times this energy of excitement optimizes success in ways that are simply extraordinary. There is, for instance, a well-documented phenomenon called 'hysterical strength,' the classic example being a woman who lifts an automobile off of her trapped child in a single, unthinking moment of stark terror. In all such reports, the events happen to ordinary people who can in no way repeat their actions later. They simply did the inexplicable, spontaneously, and quite contrary to their rational minds and to their day-to-day physical capabilities. What I am suggesting is that it is the strong jolt of bio-energy, the rush of excitement that surges through a person's body as a result of the extreme threat to her well-being, that empowers such 'impossible' feats.

I have, over the past few years, collected many such stories, admittedly anecdotes, but compelling in their numbers, in the sincerity of the tellers, and in the single current of excitement that I see running throughout. A woman runs barefoot through a parking lot full of broken bottles and glass to avoid an attacker, and later discovers not the slightest scratch on her feet. A man jumps into below-freezing waters to help the passengers of a plane wreck, and steps out of the water fifteen minutes later, his body pulsing with strong heat. A child simply stops the bleeding of his severely cut arm because his father told him that "we just have to stop this bleeding." In all such cases it is the energy of excitement that empowers the person, the energy which is always there in potential but which ordinarily only comes into play when the person experiences a strong threat or challenge to his or her well-being.

People who have been in combat situations, along with firefighters and police officers, often have 'impossible' experiences that defy simple explanation, which are written off as hallucinations or just not talked about at all since their worldview is incapable of encompassing such events. Likewise, professional athletes. In his book, *The Ultimate Athlete*, George Leonard says that if you can get professional athletes beyond the locker room cliches, and to trust that you will not have them carted off to the shrink, they will often report experiences which simply defy rational explanation. Again, the common thread running through such experiences is the extreme challenge to the person's ongoing survival or well-being.

Such stories should not surprise us, for as I recounted in the previous chapter, our bio-energy can and will empower us in truly extraordinary behaviors. What is different here is that these people are not Tibetan monks or yogic adepts or *chi-kung* masters or accomplished energy healers. Rather, they are average human beings in a very common state of fear. While master energy explorers typically learn to generate and utilize quantities of bio-energy at will, in ways they claim are open to all, it is also true that *the human organism is designed to spontaneously generate and utilize quantities of bio-energy when needed to support its ongoing survival*. Thus, rather than being the necessarily unpleasant experience we so often feel it to be, fear (as its first phase of excitement) is in fact an absolutely essential piece of the human equation, and has the potential of being a greatly empowering force for good in our lives.

Unfortunately, we all too often fail to use the energy of

excitement. Instead, we actually impede and inhibit its function, and in so doing we change it into the second phase of fear which I call *contraction*. While excitement is the generation and release of vital bio-energy to meet a threat or challenge, 'contraction' I define as *the constriction and inhibition of bio-energy which occurs anytime we fail to act in its presence*. When a situation occurs which we perceive as threatening, we immediately begin to experience an increase of energy to meet the challenge. If we fail to fight, or take flight, or take some other action, or use the extra energy in our system, then that energy begins to collapse inward and tighten, or harden within us, constricting and inhibiting, becoming the stuff of contraction, the second phase of fear.

In time, this constriction and inhibition of bio-energy wreaks havoc within our bodies. It becomes muscles tightening into rigid knots, and joints stiffening and losing flexibility. It becomes stress-lines etched into a person's face, arteries hardening within a person's heart, and holes burning into a person's stomach. It can crystallize as stones within a gall bladder or kidney, or cause a blood vessel to burst inside a skull. It very definitely can depress the functioning of the immune system. It can precipitate the onset of cancer *anywhere* within the body. The medical community refers to this whole phenomenon as 'unresolved stress and tension,' and the list of the diseases and illnesses which are considered to be 'stress-related' is constantly growing longer. (It also must be conservative, given Western medicine's pronounced reluctance to assign non-physical causes to bodily problems.)

It was the pioneering work of Canadian physician and researcher, Hans Selye, which first introduced and largely sub-stantiated the notion of stress for the Western world. Selye began his investigation of stress in the 1930s and published his major book, *The Stress of Life*, twenty years later. The core of Selye's work is that living organisms display a General Adaptation Syndrome (G.A.S.), or three-stage response to any stresses (challenges or threats) placed upon them. The first stage he called the alarm reaction, and it correlates closely with what I have been calling excitement. The next stage he called resistance, and in my terms it has aspects of both phases of fear. The third stage he called exhaustion, and it describes the culmination of what I am calling the second phase of fear — contraction. Selye called this syndrome general because it was displayed by all living organisms in response to any stresses placed upon them. He then went on to demonstrate that a great many specific problems can be traced to this general living response. Thus the idea of unresolved stress and tension, the energy of unsuccessful adaptation, made its way into our medical model.

Selye was very adamant in stating that stress itself is not the problem, that in fact stress is an essential feature of all biological activity. He titled his book as he did because he wanted people to know that stress is not an evil invader and body destroyer which needs to be fought and overcome, but that it is a very basic aspect of life which through better understanding could enhance our lives. All living organisms face an unending chain of challenging or threatening situations to which they must adapt if they would go on living and all living organisms display a General Adaptation Syndrome. They automatically generate and mobilize energy to meet the challenges of life, and to support their ongoing successful adaptation. To the extent that they are successful, they mostly do not progress beyond Selye's alarm reaction or the more energizing aspects of the stage of resistance. The generation of stress/energy is well used and the organism lives on, possibly stronger and wiser for the experience. To the extent that they fail, they tend to deteriorate into the stage of exhaustion, the energy of stress now working very much against them.

For most living organisms, I use the word 'fail' to mean that they have failed in their efforts to adapt. For the individual, that usually means loss of life, loss of food, loss of territory, etc. If this failure is characteristic of an entire species then the species will die out, for evolution tends to favor adaptability above all else. As cruel as it may seem, there is a sense of natural justice about it all, and if a creature or a species dies, then it does so because it simply is not able to meet the challenges of a changing environment, and such is life. Still, I think it is important to note that the creature or species did not fail in terms of its own design, that it truly did the very best that it could, that it met the challenge of its changing world with the full force of its General Adaptation Syndrome, but that it failed because its own unique way of being was no longer integral with its world. Thus, we do not think that dinosaurs screwed up, or that the bald eagle is in the process of doing so. Rather, the world changed, and their very best efforts to adapt were not enough.

When we get to human beings however, we discover that we are creatures who are probably the most adaptable of all (though rats and cockroaches deserve some consideration) and yet, paradoxically, through our own special mode of consciousness we manage to greatly inhibit our natural energy of adaptation. Thus, while we certainly have our failures to adapt (i.e., we do the best we can but we are not integral with our world), we much more tragically tend to foul up and fail at the right use of our energy, and thus to fail unnecessarily. It is only with humans that we begin to feel the missed opportunity, the broken promise, the thwarted possibility. It is only ourselves, as humans, that we can see as clearly failing to live up to our potential, and only ourselves that we too often think have failed to do the best that we could. It is both the good news and the bad about us, the blessing and the curse, that yes!, we are co-creators of this world, and that Oh no!, we still do it so poorly.

I believe that much of our problem stems from our conscious and unconscious interference with the General Adaptation Syndrome. *We are causing the potential of excitement to become the debilitation of contraction,* and are misdirecting the energies of Selye's alarm reaction, habitually bringing ourselves into the stages of resistance and exhaustion. To the extent that this is true, we are not only failing to adapt, or to successfully integrate with our changing environment, we are failing to realize our potential, or to use our creative energies to the very best of our evolutionary possibilities. This is a problem which is woven into the very fabric of what it means to be human, and it is a problem which tends to increase in intensity the more civilized we become.

Think back to our ancestor confronting the saber-toothed tiger. The moment she saw the tiger, the powerful energy of excitement kicked into gear and she either ran very fast or fought very hard. If she got away or won the fight, then she successfully adapted to a change in her environment. If the tiger got her, then she failed to successfully adapt. Either way, she clearly experienced the energy of excitement and used it to the very best of her capabilities. It is very unlikely that she stood and worried anxiously over what she should do, or that she broke inappropriately into tears, or in any other way misused the excitement energy.

Rather, she perceived the threat, she generated the energy, and she acted.

Even civilized humans tend toward healthy and intelligent responses when the challenges are as clear and incisive as saber-toothed tigers. The problem is that they rarely are anymore. The things and events which challenge and threaten us are generally more abstract, more nebulous, more distant, and much more complex. While they certainly frighten us, stirring and stimulating the energies of adaptive response, they too often do not inspire obvious and immediate courses of action such as RUN FOR IT!, leaving us habitually collapsing into the state of contraction.

For instance, imagine sitting in a bank, on a Monday morning, the loan officer saying, "I'm very sorry, but we simply will not be able to give you that money you so desperately need." You will surely experience the energy of excitement at such a moment. You have been threatened; your ability to adapt to a changing world has been challenged; adrenaline will be released, your heart will beat faster, your blood pressure will rise, tension will mount, and the alarm reaction will be ringing away inside of you. However, you cannot punch the guy in such a situation, and it really does no good at all to go running out of the bank faster than you have ever run before.

Instead, what you usually do is shake his hand with a very polite "Thank-you," tighten up your tie, and walk out of the bank as coolly as you possibly can. Meanwhile, inside of you furiously rages that insidious bane of civilized man and woman — money worry. (WhatamIgonnado!WhatamIgonnado!WhatamI gonnado! . . .) For most of us, this particular challenge to our ability to adapt never goes away. Money has been shown to be the number one cause of divorce, which means that it is a very heavy pressure upon all relationships. Even as children (and some studies have indicated as fetuses), we are affected by the unresolved stresses and tensions of our parents' financial reality. From the time that we leave our parents' care and begin worrying for ourselves over that first 'first of the month,' on through our elderly years of social insecurity, our money fears rarely go completely away.

Thus, a common current running throughout our lives is the generation and release of our creative energies to meet the ongoing challenge of surviving financially. Those who experience such energies as excitement tend to be highly-motivated achievers. They feel the threat of financial problems and are stimulated — mentally, emotionally, and physically — into action. Other people, however, encounter the same financial threats, and experience the same stimulation of energy, but somewhere along the way they become habituated to feelings of powerlessness and hopelessness, and to ideas of limitation and lack. Instead of an excited "How am I going to get through it this time!" the habitual response to the money challenge becomes a collapsed and stuck "Oh God, why doesn't this ever go away?" Given enough time, we cease to even feel the phase of excitement; we simply live in a state of ongoing contraction.

Let us say you have now arrived home from the bank and you sit down to read your morning paper. There it is, in big, black, screaming letters: something that really pushes you into fear these days. Nuclear waste! Acid rain! The Middle East! Third-world debt! The arms race! AIDS! You feel some degree of threat or challenge, and some measure of excitement. But again, it is hard to see any obvious course of action. You may well feel powerless in the face of all of those problems, and so many more. You feel the threat but fail to act, and the energy of excitement collapses into chronic contraction.

The low-riding anxiety, the constant worry, the creeping, quiet desperation, the undercurrent of pessimistic doubt, the dark and heavy depression — these psycho-emotional states which are taken for granted by so many in our world — all begin with a challenge to adapt and the implicit arousal of bio-energy to meet that challenge. Our world presents us, from the moment of our birth, with an endless flow of changing variables to which we must successfully adapt, or suffer unwanted consequences. This is true for all living organisms. Our world also gives us, free and abundantly, the energy with which to meet each challenge to the very best of our unique and characteristic capabilities. When we fail to use this energy, and we constrict and inhibit its flow, stifling it and tightening it, then the energy literally constipates within us, becoming a poison to our system. If we do this chronically, and it becomes our lifestyle and our habitual way of reacting to the stresses of life, then we will eventually lose our ability to even feel excitement, and become inured to the experience and effects of contraction

Since the cause of contraction is the failure to act in the presence of excited energy, the most damaging situations are those that seem to offer no options or choices, situations that leave us feeling stuck and hopeless, unable to act. Such situations have become the norm of modern life. We are the world that grew up with the bomb, with the image of an anonymous finger poised upon a button that could destroy our entire planet — and nothing we can do about it! Talk about long-term, unresolved stress and tension! Add to that the realities of toxic waste, acid rain, the deforestation of the Amazon, the depletion of the ozone layer, the Middle East, the world economy, the 'greenhouse effect,' and AIDS, to name some awesome threats which seem to offer few options for constructive action, and you have all of the ingredients for a life of chronic contraction.

Part of our difficulty is that our age-old, instinctive responses of fighting or flighting when excited are simply no longer valid or viable. It is becoming clearer and clearer that we must give up the fight, that we must stop responding to our fears by bashing them with a club, that human beings must finally evolve beyond their ancient hostilities and violent interactions. It has always been true that those who live by the sword inevitably die by the sword; the hard yet ultimately liberating truth of our time is that if *any* people continue to live by the sword then we shall *all* perish by it. While governmental actions still make the largest splash and the media still gravitates toward the most unpleasant news, at the grass-roots level, where it *matters* most, more and more people are aware of this new truth. Thus, the choice to fight when in the state of excitement no longer works for most human beings.

Nor does the option of flight, for there is nowhere to run to escape the dangers and threats of our modern world. There are no more New Worlds to colonize, no more frontiers to settle. Most of our challenges are world-encompassing: polluted air and water, dwindling resources, economic tension, sexually transmitted disease, and planet-sized bombs. We cannot run from such threats for they are truly omnipresent. And we know it. Ironically, our fractional worldview has brought us such awesome threats that we are now compelled to begin thinking wholistically.

All of this adds up to a world in which the challenges are far more frightening than ever before and the options for con-

structive response are seemingly nonexistent. This in turn gives
us a world of men and women who are stimulated with the
energy of unceasing excitement while invariably collapsing toward
a state of chronic contraction. The bad news is that fight and
flight are outmoded and self-defeating responses to the threats
and challenges of life. The good news is that there are in fact
two other responses that are always available to us. *They are:*
grow or die.

We can surely die from this process. We can gape at the
personal and planetary terrors of our world, feeling helpless
and hopeless, contracting away from it all, constricting and
inhibiting our vital bio-energy. We can constantly hold back
and stifle ourselves, losing our capacity to truly feel excited,
until we are numbed to the many challenges, and joys, of this
life. We can become tightening knots of unresolved stress and
tension, hardening our muscles, stiffening our joints, impeding
our circulations, and depressing our immune systems. We can
cripple ourselves mentally, emotionally, and physically; we can
suppress ourselves sexually; we can create for ourselves a social
environment of manic unease. Ultimately, we can age prematurely
and die, for such is the means and the end of chronic contraction.

Or, we can grow. We can open ourselves totally to the
threats and challenges that surround us, feeling the excitement of
it all, reveling in the energy that is generated and released within
us, and then using that energy to act, to grow, to evolve, to
change, to become. *We can realize that this most fear-ridden of*
all ages is also the age of an unprecedented evolutionary leap,
and that the fear/energy/excitement we are feeling is the leap
itself in progress. The energy of fear can become the raw material
of our response, the very stuff of our adaptability, the leading
edge of our evolutionary growth. We can tremble in fear, surely,
and we can allow the trembling to increase and expand and to
carry us into and through empowered action.

This is exactly what I see happening at firewalks. Most
people do experience fear — a deep, visceral, instinctive fear —
at the thought of stepping forward onto hot coals. The rising
energy in a group is quite palpable as the moment for walking
nears. Those who flow with the rising energy, and grow with
excitement, either walk joyfully and successfully, or choose
not to walk but still feel awed by their experience. Those who

constrict and inhibit their energy, contracting inwardly, either walk with some degree of burning, or choose not to walk and feel that they have failed. The difference between success and failure at a firewalk, as in life, is not in our actions but in our chosen response to the energies inherent within the situation.

Most of us have grown up with and become accustomed to the idea that fear is the boogie man, something to be avoided as much as possible. We think that when we are afraid it means we are either doing something wrong or something wrong is about to be done to us. One way or another the feeling of fear is a bad and unwanted sign. We carry the ideal of a life without fear — enough money, a good marriage, the right job, a perfect home with state-of-the-art locks and alarms, a few I.R.A.s in the bank — and finally, at last, we will feel fear no more. Or we think of our fearfulness as a sign of weakness, or lack of enlightenment, and that we should be brave and strong, and able to calmly smile in the face of any adversity.

It does not seem to matter that we can find little evidence of anybody, anywhere, who has managed to fashion such a life. Common sense tells us that as long as people continue to age and die, as long as the weather continues to have its way, as long as 'the unexpected' still intrudes upon us, as long as we dare to fall in love, as long as our world in any way presents us with challenges or risks — as long as our world in any way asks us to change and adapt — the experience of fear, with its options of excitement or contraction, will surely be an important factor in our lives.

Though I can only guess, I would venture to say that Gandhi felt fear in his prison cell, that Armstrong felt fear in his 'one small step,' that Lindy felt fear in his cockpit, that Nightingale felt fear in her battlefield ministrations, and that Christ felt fear in Gethsemane. The great and inspirational people are those who discover that true courage is not the absence of fear, but *learning to act in the presence of fear.* The first phase of fear is excitement, a generation and release of vital bio-energy which is the actual fuel of courage. Excitement is a strong and abundant force which can empower a person through the long, dark nights and hard, lonely paths that living courageously so often demands. It is only when we fail to take constructive action, and when we stifle and inhibit ourselves, that the energy begins to contract, and fear becomes such a terrible and debilitating condition.

The initial movement toward contraction, the very first act of constriction and inhibition, is a reaction to our prevailing notion that fear is bad, and wrong, and to be avoided. It is our chronic habit of saying 'no' to fear, of resisting and denying and refusing fear, which is the primary cause of our chronic contraction.

The most important step which I try to get people to take at firewalks is to reverse a lifelong habit and to begin saying 'yes' to fear. This means to actually rewrite the definition of fear, to remove it from the list of four-letter words, to reframe it, to cast it in a new image, to form such a strong context of positive associations that in that first moment of FEAR!, the body-mind resounds with YES! and the energy is allowed to flow into excitement. We learned to fear fear, and fortunately we can just as well learn to embrace it.

There is a Yaqui Indian teacher named Don Juan who has been tripping through time, and several books, with a man named Carlos Casteneda. If you could take everything that Don Juan ever said to Carlos on the subject of fear and condense it into one paragraph, it would go something like this: "Carlos, you think I have no fear. You're crazy. I feel fear. In fact, given the life I choose to live I feel much more fear than you. The difference between you and me Carlos is that for you fear is a jailor, a limitation, a stop, it is a reason not to. My fear is my friend, my advisor, my counselor. I let my fear sit up here on my shoulder, very close to me, where it whispers in my ear, 'Wake up! Pay attention! Peak performance right now!'." Don Juan is one who has learned to say 'yes' to fear, and to reap the resulting powers of excitement.

By the time that I had finished my training in firewalking, I had signed five release forms of the sort that I ask people to fill out when they come to a firewalk. I had signed a release form for firewalking, a release form for leading others through firewalks, a release form for rapelling down a rock face, a release form for crawling through a cave in the ground, and a release form for sky diving. Every few days my teachers would have us do something that would put us back into the direct experience of fear again. As I was filling out the last one, in preparation for jumping out of an airplane, I noticed I was smiling, breathing deeply, and thinking, "Here we go again!" This was not about macho, or bravado, or drinking a six pack and driving fast — the "I'm not afraid of anything" approach to fear. Rather, I had made a firm connection between the excited energies of fear and the possibilities for inspired and fulfilling behavior, so that the psycho-physical experience of fear had become more of a positive promise than a negative threat. I had learned to say 'yes' to fear.

Those who regularly take risks in their lives have all learned to say 'yes' to fear. High-speed racers, daredevils, skydivers, skiers, white-water river rafters, and others all have made some positive connection between the threatening situation and its benefits to their overall sense of well-being. Risk takers discover, paradoxically, that the best way to guarantee their ongoing well-being is to challenge it on a regular basis. They come to feel very uncomfortable with the comfortable life. They look forward to the 'adrenaline rush' of challenging situations. There is evidence that people do, in fact, become addicted to the energy of excitement; that having felt it once, they discover a need to feel it more and more and more. The good news is that life in the latter half of the twentieth century is providing an abundance of challenging situations and thus an abundance of excited energy. Saying 'yes' to fear, and really meaning it, is the way to keep that energy flowing toward positive good.

It really comes down to seeing and believing that fear always shows up for good reason, and that it is an important factor in any happy and successful life. Furthermore, it means affirming that we live in an absolutely benign universe, that things are evolving according to divine intelligence, and that if fear is so abundantly present in our world, then perhaps it is not all a big mistake, or a divine drubbing of the human condition. *Indeed, fear must be a vitally important key to human evolution.*

For instance, imagine that you are standing outside of a burning building, and it is not your building, so you have no emotional or financial attachment to it. Inside of the building is an old sweater of yours. Probably, you would be able to stand and watch the building burn quite calmly, with no fear at all.

Now imagine that it is your two-year-old child that is in the burning building. You will experience, immediately, the most pulsing, surging, raging rush of stark, raving fear that you have ever experienced in your life, a gift of bio-energy that might empower you to take 'impossible' steps and do the extraordinary. You would not want to be placid or unemotional at such a time, and certainly not contracted. You would hope to be fear-driven, terrified, and exploding with excitement. Thankfully, life has evolved so that the energy of fear is always there when we need it.

Indeed, it is the things which we care most about, the people and places, the goals and outcomes, the intentions and desires that matter to us the most, that cause us to feel the most fear. We lose very little sleep over the old sweaters, and the half-hearted desires give us few ulcers. But the more important someone or something has become to us, and the more that we have included them in our definition of our ongoing well-being, then the more energy that will be generated and released, and the more fear that we will feel, upon any threat or challenge to their ongoing well-being. This is wondrously intelligent design. The energy of fear always rises to meet a challenge, and the more serious the challenge, the more energy is available. Certain teachings, such as Buddhism, have recognized this dynamic and advised the giving up of attachments and desires, thus curtailing the arousal of fearful energies. I am saying: Want, desire, intend, form strong attachments, *and* learn to responsibly use the energy you are thereby eliciting.

Now imagine that you are standing around a bed of glowing, red, hot embers, barefooted. Suddenly the firewalk begins. Generally speaking, there is no part of you that wants to step forward at such a time. Indeed, what you would like to do is take three large steps in the opposite direction! This is your body's wisdom speaking — its instincts — the results of millions of years of evolutionary experience which has taught human beings, and virtually all other life forms, to move away from fire. Ordinarily you would do precisely that, quite simply, and without fear.

But tonight is different, for tonight you have, for whatever reason, formed an intention and desire to walk on the fire. The moment you begin to seriously consider that intention, you also begin to seriously experience the rising and excited energy of fear. It is important to understand that it is your *intention* that causes the fear, and not the fire. We have all sat around fires plenty of times in our lives, feeling quite at peace and with no fear at all. The only difference between this fire and all the others is that you have been entertaining the notion of walking on this one. The moment that the desire to walk on the fire really fixes in your consciousness, life says, "Well, that's a pretty extraordinary thing to want to do, so here's some extra juice to do it with!" You are suddenly filled to the brim with excitement, the energy needed to do your very best at the task before you.

The lesson of the firewalk is this: if you are willing to step forward in the presence of your fear — if you are willing to feel the energy of excitement and act — then the energy will support and empower you, and you will stand your very best chance of succeeding. The challenge of life is to openly face the constantly-changing landscape of our world, knowing well that there will always be demands upon our ability to adapt, and that we will always have our moments and hours and sometimes days of fear, and choosing to say YES! to the challenge, to the fear, and to the always-arising gift of living-excited-energy.

nine

BOILING ENERGY

Here the women, without a pause, grouped themselves
singing in the centre of the clearing. Quickly they piled a fire
there, lit it the classical way, and then an uncle of Nxou's led
the men in a ring dancing around the fire. They danced the first
Bushman soul setting out in the darkness, before mind or matter,
to look for substance for the fire. They looked in vain for its
spoor in the sand as if fire were some subtle animal. Hour after
hour they went round and round in the same circle without
finding it. They called on the sun, moon and stars to give
them fire ˙

How the dancers found the power to go on ever faster and
faster, hour after hour, seemed beyond explanation or belief.
They danced so hard and long that the circle in the sand became
a groove, then the groove a ditch high up to their calves. Long
before the end they seemed to pass over into a dimension of
reality far out of reach of my understanding, and to a moment
and a place which belonged only technically to the desert in
which we were all gathered. Indeed, so obsessed did the men
become by this search for fire that they were drawn nearer and
nearer to the flames beside which the women sat. Then, suddenly,
they halved the circle and went dancing with their bare feet
through the middle of the flames. But even that was not the end
of the quest. Now, the longing became so intense that two of
the older women were kept constantly busy preventing some
fire-obsessed man from breaking out of the circle and hurling
himself head first straight into the flames, like a moth overcome
by excess longing for the light. Indeed one man did break through,
and before he could be stopped had scooped up a handful of
burning coals and attempted to swallow them whole . . .

At last, here and there, a dancer began to fall in his tracks . . .
Then, almost on the second of midnight, the hero of the dance,
Nxou's slender and comely uncle, suddenly found fire the way it

119

was meant to be found. He knelt down reverently beside it, the singing died away in one last sob of utter exhaustion, the dancers sank to the earth while the man picked up the coals in his naked hands and arose to scatter them far and wide for all the earth to share ... At the back of the heroic dancer, the lightning struck with a savage, kriss-like cut at the trembling earth, so near that the crackle of its fire and the explosion of the thunder sounded simultaneously in my ear. And at that moment the rain fell.

It rained all night ... [1]

I consider it a wonderful irony that the most concise of explanations for how firewalking is actually possible comes from the most primitive of cultures on our planet, the Kung of the Kalahari desert, in southern Africa. The Kung's firedancing has been observed and reported upon by several Western scholars, always with a sense of awe and amazement, for their demonstrations of what is possible go way beyond the 'typical' firewalk. They dance through fires that have been burning for hours, standing still in the fire, picking up coals in their hands, putting their faces and heads into the flames, rubbing coals into their bodies, swallowing coals — all with an incredible sense of freedom, and without any of the equivocal factors that skeptics so often seize upon.

One very vivid account has come to us through Harvard Medical School professor, Richard Katz (*Boiling Energy*, 1982). Katz spent his time among the Kung focusing specifically upon their approach to healing, and their experience with altered states of consciousness. Central to the Kung's philosophy and healing practices is their belief in an all-pervasive spiritual energy which they call *num*, and the high-energy-enhanced state of consciousness called *kia*. Their major way for activating *num* and going into *kia* is the ritual of the healing dance, an all-night ecstatic ceremony which often inspires dancers to 'work with' the fire in extraordinary ways. Thus, the Kung have developed a very powerful experience of firedancing and have done so within a consistent and well-reasoned philosophical context. (Rather than the strictly religious explanations of so many firewalking cultures.)

For the Kung, the purpose of the healing dance is to arouse or activate *num* so that certain members of the community will go into *kia*, which in turn promotes healing for individuals in

need, and for the community as a whole. According to Katz,
"The Kung also practice extraordinary activities during kia.
They perform cures and, as part of their effort to heal, may
handle and walk on fire, see the insides of people's bodies and
scenes at great distances from their camp, or travel to god's
home — activities never attempted in their ordinary state."[2] In
the words of a Kung healer, "When we enter kia, we are different
from when our num is not boiling and small. We can do different
things."[3] Another Kung comments, "If a 'big' healer wants to go
into the fire, we would let him, because he is an owner of num.
He may kneel and stick his head in the fire and hold it there."[4]

As extraordinary as such activities may seem to us, they
make perfect sense to the Kung. As Katz puts it, "The Kung
do not see working with the fire as extraordinary; they are not
surprised that they are not burned. Their explanation is simple:
when the num in their body is boiling and as hot as the fire,
they cannot be burned when working with the fire. When their
num is dormant or cold or cooled down, they can be burned."[5]

Just as their actions in the boiling *num* state of *kia* do not
seem especially extraordinary to the Kung, neither does the actual
experience of having *num*, boiling or cold, nor the experience of
going into *kia*. The Kung's experience of *num* is not at all abstract,
esoteric, or merely mental. It is in fact very real, very tangible,
and very physical. They speak of the boiling of *num* in the
same way, and with the same word for 'boiling,' as they would
speak of boiling water, or cooking food, or the ripening of fruits
and vegetables, or the first menses of a young woman. In each
case they are describing a physical event in which essential
spiritual energy has been excited, aroused, and 'boiled' to
perfect fruition.

One Kung healer describes the boiling of *num*: "You dance,
dance, dance, dance. Then num lifts you up in your belly and
lifts you in your back, and you begin to shiver. Num makes
you tremble; it's hot ... you're looking around because you see
everything, you see what's troubling everybody. Rapid shallow
breathing draws num up. What I do in my upper body with the
breathing, I also do in my legs with the dancing ... Then num
enters every part of your body, right to the tip of your feet and
even your hair."[6] Another healer says: "In your backbone you
feel a pointed something and it works its way up. The base of

your spine is tingling, tingling, tingling, tingling. Then num makes your thoughts nothing in your head."[7] It is very real, very tangible, and very physical. It is attainable according to a prescribed methodology, constantly repeated for thousands of years, and observed to have concrete, practical benefits to the community. It is truly an ancient experiment, and the very best explanation of what is actually happening at a firewalk and how the experience can be applied to life in general.

While Katz strictly avoids drawing any parallels between the Kung's concepts of *num* and *kia* and similar concepts from other cultures, I must offer any necessary apologies and plunge ahead in that direction. It is, however, not so much a matter of drawing parallels as of simply noting the similarities that clearly exist. The placing of the energy source in the lower abdomen and the base of the spine, the feeling of energy rising up the spine, the use of rapid breathing, the experiences of heat, tingling, and vibration, the empty mind, the clearing of vision, the expanded powers, the ability to heal, the sense of being fully human and spiritually inspired — we could as easily be listening to a Chinese *chi kung* master or a Tibetan yogic adept or a Sufi whirling dervish or an ecstatic Christian faith healer. Or to Wilhelm Reich or Anton Mesmer. Or to so many of the firewalkers I have spoken with.

"When the num in their body is boiling and as hot as the fire, they cannot be burned when working with the fire. When their num is dormant or cold or cooled down, they can be burned." *When bio-energy is aroused, activated, boiling over, and excited to its fullest, then we are fully empowered and capable of extraordinary behaviors.* When our energy is dormant, cold, and tightly contracted, then we are diminished and limited, and far more prone to failure and disappointment.

————————————————

Most of our firewalks begin with my wife Penny leading the group in a wonderful Russian folk song and dance called "If the People." She has this amazing talent for being able to take a roomful of adults, most of whom are thoroughly convinced that they can neither sing nor dance and who are excruciatingly embarrassed at the mere suggestion that they do so with a bunch of strangers, and in a matter of minutes have the whole group holding hands and spinning around the room, singing

their hearts out and enjoying each and every silly moment
of it.

I know there are always some people who are perplexed
with it all, wondering what this has to do with learning how to
walk on fire. Their confusion tends to mount when we sit down
and I tell them that they have just learned how to walk on fire.
I say to them that the singing, the dancing, the holding hands,
the being willing to take a risk, the being willing to act like a
child — that these are all excellent ways to walk on fire, and
that if we had had a fire before us just as we finished singing,
we all could have danced right through it, easily.

There is something in most people that rebels at this statement.
I am making it all too easy. There must be more to it, some
magic mantra or super meditation, some state of the art human
potential technology. Somehow we have to change ourselves
from people who burn into people who don't burn, and the
technique for doing so in three hours must be pretty complex.

In fact, the way we do it is that we get our *num* to boil
over. While there are a great many highly complex and deeply
esoteric ways to boil one's *num*, all of which are very effective
ways to walk on fire, it is also true that some of the best *num*
boilers are quite simple and already known to most people.
For instance . . .

LOVE

Love is the most powerful *num* boiler of them all. It is a
very common-sense observation that the experience of falling
in love can be both healing and empowering. We seem to stand
taller, and walk lighter; our eyes sparkle; we radiate well-being;
we feel better than ever. Such is the simple power of love, recognized beyond question by people throughout time and space.
People have always known the power of love, which is why it
is the stuff of so many of our songs and myths, the foundation
of most of our philosophies and religions, and the single most
wanted commodity on our planet.

In the past few decades, science has begun to substantiate
this intuitive understanding of love. We now know that rats,
monkeys, and human beings all respond better when exposed to
basic tender loving care. We know that fetuses will grow stronger
and healthier when they are loved by their parents, and when

they sense that their parents love each other. We know that the most negative of all stresses that a human being can be exposed to is the death of a loving spouse. While we are just beginning to understand the immune system, it is already apparent that this system is definitely and positively effected by the experience of love.

One thing which is becoming clear about the immune system is that the long-misunderstood thymus functions as the master gland. The thymus gland is located in the center of the chest, which of course is exactly where human beings have always located the experience of love. We do not find any cultures talking about the loving brain, or the loving nose, or the loving throat, or the loving solar plexus, or the loving belly. Rather, we always talk and sing of the loving heart. Our feeling of love is always a movement, a flow, a radiance, an expansion, a presence that occurs in the center of the chest. Scientists may well be reticent to draw a connection between the warm wonderful feeling that fills your chest when you experience and express love, and a positive effect upon the thymus gland which is sitting right there in the midst of that warm wonderful feeling, but I have no such reservations. This positive effect then extends from the thymus gland to the whole immune system, and thus affects the overall state of health. Love *is* good health.

Viewed from the perspective of bio-energy, love is a free expansion of our essential life-force, a wondrous boiling over of our energy to the object of our love. *When we love, our energy is encouraged to excite us into connection with another, so the more we love the more connected to life we become, and the more we experience our basic unity to greater energies and larger possibilities.* When we love, we open ourselves to all of the benefits of excitement, while freeing ourselves of the varied aches and pains of contraction. This excited expansion of energy may well explode into sexual union, with its magnificent potential for healing and co-creation. Nurtured over time, it can lead to such a strong bonding (energetic connection) between lovers that communication through energy, without words, becomes quite ordinary.

BREATH

Most every culture that has developed an understanding of

energy has also become aware of the connection between energy and the breath, and has found specific ways of breathing to explore that connection and 'boil energy.' (Conversely, in American culture, which has very little experience of bio-energy, breath is taken totally for granted and only studied when something has gone wrong with it.)

To begin to understand the importance of breathing, we must first understand that there is more to the air that we breathe than oxygen and various other chemicals. The air around us is replete with energy, and is in fact our primary source for replenishing and nourishing ourselves with vital energy. The power of breath begins in purely quantitative terms: the deeper and more continuously we breathe — inhaling to the fullest and not pausing, holding, or in any way stifling the breath — the more air/energy we take in and the more alive we become. It really is that simple. To breathe in deeply is to deeply inspire oneself (Latin *spiritus,* "breath, courage, vigor, the soul, life") and to deeply fill oneself with energy. All of the languages of our world indicate this same connection between breath, spirit, life, and energy.

The respiratory system is also responsible for the circulation of energy throughout the body, the way that we breathe being the primary director of energy movement and flow. Just as on a physical level the breath/blood flows throughout the body, so on an energetic level the breath/energy goes out to touch the heart of each and every cell of the body. When the breath is in any way stifled or constricted, the rest of the body suffers, for the circulation of bio-energy is also stifled and constricted. *Thus, the power of breath is first in bringing energy into us — the more we breathe, the more energy we have available — and second in circulating the energy throughout the body — the more fully and freely we breathe, the more the energy can flow to the various parts of our bodies.*

Such a simple thing as breath and so much benefit to be derived. How then does there ever come to be a problem with our breath? Why don't people just naturally and automatically breathe in the most optimal way?

The problem has to do with the way we learn to experience our emotional nature. Our feelings are comprised of bio-energy, and are in fact energy in motion (e-motion). They are energy which is excited, stirred, aroused, and moving. In a healthy life we experience certain events that excite the energy of response, which we gratefully feel and fully express to the best of our capabilities. When something happens, it causes us to feel specific emotions, and we respond to the event by fully experiencing the emotions and by allowing the excited energy to move.

When we are threatened, we experience a surge of fear. We respond to the threat by using the fear/energy to fight, run, or grow. Someone has died, we feel great sadness, and we respond by appreciating the hurt and allowing the energy to flow through tears. We grow. We have been wronged, we feel a rush of anger, and we allow the energy of the anger to move us toward redressing the wrong, externally and/or internally. We grow. A healthy life is not a life without these and other 'negative' emotions. A healthy life is one which recognizes the enormous power in human feeling, the thrust of vital current in every emotion, and which is always allowing and encouraging the feeling/energy to excite, to flow, to move, to boil over into positive expression and evolutionary growth. The fear/energy carries the solution to the threat; the sadness/energy carries the solution to the hurt; the anger/energy carries the solution to the wrong. This is always the case. All of our emotions arise as energetic balances to the events of our lives, providing us with the raw material of positive evolutionary response.

Unfortunately, humanity as a whole, and Western culture in particular, is still struggling to fully integrate its emotional nature. Our species somewhat resembles a clumsy and stumbling adolescent, plagued with these strange and powerful new energies and virtually incapable of anything even slightly resembling a healthy and balanced emotional response. Human feelings have been the wild card curse of our philosophies and religions for eons, the messy and unpredictable piece of our nature that has never quite fit into any rational system of thought. Indeed, it has been the challenge of our rational self to somehow suppress our emotional energies out of sight, and to a large degree the measure of any civilized culture has been the manner in which it has engineered this vital suppression ("big boys don't cry," "women faint when emotionally stressed," "outward displays of anger are uncivilized," etc.)

This brings us back to the breath. *Contraction is excitement deprived of breath.* However a culture goes about actually suppressing the flow of emotional energy, the individual person involved within a specific exciting event accomplishes the required suppression by first suppressing the flow of breath. Feelings are comprised of energy. Breath is our most immediate source and circulator of energy. If we are in the midst of an event which we would prefer not to feel, or if we are going through an emotional experience which we would like to suppress from conscious awareness and/or visible expression, then we suppress our breathing, which constricts the flow of energy, which contracts any of the feelings involved. This pattern of stifled, constricted breathing in the midst of emotional stimulation is the first movement of our essential energy away from the possibilities of excitement and toward the collapse of chronic contraction. It is an automatic, subconscious, instinctive reaction which we learn from the modeled behaviors of those around us. Each generation passes it along to the next until it feels so natural, and so biologically normal, that we cannot even notice that we are doing it.

Imagine a roomful of people all awaiting news of their relatives after some disaster. They are barely breathing. Or a movie theater filled with people watching a horror show. Or a little boy trying very hard not to cry. Or an oncologist's waiting room. Or the incredible hush that can fill a packed sports arena during a very suspenseful moment.

Or remember your own breathing during rush hour traffic when you are in a real hurry. Or when you are sitting in the dentist's chair. Or attempting not to get angry at someone you love. Or trying not to laugh at an inappropriate moment. Or waiting to find out if it's a boy or a girl.

With just a little bit of attention, we notice that people stifle and constrict their breathing *all the time,* and that the contraction of breath in reaction to excited feelings is virtually a given for late twentieth-century, civilized human beings. We do it because it is a very effective short-term strategy for dealing with unwanted feelings. If we do not want to feel a certain emotion, we can contract the flow of breath and thus effectively suppress the feelings by contracting their vital energy. It works! As described in the previous chapter, if we do this for long enough around a specific emotional situation, the state of contraction will become such an ingrained habit that we will no longer even register the feelings of excited energy.

Unfortunately, while providing a short-term escape from the problem of unwanted feelings, the contraction of breath/energy kills us in the long run. We simply cannot escape the negative effects of contracted energy as a result of contracting our breath. We simply must come to terms with our emotional nature, must fully embrace a lifestyle of powerfully excited feelings, and must discover the ways of using our breath to 'boil energy' into excitement with all that this brings.

The firewalk, of course, provides a wonderful example of all of this. Talk about a group of underbreathers! A firewalk is *much* worse than your typical doctor's waiting room. Just mention the word 'burn' and you could truly hear a pin drop on the carpet, so quiet does the room become. As the minutes tick away and the time for walking comes closer and closer, the energy of the group tangibly contracts, as the participants breathe less and less. Throughout the evening I exhort and remind them to breathe, over and over again — to breathe loudly, to breathe obviously, to yawn, to do whatever they can to keep their breath deep and flowing. As we approach the fire I remind them again, for my experience has shown that firewalking with excited breath works much better than firewalking with contracted breath.

Ultimately, learning to 'boil energy' with the breath is not something that we pick up in an evening, or by reading a book. Because we have used our breath to put a lid on so much emotional energy, opening our breathing means taking that lid off and therefore beginning to deal with a lot of heavy feelings and intense energies. So it can, and should, be a slow process. It is truly a life process, something to be worked on as a condition of being fully alive.

There are many ways, ancient and modern, to do the work of reclaiming the breath. However we go about this, the basic lessons of 'boiling energy' with the breath remain pretty much the same: *to bring conscious awareness to the process of breathing, paying attention to the way different circumstances impact the breath, and choosing again and again to breathe deeply, fully, and freely.* It must become an ongoing conscious practice, especially at times of unwanted feelings, when our psycho-physical energies

are contracting, to let the next breath be a deeply-inhaled af-
firmation of expanding energy — a moving, flowing, boiling
over into excitement.

POSITIVE ATTITUDE

This is a tricky one. Most of us have at one time or another
been pursuaded by the 'power of positive thinking' that if we
could just keep our thoughts perfectly positive, only good things
would happen in our lives. Then it seems, inevitably, that we
have eventually found ourselves rolling down a hill in a runaway
truck, our minds screaming, "I'm not gonna crash, I'm not
gonna crash, I'm not gonna crash!" Later, as we are picking
up the pieces, we sagely conclude that all that 'positive thinking'
stuff was a bunch of baloney.

Likewise, I observe a lot of 'positive thinkers' at my firewalks
sitting there all night thinking, "I'm not gonna burn, I'm not
gonna burn," and I have to grimace because statistically they
are so often disappointed. How can this be?

First, let me stress that I personally am an ardent devotee
of positive thinking. In addition, I have found that our current
train of thought is only one piece of the puzzle. If we are thinking
positively within a tightly contracted body, or in opposition to
our most deeply held beliefs, or while suppressing unwanted
feelings, or while strongly intending otherwise, or while hardly
breathing, then our thoughts are truly crippled, and not at all
powerful, and we tend to manifest the precise opposite of what
we are thinking. As powerful as our thoughts surely are, they
are like extremely potent seeds which can ultimately be only
as good as the soil into which they are planted.

The 'soil' in the human creative process is the overlying and
underlying attitude through which we approach a situation. It is
comprised of our thoughts and feelings, our ideas and opinions,
our mood, our disposition, our manner of acting, and the way
we hold our body. Our attitude at any given moment is the sum
total of all of our various parts, both giving expression to our
whole nature and at the same time operating as a pattern for
future interactions. It is an all-encompassing field of energy, the
precise mixture of excitement and contraction which we bring
to a specific event, and it thus has everything to do with our
success or failure.

I have already described the posture of skepticism, a very negative, counterproductive, and yet widely-accepted attitude. When we approach life with the attitudes of doubt, distrust, and disbelief, we invariably contract ourselves on every level, leaving our energy very unboiled, and very uncreative. This is true with all negative attitudes: hostility, paranoia, boredom, disrespect, low self-esteem, rigidity, indecisiveness. All involve an essential contraction from life and thus can only cause destruction in our world.

Positive attitudes, on the other hand, contribute to the creation of positive results. The all-embracing attitude, "I will love," can excite outwards like a great wave, transforming everything in its wake. The sharply focused attitude, "This is what I want," can be a guided missile of energy, carrying us out into our manifested dreams. The unquestioning attitude, "I believe in . . . ," can, and has, moved mountains. All of the positive attitudes available to us — trust, faith, confidence, clarity, respect, devotion, flexibility, enthusiasm — involve an essential excitement toward greater connection with life, and thus can only enhance our creative possibilities.

An especially destructive attitude, for it supports and strengthens all of our negative attitudes, is the one which says/feels/believes/embodies that we are victims of the world, and that the attitudes which we hold, positive or negative, are caused by the events of our lives. This attitude says, for example, that my unhappiness, my depression, and my negativity is the inevitable result of my unfortunate circumstances. Having been through what I have been through, or to be facing what I am facing, I must feel this way; I must have these gloomy thoughts; I must have a negative attitude. It is only human, after all.

In fact, what is so wondrously human is that we have the capacity and the responsibility (the ability to respond) to choose our thoughts and feelings and beliefs and intentions, to choose our manner of breathing, to choose our posture, to choose, regardless of the circumstances that we are living through, to respond with a positive or negative attitude, and to move in the direction of excitement or contraction. Human beings have free will, and though it too often seems otherwise, we freely choose, from moment to moment, our happiness and unhappiness, our love and hatred, our trust and doubt, our faith and disbelief,

our optimism and pessimism. Receiving injury, we can turn the
other cheek. In the midst of disaster, we can whistle a happy
tune. Fatally diagnosed, we can see ourselves living on in good
health. Anxiously kept waiting, we can breathe deeply and
expect the best. Financially ruined, we can find a lucky penny
and start all over again, wiser for our mistakes. Lost and abandoned,
downtrodden and forgotten, we can turn to love, we can open
to God, over and over again. The positive choice and attitude —
thought, felt, believed and embodied — always boils our energy
outwards toward positive possibilities.

LAUGHTER

Several years ago the writer Norman Cousins (*Anatomy
of an Illness*, W.W. Norton & Co., Inc., 1981) made a major
contribution to Western medicine with his account of his recovery
from an 'incurable' disease. He says that when it became clear
that the standard medical prognosis for his problem was not
at all hopeful, he decided (inspired by his investigation into
alternative healing practices) to leave the hospital and to set
about a treatment program that involved massive doses of vitamin C
and nonstop viewing of old "Candid Camera" and Marx Brothers
films. He says that whenever he was laughing, especially when
he was having good, rolling (boiling over) belly laughs, he
experienced less pain and felt intuitively that his condition
was improving. Of course, he lived to tell the tale.

Laughter is a great excitement of energy. It will often accompany
a positive attitude, and a happy release of the goodness that a
person is feeling. More importantly, laughter thankfully arrives
at those times when our energies are contracting, when embarrassment, anxiety, fear, or terror are just beginning to grip us,
and when the tension of a situation is hardening. At that point,
a joke is cracked, the grip is broken, and the energy chuckles
out in free and spontaneous laughter.

I feel that I have proven the power of laughter, to myself
at least, at firewalks. I try to weave a lot of humor into my
presentation, especially in the last half hour before the walk,
because I am convinced that laughter is a very effective energy
boiler. For whatever reasons, though, on some nights I feel like
the consummate bombing comedian, for despite my best efforts,
nobody laughs. On such evenings the tension in the room seems

to grow thicker with each passing moment, and with each failing joke. (And with the lack of breath, which invariably goes with the lack of laughter. A person who is breathing deeply and fully will be much more inclined toward laughing. A person who is laughing *is* breathing.) It is an indisputable fact that there are more burns experienced during unlaughing firewalks, so much so that I usually warn people that if they haven't been laughing, they should seriously (how else?) consider not walking.

LOVING SEX

The world's favorite energy boiler!

Sexual energy is bio-energy aroused and expressed through the specific practices of sexual intimacy. Much of what I have been saying about energy is clearly and quite naturally encountered in the sexual experience. Sex involves the incredible rush of excitement, with all of its potential for healing, releasing, and balancing energies, and for bringing forth the most wondrous of all creations. It reveals the undeniable connection between intention (I want her! I want him!) and the immediate arousal of vital energy to meet the challenge. It proves that the mind and the body are linked through energy (just try making love when your mind is somewhere else). It demonstrates that where consciousness goes, energy flows. It shows the obvious importance of the breath to the flow of energy. Finally, it illustrates the well-documented and painful truth that to in any way suppress, stifle, deny, abuse, or contract this living energy is to cause extreme harm to the human body, mind, and spirit involved.

When sexuality is held within any of the negative attitudes of contraction (guilt, denial, suppression, repression, hate, violence, embarrassment, self-hatred, pride, superiority, inferiority), then the very creative strength of sexual energy is turned against the human condition and great injury results. Rape, incest, pornography, torture — all such aberrant behaviors are initiated with the contraction of vital sexual energy on an individual and cultural basis and are misguided attempts to release this suppressed and stifled energy. Tragically, like a bomb exploding inside of a steel box, the energy never excites outward in truly healthy expression, but is instead greatly intensified and driven inward against the person, causing further contraction, and further need and tendency for aberrant release. When an entire culture engages in such contracted sexuality for a long enough time, it should not surprise us to find the sexual energy of that culture becoming contaminated and diseased.

This is why I say 'loving sex.' When sex is shared in the spirit of love, and when the energy of the lovers is already boiling over and expanded with their love for one another, then sexual play is a vast and wonderful intensification of that expansion. The lovers are increased, lifted up, and blessed through their sharing. Sex is truly a godsend; it requires of us that it also be God-received.

MOVEMENT

At the molecular and submolecular levels, life is a dance. It is a constantly flowing, swirling, pulsing, gyrating, vibrating, thrusting, orbiting of particles and waves; an unceasing play of motion; an endless and untiring dance. Even a most solid and unmoving piece of rock, when viewed through an electron microscope, is seen to be a gathering of infinitely small and wondrously ephemeral particle/waves, spinning their way through very large volumes of open space. What we are learning to see through such microscopes is energy itself. What we will eventually come to see is that energy is vibration, and that physical reality is the manifestation of energy according to different levels and rates of vibration.

Human beings have found that it is generally healthy and empowering to support and expand this essential vibration, that it is good to 'boil energy,' and that exciting energy to a higher rate of vibration is better than contracting it. One of the easiest most natural, and most enjoyable ways to do this is to actually vibrate the physical body — to shake it, bounce it, spin it, and twirl it — to dance.

This dancing of energy can be performed as very slow movement. Systems such as yoga, Tai Chi, and Feldenkreis all involve moving the body in a very slow manner while focusing consciousness on a gradual awakening (boiling) of energy. More often, and more instinctively I think, we find the arousal and boiling of energy through fast movement, such as with the more forceful martial arts like kung fu and karate, the spinning of whirling dervishes, the rapid motions of belly dancers, hula dancers, and rock 'n rollers, and the wild, abandoned dances of so many different cultures. One does not need a philosophy of energy to know that twenty, thirty, or forty minutes of such free and spontaneous movement will cause a definite shift in awareness with exciting benefits for the dancers. Indeed, it is difficult to delight in being alive, to rejoice in one's humanity, to feel real excitement in the moment, *without* feeling one's body wanting to move around and express its joy through dancing.

I have found that there are more cultures which approach the firewalk through slow walking than through dancing, which is why I have chosen to continue to refer to the experience as firewalking. I have also found that the people who have gone the furthest with the experience, in terms of prolonged contact with the coals and exceptional demonstration of what is possible, are those, such as the Kung and the Greek Anasterides, who approach the fire with ecstatic dancing. Likewise, while my firewalks began as walks, I have gradually developed more and more of a dancing style, resulting clearly in a greater sense of enjoyment and more positive benefits.

I have also found movement to be very important during the time leading up to the walk. There are moments in every evening when the energy in the room is very contracted. As I tell the group itself, this is probably unavoidable. It is impossible to spend a few hours feeling the pending threat and challenge of a bed of hot coals without having energy aroused to meet the challenge. However, it is difficult to keep the energy moving toward excitement while sitting in a room listening to a lecture, so many people find themselves getting rather contracted as the night continues. Therefore, several times during the evening I get the group up and shaking. This is nothing difficult, esoteric, or even prolonged — we just stand up and shake it out. Thirty seconds of such movement always leaves the group feeling lighter, freer, happier, and more optimistic.

So often that is all that it takes when we find ourselves contracting: to feel the energy at a visceral level and cause it to boil by physically moving the body. Unfortunately, we too often do precisely the opposite when contracting: we sit still, stuck and unmoving, thinking and worrying, arguing with our fear, the energy becoming tighter and tighter.

SOUND

Everything that has been said about movement applies also to the experience of sound, through singing, making and listening to music, and the use of percussion. Like movement, each of these activities is a vibratory practice, or experience, which 'boils energy' by increasing the rate of energetic vibration in a person's body, or within an environment. We know, for instance that a high-pitched song can raise the rate of molecular vibration of a glass on the other side of the room and cause it to shatter. We know that prolonged use of a drumbeat can entrain a group of people within a high-energy-enhanced trance state. We know, in the simplest of terms, that music has universal appeal, that it can soothe all manner of unhappy beasts, and that it heals, empowers, inspires, and excites.

I start my firewalks with singing and dancing, and I include further movement and song thoughout the evening. I have found it especially important to sing during the actual walk for several reasons. First, on an individual level, it allows one to release pent-up contracted energy. Second, it enables the group to feel connected as our voices join and harmonize. Finally, if we weren't singing we would probably be holding our breath! In fact, at this point the idea of having a firewalk without singing is far more weird, threatening, and difficult for me to imagine than the idea of firewalking itself.

———————————————

There are other good 'energy boilers' which I have not mentioned. One of these, for instance, is touch, as demonstrated by the efficacy of laying-on-of-hands. The strong and unshakable belief in God; the willing giving of oneself in service to others; the many avenues of creative self-expression; fulfilling labor; firm commitment to a person, place or ideal; taking risks; the practice of meditation — these are all powerful energy boilers. Each one tends to have an expansive effect upon the human energy field, helping to generate the shift from contraction to excitement.

The common denominator in all of the energy boilers that I have listed is that they are the practices, activities, and experiences which human beings everywhere would agree upon as being good and desirable. That is, if one were to survey a wide mix of cultures throughout the world, and ask, "What are the aspects of living that you consider to be most important?" certain 'wants' would show up everywhere near the top of the list: to love and be loved, to know God, to have positive thoughts and feelings, to breathe fully and freely, to sing, to dance, to enjoy music, to make love, to have good and fulfilling work, and to express creative possibilities. We find the active pursuit and ongoing development of these common energy boilers within all human cultures, past, present, and future. Why? Because these are the activities, practices, and experiences which work the best for us; because whether we are aware of bio-energy or not, we are intuitively drawn to our most energy exciting behaviors and possibilities; and because, ultimately, we are intelligently designed creatures destined to realize our full evolutionary potential.

This is not to deny that for most of our history we have been working at least as hard, and at times much harder, at the development and practice of 'energy destroyers.' We have maimed and killed each other for eons. We have hated with great passion We have doubted and distrusted and disbelieved and denied. We have feared deeply, and we have enforced and defended our fears suicidally. We have invested very heavily in the ways of contraction, closing our eyes and ears and hearts to exciting possibilities, stifling any voices of optimism, discounting all hope, and crucifying those who have had the audacity to suggest that we are capable of positively directing the course of life on this planet — that we are capable of co-creating heaven on Earth, and more.

The fact remains, however, that if we were to take the average human being and say, "Assuming that you are now free of social constraints and necessities, and are free to create your life just as you choose, how would it look?" most people would design a lifestyle of boiling energy, a life filled with excitement and free of contraction. Most people will gravitate very naturally to the ways which I have been describing when they begin to truly feel their freedom and power as co-creators of this world.

The solutions to the problems facing us today are not nearly as complex as we would fear them to be, and are truly as simple as love, breath, singing and dancing, bodies touching, faith, trust, and belief. Which is not to say that this is easy! The establishment of an ongoing and sustaining lifestyle of excited energy, expanded awareness, and self-realization is hard work, to be sure. But too often when something is hard, we decide that it must also be complex, which easily leads to the idea that it is beyond our understanding, unfathomable, above and beyond us, and impossible.

We are just beginning to see how much is possible, to feel how much further human beings can go. Let us also begin to appreciate the simplicity of the path before us, and to commit our energies to the fires of love and breath, of faith and belief, of singing and dancing and happy laughter. There is much to be excited about.

ten

THE POSSIBLE
HUMAN

There is therefore no reason to put a limit to evolutionary possibility by taking our present organization or status of existence as final. The animal is a laboratory in which Nature has worked out man; man may very well be a laboratory in which she wills to work out superman, to disclose the soul as a divine being, to evolve a divine nature.[1]

The intention of the universe is evolution. Each of us is involved in the grand enterprise . . . . To further evolutionary purposes, human intentionality will some day use tools that do not now exist and will operate in dimensions that confound our present day science.[2]

The universe bestows on us fire from the beginning of time, simultaneously evoking our profound reverence for this fire. The universe demands our response: Do we awake, dedicating ourselves to a vision of beauty worthy of our fire's origins? Do we shape this fire as it has shaped us, aware of the awesome work that has gone into providing it?[3]

I was first exposed to the idea of firewalking in 1976 through the book, *Exploring The Crack in the Cosmic Egg*, by Joseph Chilton Pearce.[4] In a very thorough and scholarly investigation of the firewalk (and other non-ordinary events), Pearce deals with the practice mostly as it occurs in Bali, where it is a coming-of-age ritual for seven-year-old girls. He gives some description of the ceremony leading up to the Balinese firedance, and suggests that the young women attain their ability to dance on fire through observing and then mimicking the experienced dancers. He further suggests that they are able to do so because they have seen it done for their entire lives and thus always knew they would do it when their time came. As part of his thesis for the occurrence of non-ordinary events, Pearce builds a strong case for the necessity of a surrounding culture which is supportive of the event, and, in this instance, of the special receptivity, or suggestibility, of the seven-year-old mind. (I would later discover Pearce's earlier work, *The Crack in the Cosmic Egg*, in which he cites several other firewalks and offers slightly differing explanations.)

Upon reading Pearce's book, I can remember that while I certainly did not feel ready to plunge into the next fire that came my way, I was at the same time quite certain that not only could I and would I one day walk on fire, but that it was a possibility or trait open to all human beings. My feeling was that if a seven-year-old Balinese girl could do it, then surely I could do it, and surely all people could do it, for I just could not believe that there was some essential genetic difference between me and the Balinese girl which enabled her flesh not to burn while mine would. Rather, I felt certain that the difference was in mind-set — a basic difference in how we looked at and thought about the world; a specific psycho-emotional approach to life that allowed her to experience reality in this special way. I further believed that, while I was somewhat past my seventh year, and had grown up in a clearly backward culture (ask any firedancer), it still must be possible for me, and anyone else, to learn this way of thinking, and this approach to life, and thus to be able to walk on fire without burning.

As I was very involved in exploring alternative approaches to healing at that time in my life, the whole idea of firewalking immediately grabbed me, for it was such a graphic demonstration of a mind-body interaction that went way beyond the commonly agreed-upon limits of my culture. According to all of the known laws of human biology, the Balinese girl was doing the impossible, and yet I was convinced that not only could she do so, but that I could do so also. I began to wonder if there were other biological 'laws' which were in fact mutable, if there were other impossiblities which were in fact possible, and if there were other human abilities or talents or traits which my culture had neglected to tell me about. I looked to my everyday life, my everyday assumptions about how things had to be, and began to question all of them If, I wondered, fire does not necessarily burn, but it burns or not according to the subjective experience of the individual interacting with it, then perhaps sugar does not *necessarily* cause tooth decay, and carcinogens do not *necessarily* cause cancer, and germs do not *necessarily* cause colds, and calories do not *necessarily* cause fat.

In other words, if 'fire burns' is not the simple cause-and-effect relationship that we have always assumed it to be, and if true cause rests somewhere and somehow within human consciousness, then should we not re-examine and re-vision many other assumed cause-and-effect relationships? Furthermore, if human beings can do this 'impossible' thing, then why shouldn't we *expect* that we have other undiscovered potentials, and realize that *our whole notion of what it means to be human might be inadequate and counterproductive?*

For me, firewalking became a very good example, a model, for what I now like to call the 'possible human' (after Jean Houston's wonderful book of that title).[5] The possible human is the embodiment of our very best, the unfolding realization of all of our potential, and the rising into expression of all of our suppressed, forgotten, and/or latent abilities. The possible human is a growing, living, breathing, evolving miracle in the making, reaching far beyond the commonly accepted limitations of our race. The possible human declares that we are as yet unfinished, that our shortcomings and failures are the stages of a work in progress, that we will surely grow into greater beauty, greater wisdom, greater health, and greater love. Truly, the possible human is a being of mythic proportions, sensed and dreamed for many centuries in strikingly similar ways by all of the people of our planet. Most exciting, for so many people alive today the possible human is a small, quiet voice whispering, "Yes, you can, the time is now."

As Jean Houston puts it: "They feel that as of now the future is wide open, and that what we do truly makes a difference as to whether humanity fails or flourishes . . . . They have a healthy and spirited appreciation of the complexities and capacities of their own being, and regulary spend time in discovering, refining, and applying the latent potentials of their own body-minds. There is little of narcissism here, as daily they rid themselves of unneeded rancor and deliberately pursue ways both mental and physical of deepening into the Depths of which they are a part. In this they become in some sense citizens of a larger universe, who take time to prepare themselves so that they can listen to the rhythms of awakening that may be pulsing from a deeper, more coherent Order of Reality."[6]

Basic to the possible human's character is the experience that we are connected to one another, that humanity is essentially of one body, one mind, one spirit, and that each individual is thus born with similar potential. While celebrating our individual differences, the possible human views the really important talents and abilities as being universally accessible. Rather than living in a world of 'special' people with 'special' talents, the possible human sees one person's peak performance as a pattern for all people. If trance dancers in Fiji and Bali can walk barefoot over hot coals, then I can do that too. If a stricken cancer patient can wake up one day and heal against all odds, then I can do that too. If Tibetan monks can sit naked and warm in the snow, then I can do that too. If a 50-year-old housewife, in a moment of unthinking desperation, can lift a 2,000-pound automobile off of her trapped child, then I can do that too. If Chinese *chi kung* masters can move objects at a distance, then I can do that too. *One person's extraordinary steps stake out territory for others to follow, yesterday's miracle becoming today's regular event.*

Rupert Sheldrake (*The New Science of Life*),[7] a Cambridge-educated biologist, has given us a beautiful theoretical framework for how this shift from the extraordinary to the ordinary may occur. His Hypothesis of Formative Causation states that every organism has an associated morphogenetic field (*morphe* = form, and *genesis* = coming into being), or m-field, a non-physical structure such as a magnetic field which governs the growth and development of each organism, guiding it into its characteristic form. Each species would have its own m-field, invisible and existing across space and time, which would carry the pattern of development, or rules, for its members. Upon conception, an individual organism of that species would 'tune in' (through a process which Sheldrake calls 'morphic resonance') to its governing m-field, thus receiving its blueprint for growth and behavior

Sheldrake's theory gives a very elegant explanation for a long-annoying puzzler of science: the problem of how a greatly complex organism, such as a human being, can grow from a single cell. Scientists have tried in vain to locate within that single cell the vast quantities of information that must be available to guide the growth of the human body. Sheldrake says that the information is not located in the cell but in the human m-field, and that the single cell has at conception the capacity to tune into and receive guidance from the m-field. His theory also explains how there can be such remarkable stability within a species over enormous spans of time and space, since the m-field is non-physical (i.e., non-corruptible) and can therefore exist across time and space. Most important for our purposes is that he offers an enticing framework for how evolutionary change toward the possible human can occur.

Sheldrake sees the m-field/individual combination as a two-way interaction. While the m-field acts upon the organism, giving it its pattern for growth and behavior, the organism also acts upon the m-field, feeding back into it the individual's actual life characteristics. The m-field forms as a summation of all the data from all of the individual organisms of a species taken throughout space and time, and then reflects that data back to new individuals. The individual grows according to the collective pattern of all of the past organisms of its species, and then feeds its actual living data back into the pattern for individuals to come. Thus, the m-field is not so much a law, etched in stone, eternal and unchanging, as it is a collective habit, things being the way they are because that is the way they have mostly been in the past.

When an individual, through exposure to new environmental demands, or, in the case of human beings, through an act of conscious volition, learns a truly new behavior or takes on a truly new characteristic, this also feeds back into the governing m-field. A case of one instance of such new behavior will have little or no effect on the m-field though, just as a single moment of determined change will usually not overcome a long-ingrained habit. But if the behavior is repeated, and if it is successful enough to be adopted by other individuals, then eventually it will feed into the m-field enough to change it, and then change for the species will occur — the evolutionary leap.

The few studies of Sheldrake's theory which have been thus far undertaken have had favorable results. It was found, for instance, that children learn common, old nursery rhymes, such as "Mary Had A Little Lamb," much easier than newly created ones. Likewise, people learn legitimate foreign languages much faster than invented ones. In each case, the suggestion is that something which is already well-established in the human m-field is more readily received than some newer piece of information. Another example, widely used to illustrate his ideas, though disavowed by Sheldrake himself, is that of The Hundredth Monkey. (There is a great deal of controversy surrounding this account, and serious question as to whether it ever actually happened. I include it for its value as a helpful metaphor in our understanding of the possible human.)

The story goes that a group of Japanese scientists were observing a population of monkeys spread throughout a chain of islands in the South Pacific. As part of their experiment they began dropping a variety of sweet potato onto the islands, which the monkeys liked very much. At some point, they observed a young female monkey (who they named Ibo) take her potato down to the ocean and wash it off before eating it. Sandless and salted, she seemed to like it much more, and soon was urging her friends and family to do likewise. Eventually she succeeded, and most of the monkeys on her island began washing their potatoes also. At this point the scientists observed something totally surprising, for suddenly all of the monkeys on all of the other islands began also washing their potatoes. As there was no way for any physical communication to have taken place, the notion of a non-physical field through which behavioral patterns and changes could have been communicated made some sense.

The Hundredth Monkey refers to an arbitrary number of individuals; the theory is that change for the whole species seems to occur when a critical mass of changed individuals is reached. When there are, say, 95 potato washers, they are merely aberrants and weirdos doing things differently than everyone else. But at the moment that the hundredth monkey makes the shift, a critical mass is reached, the m-field changes, and the entire species shifts. The aberrants and weirdos then are those who stubbornly cling to *not* washing potatoes.

This is a very powerful model of change, for it suggests that the individual who takes determined steps to change herself is making a valid and valuable contribution to her fellow beings, even if she is working in isolation (the monk on the mountain), or even if her best external efforts (voting, organizing, etc.) seem to be for naught. Furthermore, it is very reassuring to think that those of us working for change do not have to somehow influence and change the entire population, person by person, neurosis by neurosis, but that the change and evolution of an inspired few can substantially support the evolvement of everybody. (Those who have observed this phenomenon in human populations place the critical hundredth-monkey mass at five to ten percent of the population. This is the percentage of changing beings needed to create change for the whole.)

The possible human is like a monkey on one of the other islands who senses the possibility of clean and salted potatoes soon after Ibo's breakthrough, but way before the m-field shift. The possible human intentionally opens to and resonates with the most positive and exciting portions of the human m-field, learning to attune to new patterns in advance of the m-field shift and thus contribute to the gathering of momentum toward critical mass. With the vast and varied ocean of humanity that has inhabited this planet through so many centuries, the m-field governing our race is surely bursting with possibilities that go beyond the typical cultural norms. *The possible human is one who enthusiastically acknowledges the extraordinary models who have gone before and desires to be touched by their examples, to be moved by their patterns, to be governed by their very special contributions to the human m-field.*

This is a matter, again, of intention and belief, and the excitement of energy. The possible human is one who urgently wants to know and experience the highest of human possibilities while believing firmly in her own capacity to bring forth such states and abilities. This, in turn, allows for an expansion of the person's energy, connecting her to the infinite sea of human potential.

A very certain fact within the m-field of virtually every species on this planet, humans included, is that an organism coming into close contact with extreme heat will be burned, instantly. Yet, at some point in early human history, some brave soul discovered that fire, when approached with the proper attitude, could be safely handled, walked upon, and danced with. (Leonard Nimoy, in an episode of "In Search Of" on the subject of firewalking, hypothesized that it arose as a survival trait for people retreating from lava flows.) It was then discovered that if others viewed the firewalk, wanted that behavior for themselves, and believed they had properly follo red their model, they were also able to do it. Thus did the possibility for firewalking enter into the human m-field, allowing the firewalk to be passed down through time by so many different cultures. When a late twentieth-century housewife from the Midwest steps toward the fire, she is crossing a path that has been prepared by thousands and thousands of others who have gone before, and she will be greatly empowered to the extent that she can feel connected to and resonant with their experience.

Of course, the human m-field patterns governing our relationship to fire have only been broadened within the context of the firewalk. It is very important to all of the people of our world that fire continue to burn, for so much good comes from fire burning. When people contact high heat accidently (i.e. outside of the firewalk and within the primary patterns of 'fire burns') they still get badly burned and probably always will.

For myself, the firewalk served as an introduction to what could be called the m-field of humanity evolving beyond set limitations, or the possible human. What I found was that the moment I opened my mind, eyes, and heart to the possible human, the moment I began to really believe that there were ways of being that went way beyond dirty potatoes, then I began to see examples of possible humanity dancing around all over the planet. I started to gather some possible human stories, both to keep myself inspired and to share with others. As a way of demonstrating that the firewalk is just one of many fingers pointing toward our possible future, the following stories are a few of my favorite examples.

In the early 1960s, a couple named Peter and Eileen Caddy,[8] along with their good friend Dorothy McClean, made a firm commitment to follow the inner guidance that they were receiving in the form of 'small quiet voices.' They were not strangers to the spiritual path and had been trying to align their lives with God's will for a number of years, so they were receptive to the idea of God speaking to them from within, and were ready to live as directed. First, they were led to give up their very successful hotel business and move to an empty, barren stretch of land in northern Scotland. They were told to establish living quarters in an old caravan trailer. Then they were told to begin planting a garden.

The land was barren indeed — sandy, mineral poor, organically depleted, and windswept on three sides. Also, the three friends had virtually no gardening experience between them. But they held true to their commitment, tilling the soil, sowing the seeds, working the land each step of the way according to the inner guidance they were receiving. They perservered through a couple of very hard years when all of their external guidance told them to give up their craziness and start living sensibly. Within three years they began to bring forth what became internationally known as the magic of Findhorn garden.

Stepping into the garden at Findhorn in its early days[9] was like stepping into the extraordinary: an overflowing abundance of fruits, vegetables, and flowers which quite literally vibrated with aliveness, including some which were accustomed to much warmer climates. Everything seemed to grow bigger, taste better, and look more colorful. There was a magical quality to the garden, a tangible sense of the impossible on display.

When scientists and experienced gardeners went to Findhorn (and several hundred did), "Impossible" was always their first comment. Looking at the location, and knowing the soil and climate of the region, they knew there was no way, even with the most sophisticated of composting and fertilizing techniques, that such soil could have produced such bounty. Yet it was clearly doing so. Whenever the soil was actually tested, it proved to be perfect on almost every count, and did not even vaguely resemble the soil from surrounding farms. Again, the reaction was, "Impossible! Even with the most advanced of gardening techniques — impossible!" Yet there it was, for all the world to see, and taste.

When the people of Findhorn are asked how they did it, their answers are always quite clear and very simple. They say that they learned to listen to the spirits of the land; that there are different sorts of nature spirits, or subtle energy beings, variously known as angels, devas, fairies, and sprites, who are responsible for governing the growth of living things on the planet, and who will help any of us in our work if we will only learn to communicate and cooperate with them. The people of Findhorn claim that it was through the help of the nature spirits that the soil was made so rich, that so many intelligent choices in the design and planning of the garden were made, and that the plants received such special good fortune regarding bugs, disease, wildlife, etc. They see the garden as a demonstration of what can happen when humanity learns to cooperate with the living consciousness of the Earth rather than blunder on in ignorance of it, or engage in hostile warfare against it.

The skeptic, of course, goes quite crazy at this point. What could be more impossible, more out of the question, more rationally ludicrous and logically ridiculous, than claiming the existence of, much less the help of, angels and fairies?

Yet unless a better explanation for Findhorn can be offered, and none has, does it not make sense to listen to the people who have been living through the experience for more than twenty years? Given the ongoing failure of industrial-chemical agriculture, the monumental stupidity of eradicating our tropical rain forests, the dangers of acid rain, toxic waste, poisoned oceans, and depleted ozone — given that our world is going environmentally and ecologically berserk in so many ways — is it not reassuring and inspiring to think that such deep connection with the living consciousness of our planet is possible, and with such wondrous results? True, a bit of humble pie may be in order for many of us; an allowance that the animistic teachings of the Native Americans, and so many others, have had some validity all along. Certainly this will necessitate some major changes, for the nature spirits cannot coexist with the man-versus-nature philosophy of Western people, nor with the industrial brutality that it has spawned.

One of the earliest messages that the nature spirits whispered to the Findhorn gardeners was, "One garden can change the world." The continuing message has been: The Earth is a living, conscious being, humanity is just one of the many different kingdoms, physical and subtle, which reside within her consciousness, and if we learn to truly work in concert together — humans, animals, plants, spirits, and technology — then our world can be transformed into one garden. Such is the magic and message of the Findhorn Garden: that the Earth is alive, that a deep connection with her living consciousness is possible, and that our planet is a very possible garden for the possible human to come forth.

———————————————

Barry and Suzi Kaufman are the founders of a school called The Option Institute, now located in western Massachusetts.[10] Throughout the late sixties and early seventies, the Kaufmans

were students and teachers in the area of human potential and
consciousness development. At the time that this story unfolds,
they would have described themselves as both successful and
fairly happy. Then, in 1973, a major crisis occurred in their lives
when their two-year-old son, Raun, was discovered to be autistic.
Autism is a syndrome, usually afflicting the very young, in which
a child totally withdraws into himself, closing himself off from
his environment and especially from other people. For the most
part he ceases any learning or development, and often engages
in self-destructive behaviors, such as head-banging. Autism is
considered incurable and nobody knows what causes it.

When they realized how seriously ill Raun was, the Kaufmans
immediately began taking him around the world, from expert to
expert and system to system, to see what could be done for their
son, what hope could be offered. They saw children being treated
to a variety of drugs, children being electroshocked, and children
strapped to tables and locked in closets — all 'aversive therapies'
which aimed at stopping the self-destructive behavior but which
offered no hope for any real cure. Barry and Suzi refused to
accept the verdict of 'incurably lost' that the doctors were placing
on their son. They felt very strongly that there was something
fundamentally wrong with punishing their son as if he were
fundamentally bad.

Finally, they returned with Raun to their home in New York.
They knew that if Raun was going to get better, they were going
to have to work with him themselves. They felt quite certain
that now was the time to start practicing what they had been
preaching for so long: that love is the greatest power in the
universe, a power which can surely heal all wounds. Great words
when written in a book or spoken from a podium, but a very
different matter when it is your own son who is 'incurably' ill.

Barry and Suzi knew that they would have to love their son
unconditionally, with the kind of love that says, "I love you just
as you are. You are perfect now. I love you now," rather than
the typically conditional love that says, "I'll love you when you
live up to my expectations." They knew, with Raun's deep state
of withdrawal, that it would certainly not be enough simply to
say, "I love you." They would somehow have to communicate
their deep love to Raun in a way that he would be able to receive
it in his world. It was a cornerstone of their philosophy that

"Love is to be happy with," and that people only really experience your love for them when you are genuinely happy in their presence. Thus, they felt that their challenge was to be happy with Raun, unconditionally, as he was, and in a way that he would be able to experience given his special state of consciousness.

They set up a program which involved having someone be with Raun at all times, and totally enter into his special world. If he rocked for hours, someone would sit and rock for hours with him. If he stared vacantly off into space, someone would sit and stare vacantly off into space with him. If he drooled, someone would sit and drool with him. During his every waking moment, someone was with Raun, stating explicitly through their actions, "What you're doing is good. What you're feeling is good. I'm happy to be with you just as you are. I love you."

It took about eight months, but Raun finally came out of his withdrawal. He continued to come out, and is now an extremely precocious and intelligent teenager with a genius level I.Q., who has gone way beyond his peers in all of the ways that we have of measuring people. He is now helping his parents to perform similar miracles with others. The Option Institute has become an ongoing story of miracle after miracle, with the same simple lesson running throughout: it is possible to respond with the option of happiness and love to even the most dire of circumstances, and when we do, the 'impossible' may very well happen.

The Kaufmans have had success with a variety of problems, organic and psychological, and their treatment program is always very much the same. When somebody comes to see them with a problem, they do not respond, as most medical models typically do, by trying to figure out and name what the problem is; that is, they do not focus on what is wrong with a person. Rather, they attempt to create an atmosphere of loving happiness, a non-judgmental atmosphere in which the therapist, the person, and the person's family all defocus as much as possible from the perception of a problem and instead work toward generating a feeling of happiness in the present moment, a genuine acceptance of things just the way that they are. They have found, again and again, as with their son, that *human beings tend to move toward health, toward wholeness, toward greater happiness, when they are able to live in such an atmosphere of unconditional love, an atmosphere that vibrates with, "I am happy to be with you, just as you are."*

Since we have reached, at best, a stalemate in our war against cancer and are now facing perhaps an even larger threat from AIDS, Barry and Suzi Kaufman are a very important finger pointing toward the possible human's powers of regeneration and healing. They are saying that it is possible that there are no ultimately incurable illnesses; that it is possible that we all have the capacity to generate the healing response within ourselves and those around us; and that it is possible that the realization of this capacity does not necessitate the years of complex education we usually associate with becoming a healer, but rather that it is a direct result of our very human ability to be happy with life as it is. And they are saying, in their own special way, that *all of the wonders and miracles of the possible human derive from the simple energy of love.*

Then there is a man named Jack Schwarz, who now resides and teaches in Oregon.[11] Jack had the misfortune to get caught up in World War II and spend two years in a concentration camp. He says that as he entered the camp he had two very clear and compelling thoughts. The first was, "If I let this get to me, it will kill me," meaning that if he saw himself as a helpless victim of events beyond his control, and if he contracted negatively from his situation, then he would surely die, as so many did. Secondly, as an answer to the inevitable question about how one could *not* react negatively to such a gruesome situation, came the thought, "Practice forgiveness."

Though it would have been easy and the height of rationality to dismiss such a thought, Jack's philosophy, a combination of pure Christianity (love your neighbor and turn the other cheek) and Eastern mysticism predisposed him to the possibility of the ultimate forgiveness for any and all sins, so practice forgiveness he did. Throughout the entire experience, the words, "I forgive you. You are forgiven," were his constant mantra, repeated over and over again, and practiced, worked at, envisioned, and affirmed, until the idea of forgiveness became an actual expansion of love's energy from his heart. He forgave his captors, he forgave his jailers, and he forgave his tormentors. He forgave his fellow prisoners. He forgave his world gone crazy with war. He forgave

himself for getting caught. He forgave his God for letting the
whole thing happen.

He had one experience in which he was being tortured —
whipped — and as he forgave his tormentors his wounds healed,
instantly. They left him alone after that. When he walked out
after two years of a Nazi concentration camp, he was not only
a survivor, he was a remarkably healthy human being, given
where he had been. He had become a self-made yogi, with all
sorts of mind-body abilities.

Jack is able to consciously control many of his bodily processes,
such as heartbeat, blood pressure, respiration, body temperature,
etc. He also perceives auras (energy fields) and is able to make
accurate diagnoses according to what he sees. He has been wired
up and studied by a number of scientific institutions, most
notably the Menninger Foundation in Kansas, because he is both
a fascinating personality and a compelling rebuttal of the Western
split between body and mind.

Jack's favorite demonstration for years has been to take a
common knitting needle and calmly push it through one side of
his upper arm and then pull it out the other. Then he pokes it
into his other arm — in one side and out the other. Not only
does he not feel any pain as he is doing this, he also does not
bleed. (He has pushed the needle through his brachial artery, a
large vessel in very close proximity to the heart.) Not only does
he not bleed, his wounds heal up very rapidly, and without a
trace, as his audience is watching.

Jack says that this is the way the body is designed to perform,
that the human body is designed to heal itself, and maintain
itself always in a state of perfect health. He claims that our
physical problems stem not so much from breakdowns of the
body as from breakdowns of the mind. He says that a puncture
wound, for instance, is not caused by the needle entering the
body, but by what the mind is doing as the needle enters the
body (i.e., Oh my God, it hurts!, I'm gonna die!, This is BAD!,
I've gotta stop this!, etc.). That is typically how our minds
perform, spinning on the most negative and contracted wheels,
not only when our body has actually sustained an injury, but
also, much worse, in the anticipation, expectation, or imagination
of such injury. Jack says that when the needle is passing through
his body he feels mentally and emotionally detached; that it is

like watching a needle being pushed into sand and then pulled out, the earth easily healing its 'wound.' He adds that when we can achieve such detachment, when the mind is kept from negatively impacting the situation, then the body is capable of far more than we would ordinarily consider possible.

The possibility that Jack Schwarz is illuminating is that we can exercise some degree of control over what will be harmful to us, even with the greatest horror that human beings have ever thought up — the Nazi death camps. In essence, all harm is created within each individual heart and mind. This is certainly my experience with the firewalk, in which a situation that has always been defined as harmful becomes positive through a shift made by the individual. *It is very possible that it is our own habitual contraction of energy which causes so much pain and suffering;* that just as we can energetically depress our immune system, causing otherwise harmless viruses and bacteria to become serious threats, we can likewise depress some larger energy system that we are part of, thereby creating harmful situations in our external world (such as when animals tend to attack fearful people). And it is very possible that as we learn the ways of excitement, of hearts opening with expanded energy, that our world shall become a much, much safer place.

We can walk on fire without burning. We can connect deeply to and cooperate with the living consciousness of our planet. We can be healers to one another. We can exercise a great measure of control over our bodily processes. Through each of these possibilities, we can create a world which is much safer, and much more supportive of our dreams. These are possibilities inherent within all human beings, with the living examples of the firewalkers, the people of Findhorn, Barry and Suzi Kaufman, and Jack Schwarz each serving as inspirations toward what we could become.

I have, over the past several years, collected many such stories and examples of human potential. I have offered these specific stories for several reasons. The first is that in each case the people involved are very explicit in stating that what they are doing is no big deal. They were not struck by lightning or visited specially by God, and *the possibilities which they are demonstrating are clearly available to all people, realizable through simple shifts in consciousness.* Their behaviors are not even new. Each had already been demonstrated by other people in the past, was already existing in the human m-field as a pattern of energy which could be attuned to and 'discovered,' and thus is truly a trait inherent within all people. What is especially exciting about our current age is that when the possible human steps forward, our mass media can spread the news far and wide, greatly accelerating our movement toward critical mass in a given area.

I have also shared these specific stories because they are widely-known, well-documented, and ongoing demonstrations of human potential. Many of my possible human stories have been one-time spontaneous events, such as examples of hysterical strength, in which the person involved has done something remarkable but does not know how, and cannot later repeat it. The skeptic will dismiss all such stories out of hand as being anecdotal, unverifiable, and unrepeatable. This is a favorite refuge of the skeptical mind, the rule being that if it cannot be repeated in a scientific laboratory then it is not real.

But how many of us would care to fall in love and pursue a romance in a laboratory? And what have we come to logically understand about the process of falling in love? What songwriter could conceive and compose new music under carefully monitored laboratory conditions, over and over again? What have we scientifically proven and patented about the creative process that artists go through? Indeed, even the process of scientific discovery itself often proves to be elusive, with benzene rings showing up in dreams, and physical laws arising in bathtubs. The simple fact is that many of the best things in life are anecdotal, unverifiable, and unrepeatable (on demand), but that does not make them any less real, important, or capable of illuminating the human condition.

Along these lines, one scientist that I corresponded with suggested that I come into his laboratory and lie upon a table as he carefully applied specific measures of heat to the soles of my feet, thus providing what he thought would be a clear and unequivocal test of the firewalk. I find it very difficult to explain to such a person that without the grass under foot, without the moon and stars overhead, without a circle of people holding hands and singing songs, and radiating loving support to one

another, without our ancient friend the glowing wood fire, that
without all of these elements you would not have the firewalk
I am writing about, and therefore could not actually study and
learn anything about it. Not that these are necessary elements —
it has been done on asphalt, it has been done in daylight, it has
been done alone, it has been done on charcoal briquettes — but
in removing any of these elements you have already made some
essential changes and thus will be studying something entirely
different. *Since we are spontaneously arising and organically
grounded creatures, we will certainly derive important lessons
from the observation of spontaneously arising and organically
grounded events.*

Still, in deference to the skeptical mind, I have chosen the
examples of Findhorn, the Kaufmans, and Jack Schwarz precisely
because they are widely-known, well-documented, and ongoing
demonstrations[12] of the principles in this book. If the mind truly
wishes to be opened, then these folks can be read about in a
number of books, or visited, or studied with. But do take caution,
for once having embraced such realities you may find it harder
and harder to turn away any evidence of your potential, even
when it is 'scientifically unproven.' Give the possible human just
a fraction of an inch and you are opening up to light years of
change and transformation.

My final reason for offering these stories is that each one
clearly demonstrates the role of fear in the creative process.
Findhorn, for example, began with what many Westerners would
find unthinkably terrifying: to leave a sound financial business
and lifestyle and to step into the total unknown, with no prospects
whatsoever, and all upon the guidance of small inner voices! For
the first two years, the Findhorn members were constantly
worrying over money and bills and their lack of gardening
experience. They also found that each time they were able to
really surrender to their situation and laugh about it all, another
'miracle' would open on their path. Would they now say their
fear was worth it? Without the slightest hesitation.

I doubt very much that Barry and Suzi Kaufman would ever
have made their special discoveries if Raun had had a sore
throat. It took autism — Oh my God, he's going to be that way
forever! — to generate the very large currents of energy which
would challenge them, push them, and inspire them until they

received the insights and made the breakthroughs which have now gone on to positively touch thousands and thousands of lives. Nor could Jack Schwarz have expected to make his discoveries at Club Med. It took the unfathomable horror of a concentration camp to lead him through his transformations. He now refers to the experience as his 'blessing.' His blessing! That is what it means to say yes to fear and turn its energy toward positive creation.

The possible human consistently springs from negative circumstances, consistently arises out of the fearful energies of illness, danger, conflict, injustice, strife, etc., and is invariably a risk-taker, one who consciously chooses life on the razor's edge. The possible human is usually not comfortable with a comfortable life, but instead feels the need to be challenged every bit as urgently as the needs for food, water, and shelter. My sense is that the strong rush of excited energy provided by challenging and threatening situations somehow carries us across the gap between our current m-field realities and the m-field of possible humanity. The more contracted we are, the more our potential is limited to the world as we have lived it. Allowing our energy to expand with excitement (mostly through choosing to live with threatening and challenging situations), we can come into contact and resonance with many other patterns and possibilities.

This is the age of the possible human precisely because this is an age of so very many terribly threatening razors that life on the razor's edge is becoming the norm. When it comes to the energy of evolution, we are experiencing anything but a shortage. We are bursting at our psychic seams with more energy than we know what to do with. Our collective challenge is to be responsive to this great flow of creative energy, and to allow ourselves to be always expanding outward, into connection with others and with the highest of human possibilities. Most importantly, our collective challenge is to realize that we are participants in a vast and sweeping evolutionary process, literally poised upon a precipice as we gather the energy necessary to leap.

Since the earliest days of human history there have lived special people — sages and mystics, masters and saints, shamans and heroes — who have lived special lives, moving beyond normal human boundaries. They have stated with their lives, "This is what's possible, this is where we're going." They have made their contributions to our histories and mythologies, and they have made their contributions to the human m-field. Most viewed themselves as models for their fellow men and women while dreaming of a time when their special ways of being in the world would become the common ways of humankind. Most would agree with one such possible human who, speaking two thousand years ago, told us that the most important of all commandments is that we love our neighbors as ourselves. Yes, it is a vast and sweeping movement we find ourselves awakening to, and yes, the way remains, as ever, as simple, and as possible, as opening our hearts and offering love.

eleven

OUCH!

One of the first procedures he [Dr. Dabney Edwin, of Tulane University] performs for burn victims is making a hypnotic suggestion that they will feel a cooling sensation in the burned area . . . . This procedure minimizes damage and inflammation so well that Edwin has seen patients who would have ordinarily required skin grafts heal without them.

At the Alta Bates Hospital's burn center in Berkeley, California, burn center director Dr. Jerold Kaplan, too, has been using hypnosis. Kaplan takes patients with burns on both sides of their bodies and, after hypnotizing them, asks them to try to make the temperature of one side higher than that on the other. The patients were able to raise their temperatures by as much as 4°C; in addition, the side with the temperature increase healed faster than the unwarmed side.[1]

What to me was most fascinating about the firewalks is not the fact that most individuals come through it without burns or blisters but that some of them don't. What accounts for the difference?[2]

If someone had told me before I embarked on my firewalking adventure that my major lessons would have to do with pain, I suspect I never would have made the journey. Like most people, I neither liked pain, nor had any positive associations with it. My definition of a happy, well-lived life did not include the experience of pain, and was in fact precluded by it; to suffer pain was an indication of failure and/or misfortune, and happiness could only arise as the pain disappeared.

Besides this, it seemed to me then that the whole point, purpose, and relevance of firewalking was that one *not* experience any pain. After all, I already knew how to step on fire and get burned! The allure of becoming a firewalker was that I could

somehow prevent that from happening; that I would be able
to walk on fire and not burn; that I would not feel any pain.

Alas, such illusions were to die a quick and fairly painful
death. As described in Chapter 1, I felt a little pain after my
very first walk, and was well aware that a fellow trainee had
picked up a nasty burn that would fester and blister for the
duration of the training. The next night I would hear Kathy's
scream, see her feet thoroughly scorched, and watch as she was
carried away to a hospital. Shortly thereafter I would experience
my first really bad burn — 'really bad burn' being loosely defined
as: needing some sort of physical treatment or attention (i.e.,
aloe, cold water, wet rags, a cool breeze), making it hard to fall
asleep that night, and causing difficulty walking the next day, or
several days. One night in particular during my training stands
out as a rather lucid indicator of the path that lay before me:
two of my companions and I, wracked with pain and laughter,
are taking turns sticking our torched tootsies into a motel bathroom's
toilet bowl. Ah, the special, sacred moments of a spiritual life . .

Nonetheless, I carried on, continuing to pursue the practice
of firewalking despite the perplexing and nagging problem of
burns. While I could not and would not have denied the occurrence
of 'really bad burns' for myself and others, the prevailing and
majority experiences were so clearly of joy and personal empowerment that I was able to remain positively focused and
inspired. My underlying attitude was that burns were a mistake,
a sign we were doing something wrong either logistically or
psycho-emotionally, and that eventually, with time and experience,
we would do everything right and people would no longer
get burned.

Four years later I am not so sure. I must honestly say that
while time and experience have certainly deepened my understanding
of firewalking, and while my workshop presentation has become
clearer and more effective, while the physical logistics of the
actual walk have gone through definite improvements, and
while Penny and I and some friends have grown to truly *love*
firewalking — statistically speaking, the incidence of burns,
minor and 'really bad,' has not changed nearly as much as one
might expect. We have found that every continuing firewalker
(someone who comes to more than five firewalks) gets burned
sooner or later; that even the best of firewalks leave at least a

person or two with what we have come to call the 'ouchies;' and
that occasional firewalks seem to zap the whole group. All of
this has led me to conclude that, in terms of the actual quantity
of burns, nothing we have done, and none of the lessons of time
and experience, has really made that big a difference.

Let me try to clarify this by drawing an analogy to automobile
safety. Over the years, through the development of seatbelts,
larger bumpers, better tires, etc., the automobile has certainly
been made safer. Yet there were drivers twenty years ago who
never got in an accident, and never experienced their automobile's
unsafety, just as there are drivers today dying on the highways
in the safest of all vehicles. The deciding factor, of course, is the
human element. While improvements in the design of a car may
improve a poor driver's chances of surviving an accident, no
amount of work upon the car can really prevent a poor driver
from *having* the accident. Ultimately, it is the human element,
the consciousness of the individual driver who gets behind the
wheel of the car, that makes the creative difference.

In a similar way, we have diligently worked to improve the
safety of firewalks. For instance, when I first began I followed
Tolly's model of raking the coals out to a depth of about four
inches, and then putting the rake down and letting the walk
proceed, the path untended. What I noticed was that walking
on such a thick bed of coals was much like walking on a pile
of tennis balls — it could be a very unstable and clumsy affair.
I also noticed that when a person stumbles during the walk,
losing his balance even momentarily, he invariably gets a nasty
burn. Finally, I found that during a walk, the path would be
disturbed by one person's walking in such a way as to leave the
path more unstable for the next walker. Gradually, I developed
an approach which involved raking the path of coals much
thinner (about two inches) — allowing the stability of the earth
beneath the path to be felt — and of tending the path throughout
the walk, smoothing out any disturbances caused by the walkers.

On the one hand, I feel that such continuing improvements
have undoubtedly made a positive difference for potential firewalkers. As I remove any physical or logistical dissimilarities
which may have occurred from one walk to the next, I am
removing from the individual's path the factors which may have
interfered with the primary intention of firewalking. I view my

work as that of *physically* providing the event for which people are *psycho-emotionally* preparing. Stumbling on hot coals is very different than walking on hot coals, and may override the best of conscious preparations that a person has made. Having a flashbulb explode just as one is about to walk, or hearing loud distracting noises, or being surrounded by unsupportive people: these are all variables which are likely to intrude upon the individual's consciousness. By doing my very best to eliminate such fluctuations, I feel I have greatly diminished the occurrence of *accidental* burns, (i.e., burns which occur because the individual is stepping forward with an intention which is not in alignment with the environment in which he is moving), and in so doing have clearly made the firewalks much safer.

On the other hand, people still get burned, even within the most conscientiously engineered environment. As Norman Cousins has so cogently pointed out, this is what is so fascinating about the firewalk. If many thousands of people have walked on fire without the slightest sensation of heat or pain, then why does anyone ever get burned? If we have indeed managed to maintain the firewalking environment as a constant, then what makes the differences in individual experience? The firewalk is a finger pointing inward, insisting somehow, in some way, that each of us contributes to the creation of our body, of our world, and of our ongoing experience. It is the human element, the far-from-fully-understood co-creative process of the human being, which is the principle cause of the far-from-fully-understood practice of firewalking. *It is the human element, the co-creative consciousness of each individual firewalker, which is the principle cause of most firewalking burns.*

A caution about the word 'cause.' Once we agree to add human consciousness to the causal equation, and say that humans contribute to the formation of objective reality through the movement of subjective processes, then our classical notions of cause and effect must be altogether revised. In the Cartesian worldview, the universe is an infinity of billiard balls, planet-size to electron-size, which spin about in precise paths, have mathematically predictable collisions, and fly off on exact trajectories into further predictable collisions. The present moment is the linear conclusion of past interactions, and the future logically and inevitably unfolds from the present. Cause and effect are

absolutes in such a strictly mechanical universe: I caused my
hand to wind the clock, which caused gear number one to move,
which caused gear number two to move, which caused gear
number three to move, which caused the hands of the clock to
move, and so on. Furthermore, having observed the hands of
the clock in motion, we should be able to trace back along a
linear chain of cause and effect events to the exact instant when
I began to wind the clock — the fabled first cause.

The moment we say, "Ah, but the clock is a living, evolving,
conscious entity — a creative intelligence — comprised of mech-
anically defined movements *and* capable of consciously contributing
to the flow of those movements," then the 'laws' of cause and
effect are not only called into question, but the very idea of
cause and effect becomes at best tenuous, if not dubious. If, as
James Jeans mused, the universe is more a great thought than a
great machine, then it becomes a lot more difficult to think
about! In the words of physicist John Wheeler: "There may be
no such thing as the 'glittering central mechanism of the universe.'
Not machinery but magic may be the better description of the
treasure that is waiting."[3] Magic!? Is it any wonder that science
has so stubbornly resisted the merging of subjective and objective
realities? The inner world of human consciousness will never
yield to the mapping, sorting, measuring, and defining of the
classical scientific process; there is too much of the dream *in
there*, and always shall be. Perish the thought that the dream
be permitted to escape *out here!*

Nonetheless, as denizens of the clockwork world of Cartesian
science, we find it almost impossible to stop thinking in linear
chains of cause and effect, to stop thinking, "Here is an effect,
and this is what caused it." Observing the firewalk, we want to
say, "The man got burned *because* he stepped on that hot coal,
or *because* the fire was so many degrees hot, or *because* he
walked at such and such a speed;" or, "The man *didn't* get
burned *because* his feet were coated with sweat, or *because* he
has calloused feet, or *because* he walked on the cool spots." This
is the clockwork thinking of our clockwork worldview: any
observable effect must have a definitive cause. If the man got
burned there must be a specific cause, which we can isolate,
name, and hopefully eliminate for the future.

For the first year of our firewalking experience, that is precisely the process which Penny and I followed, especially if a walk had any 'really bad burns.' We would ploddingly analyze the evening, piece by piece, searching for the cause (What did we do wrong!?) of that evening's failure. Through that process we gradually came to make specific changes, tightening up the 'experiment' by eliminating those factors which usually seemed to lead to burns. In our second year, however, people would still get burned even though there were no longer any errant variables upon which to pin the blame. The situation was literally like grasping water with a tightened fist; the reasons and explanations would fall further away the harder that we grasped. There was a fundamental slipperiness to all of the data which we were observing. Typically, our minds would grind away for an hour or two, determined to name the cause for the effect we had witnessed — "Maybe it was this, maybe it was that" — until finally we would surrender to the futility of our grasping. The simple and inescapable fact was that we could not prevent all firewalking burns because many were being caused by the human element, the consciousness of the individual walkers.

I cannot overly stress the degree to which I struggled and still struggle with this basic insight. Despite my predisposition to such a viewpoint, despite the easy agreement of my peers and students, and despite my constant articulation of 'the co-creative process,' I still find it difficult to view a firewalk without thinking first in purely objective, cause and effect terms. Thus, if I see a person leap off the fire in pain, my first thoughts are to see if there is something about the path that is amiss, rather than to assume the workings of consciousness. Or when somebody walks especially slowly, with no difficulty at all, my mind will first note whether or not the path is really glowing, or whether or not we are at the end of the night when the path is cooling off from so many walkers. On nights when it is raining, my mind says, "Water cools fire," and I just feel safer, without a doubt.

On the other hand, two or three times per firewalk I witness or experience something which, as the saying goes, simply blows my mind. It is like diligently adding one plus one and suddenly getting fifty — clearly there is more going on than ordinarily meets the eye; there is some other important factor. I have learned to smile during such moments, releasing my need to have it all figured out, and content to mentally file the experience away in a drawer labeled 'messy data.' It is these experiences which have steadily moved me to believe so strongly in the creative power of human consciousness. For instance:

— My own 'first foot' experiences have been relentlessly convincing. I always do the raking of the coals, so I always get a close-up view of the condition of the path, and take the time to prepare it exactly as I want it. I always walk first, so the path is always a perfectly glowing, bright orange carpet of coals, undisturbed and not at all cooled down. Nine times out of ten I take my four or more steps without the slightest hint of heat or pain, but from time to time I take one or two steps and **FEEL** it! I usually *know* the nights I'm going to get burned before I ever rake out the coals.

— I always take my first step with my right foot, so, given that I sometimes take an odd number of steps, my right foot sometimes spends more time in the fire. Yet, I almost always get burned on the same spot on my left foot, and have rarely been burned on my right foot. Getting burned on only one foot is very common and, as in my case, not necessarily related to the foot which was in the fire first, or longest.

— There is a system of energy bodywork called reflexology which maps specific points (like acupuncture points) on the feet which relate energetically to specific organs and systems throughout the body. When I have compared walkers' burns with information about their health, I have found a very high correlation between the location of the burns and reflexology points.

— Many walkers have reported that their first time across the fire they felt a great deal of heat, and pain, and thought they must be badly burned. Nonetheless, they felt guided to walk again, sometimes three or four more times. Their sense was that each time across the fire their feet felt better, and that the continuing exposure to the fire was healing any burns, rather than exacerbating them. By the time the walk was over they were feeling no pain at all, nor were their feet at all blistered.

— As a walk progresses, live coals will be kicked into the area surrounding the path, which I endeavor to put out with a hose. When I miss one, and somebody *accidentally* finds it with his bare foot, he will often gasp with pain, in very pointed contrast

to his experience of *intentionally* walking across the solid sheet
of glowing embers.

— Invariably, if the first or second person who follows me
across the fire gets burned, we are in for a bad night. Those
who are sensitive to energy can feel a shudder ripple through
the whole group when someone gets stung by the fire. When
this happens to one of the first walkers, it seems to set the tone
or establish the model for everyone else. I have found that this
can only be overcome by actually stopping the flow of walkers,
doing something physically to shake up the energy, and then
starting over again.

— During my first year, I would pass around a bottle of aloe
after the walk for those who had 'ouchies.' Some nights I could
clearly see that individuals who had been feeling fine up to that
point would watch the bottle circulating and gradually develop
a serious need for it! Likewise, I have found that just talking
about 'ouchies' too much after a walk increases the volume
and intensity of pain in the room.

— There is clearly a sense of greater ease on nights when it is
raining, for psycho-emotional reasons (it just *feels* good to stand
around a fire in the rain, unconcerned with getting wet, like
children), and for the obvious reason that the rain causes *some*
physical cooling. I have also witnessed some very nasty burns
on rainy nights, including one which happened toward the end
of the walk when the path was a soaked but smoldering path
of black ash.

— During the most disastrous firewalks that I have ever led,
at least half the group was not burned! That is, the fire was
not unwalkable for some logistical reason. Indeed, it is out of
such really rough evenings that I have heard some of the most
astonishing miracle stories from those who did walk without
getting burned.

— Without a doubt, in tracing back through all of my walks,
the most common element in the 'bad' ones is the surrounding
presence of unsupportive people. This is why I stopped firewalking
in public, and it is why I take great care to communicate to, and
feel congruent with property owners, roommates, and neighbors
of the site. It is why I in no way try to persuade or convince
anybody to come to a firewalk; it simply works much better

when all of the human consciousness in attendance is *freely* participating, 100 percent.

— Most of the people who have ever announced early in the evening that they have just given up smoking (and perhaps are coming to empower that choice) have gotten nasty burns. The same is true for the vast majority of those who have been clearly sick, with colds, headaches, allergies, etc.

— Finally, there is the sheer contrast between different firewalks. One night the fire seems to pulse with danger. It is an ordeal to be somehow gotten through, a harsh force to hopefully overcome. My body shudders through the entire walk as I watch 20, 30, or 40 percent of the walkers getting painfully zapped. On such a night the fire never gives up its prerogative for burning, and I count any painless walks as true blessings. A month later — same time of night, same place, same wood, same inside presentation, *different people* — and the fire is a benevolent pool of sparkling light. People are walking slowly, and stopping, and picking up coals, and dancing with one another. The whole group is lifted up in a current of laughing wonder. I have been part of many such nights, when the energy has totally shifted, and there have rarely been any 'ouchies.' On these nights I stand there wondering how anybody ever gets burned at all.

These are the experiences which stand as my evidence in support of the idea that *something* is going on at a firewalk. They are repeated observations which have left me with little doubt that the subjective movements of human consciousness are to some degree contributing to the ongoing creation of objective reality. There have been other powerfully convincing moments which I have omitted here because of their overly subjective (for these purposes) nature. I realize that even what I have offered is hardly objective evidence by most standards. Perhaps it is just not possible to teach an old experiment new protocols.

————————————

Pain, or the surprising absence of pain, is the common thread which runs through all of my firewalking experiences, and through, in fact, the entire firewalking phenomenon. As stated in Chapter 3, it is the possibility of failure, and of suffering pain and serious injury, which gives meaning to the practice of firewalking for the Kung, the Anastenarides, the Balinese, and for firewalkers everywhere. It is the very graphic feedback of pain — it either hurts or it does not; you are either walking or you are limping — which tells the firewalker about the clarity and/or potency of his creative process or relationship to the Creator. If nobody ever got burned, the firewalk would lose much of its power and significance as a religious rite, and as a personal life-teaching.

This is easy to say, but almost impossible for me to really accept and embrace. From the very first time that my foot screamed Ouch!, through all of the times that I was burned, and through the ever-stern looks on the faces of especially 'unsuccessful' walkers and the feelings of guilt that would invariably follow, I operated under the belief that 'successful' firewalking meant not getting burned and that pain was a sign that we were doing something wrong. For the longest time I would try to downplay the whole issue, shrugging it off as a 'bug' we still had not quite worked out. It was not that I lied about it; I always told people about the possibility of getting burned. But I was purposely vague about what it meant, and failed to establish a positive or healthy context for pain. Rather, I felt, and must have communicated, that pain was an unfortunate distraction, an affliction upon the firewalk to someday be eliminated, and hopefully that night.

Slowly, I have come to recognize that the expectations I was bringing to the firewalk — that things should be totally predictable and under control, and any pain is a sign of failure — were the same expectations I was bringing to life. And slowly I have come to appreciate that such expectations were misguided, for life is ever unpredictable, we are never totally in control, and *pain is not so much a sign of failure as it is an indication that we are fully awake to life and to the unceasing growth and change that it demands.* The commitment to grow beyond set limitations and to evolve, which is the very essense of being human, is a certain opening to the lessons of pain. The happy and fulfilling life (or firewalk) is not the one which somehow manages to be painless; it is the one which understands and is enriched by any pains which happen to come.

Just as the idea that we can somehow live without fear actually intensifies our experience of contraction, so the idea that we can somehow live without pain actually intensifies the unpleasantness of pain. Just as fear serves a critical function in the growth of a healthy human being, so pain is an essential and unavoidable teacher as we travel through our lives. And just as it was helpful to divide fear into the two separate experiences of excitement and contraction, so I have found pain much easier to understand by sorting it into four different levels: homeostatic, acute, chronic, and transformational.

Homeostatic pain operates as an ever-present psycho-physical compass to guide us through our daily lives. It is a continuous influence, which functions mostly below our conscious awareness, an unceasing play of pain which carries vital information about our world and our relationship to it. It would be *impossible* to negotiate life in a balanced manner without the constant feedback of such pain to guide us. Homeostatic pain lets us know that we are gripping the doorknob with too much force, that we are pulling our shoelaces too tightly, that we are leaning with too much weight upon our elbows, that we are scratching an itch with too much intensity. As we lean back in a chair, homeostatic pain tells us when we are reaching the limit of our backbone's flexibility. It lets us know when it is time to eat, and when it is time to stop eating. It lets us know of the need for exercise, and of the need to stop exercising. It lets us know if our environment is too hot, too cold, too toxic, too noisy. And, it lets us know of our needs for love, spirituality, companionship, sexual expression, acknowledgement, creative outlets, meaningful work, and physical contact.

When we are living in a state of physical and emotional balance (homeostasis) we may not *really* feel any of these pains. Rather, we will feel just the slightest hint, the mere possibility of pain, which will only register on unconscious levels but will be enough to direct our behavior and to sustain us in a state of balance. When we behaviorally move out of balance, or when our environment changes too quickly or extremely, we begin to feel mild pain, which is our motivation to change and the guidance for our movements. This is exquisitely intelligent design, and one who is awake to the ever-shifting currents of the body/mind and at peace with the necessity of homeostatic pain will rarely encounter anything more severe than slight discomfort.

When we somehow miss the quiet whisperings of homeostatic pain, then we leave ourselves open to the dissonant screech of *acute* pain. Acute pain tells us that we are *seriously* out of balance, that we are running the risk of crippling injury or death, and that we must take steps immediately to remedy our situation. Acute pain is impossible to ignore. It is an intensely garish, flashing neon light, totally commanding our attention, and warning us of organic damage, systemic failure, and/or toxic invasion. It tells us without question that something is *wrong*. It is an alarm clock compelling us to stop, look, listen, and make effective changes.

When you attempt to move your foot through an immovable object, your stubbed toe makes you instantly aware of your misjudgement — the more so the more seriously you have misjudged. When you slip with a knife, your sliced finger cries out your error. When your tooth decays to the nerve, or your appendix explodes, or you are struck by a moving vehicle, or a virus overwhelms your immune system, or your heart fails in its pumping — you are acutely informed that something is very wrong. Likewise, when your lover abandons you, or you are fired from your job, or a friend dies, or a dream collapses — you ache deeply, and acutely. There is an irrefutable sense of things gone wrong and the need for immediate healing.

During our moments of acute pain, we all too literally *become* the pain. It is as if everything else ceases to exist and there is simply our awareness of the pain *and* our awareness of any circumstances or actions leading up to and surrounding the pain. This is the key to acute pain: as long as our attention is dominated with pain, then we will be attending to everything which may have caused or contributed to the pain and thus will, hopefully, learn for the future. To fail to learn from our times of acute pain is to insure further such hurts down the road, whereas to suffer acutely and see clearly the totality of conditions preceding our suffering is to grow more conscious, and to become less liable of repeated errors, and repeated pains.

Most of our acute pain is unnecessary. The purpose of homeostatic pain is to circumvent the need for acute pain, shifting our conscious and/or unconscious awareness to a situation before it progresses into an overly painful episode. Unfortunately, we have many ways of interfering with homeostatic function. The use of drugs, alcohol, and painkillers, while offering short-term relief, ultimately renders us less aware and less able to hear homeostatic messages. The unresolved stress and tension of chronic contraction totally inhibits homeostasis: people are statistically more prone to the acute pains of bodily illness *and accidents* when they are under too much stress. Being overly mental; living in a way that is unaware of, or unconcerned with, or unattentive to one's body; living 'out of the body;' or, even worse, openly disliking one's body, fighting it, hating it — these are all attitudes which desensitize one to healthy homeostatic pain. This is also true for the attitude of ignoring or disdaining pain — the athlete or macho-man who rigidly overrides and 'pushes past' the body's minor pains and invariably hits the wall of acute pain. In all of these ways we subvert a natural process and painfully pay the price later.

The same holds true for most of our acute emotional pains. Usually, if we had been paying attention to all of the quiet homeostatic messages, we would not have been so acutely pained when she suddenly left, or it failed, or he betrayed. Many such events are in fact preventable when we are committed to being fully awake to life and fully responsive to its ever-changing demands. Even the unpreventable emotional pains, the hurts from our past, the deaths, the rainy day inevitabilities, are weathered better by the person who has practiced homeostatic awareness than by the person who only feels the sledgehammer blows. In shutting down our moment-to-moment homeostatic awareness, we cripple ourselves on many levels. And it hurts!

Still, even more tragic is *chronic* pain. Chronic pain is created by the mind and is clearly the most difficult pain to deal with. This is not to say that such acute pains as starvation, war, and rampant disease are not difficult to deal with. They do make a sort of sense, however, and it is easy enough to see how to get such pains to stop. Chronic pain, on the other hand, can be agonizingly baffling. It can seem to have no 'real' cause, and thus frequently drives doctors and researchers to say that it is "all in one's head" or that "you're just making it up." This, of course, is asinine to one who is suffering day in and day out for months and maybe years from chronic pain.

Chronic pain is the placebo response in reverse. It is a way of using the (mostly *unconscious*) power of one's consciousness to debilitate the body rather than heal it. While the placebo response is initiated by something which pleases (i.e., a 'medicine' which the patient believes in) the chronic reaction is usually initiated by something which strongly displeases. The pain of a whiplash injury may stay around for years, finally crippling the body, if there is unreleased resentment and hostility toward the other driver (or a long-pending lawsuit). Migraine headaches can grow directly out of unpleasant thoughts about unpleasant situations. The chronic stiffening of arthritis often follows the adoption of a rigid and inflexible attitude. The appearance somewhere on the body of a small lump, discovered, palpated, thought upon, worried over, obsessed about, finally invested with the full creative/destructive power of the human mind, can be transformed from a transient cyst to the malignant tumor which was so greatly feared. The simple truth is this: human beings have a *very* easily realized capacity to psycho-emotionally create pain within their bodies. We do it all the time.

Chronic pain usually begins as homeostatic or acute pain. A slightly achy (homeostatic) feeling in the lower back one morning can be intensely and negatively focused upon, causing a *physical* tensing of muscles, a *physical* contraction of fluid circulation, and an actual pulling of vertabrae out of alignment, until there is a full-blown lower back problem that *hurts*. If the person feeling this happens to hate pain, and hates being laid up, and hates the idea of growing old, and hates spending money on chiropractors, etc., etc., then he or she can reverse-placebo the lower back into a long, suffering chronic problem. Or instead, the body may go through an acute injury, and instead of healing in one week it takes three, the mind chronically plaguing the body's natural healing process. The tragedy of it all is that while acute pain is occasionally necessary, chronic pain *never* is, except that it is our way of learning to *stop* creating chronic pain and contraction.

Finally, there is *transformational* pain. This is the pain that almost always accompanies our major changes. It is the psycho-physical feeling of changing forms: trans-form-ational. It is the pain of birth and death, the growing pains of the body becoming bigger, the pains of menarche and menopause, and the pains of growing older. It is the pain of breakthrough, the pain of catharsis, the pain of purification, the pain of falling in love, the pain of sexual orgasm. It is the pain of healthy athletic conditioning — the wall just before the 'runner's high.' It is the self-doubt just before a hard-earned success. It is the 'you can't make an omelet without breaking the egg' pain. It is the pain of leaving home, the pain of letting go, the pain of surrendering to God.

Transformational pain is much like homeostatic pain in that there is a very natural feeling to it, a sense of it being a good, worthy pain. As with homeostatic pain, the more that we accept the pains of transformation, the easier our changes will be, and the easier our pain. Transformational pain is also like acute pain in that it can *really* hurt, focusing all of our attention and awareness into the present moment and any lessons to be learned. Transformational pain is also much like chronic pain in that it is filled with mind, ripe with consciousness, and governed by the subjective processes of the individual; we all too often chronically prolong our transformational pains.

There is, of course, a lot of overlap between these different levels of pain. There are some experiences, birth being a prime example, which involve all four levels simultaneously. Every other pain also has the potential to include or move through the different levels. Moments after acutely slicing your finger with a knife, your mind will enter in and begin to push things toward either homeostasis or chronic difficulty. If you are like the little boy mentioned in an earlier chapter who told his finger to stop bleeding and it did, or like Jack Schwarz who discovered that simple forgiveness both releases pain and promotes rapid healing, then your cut finger may carry you to an experience of trans- formational pain. You may be a different person for having gone through the pain.

The purpose of differentiating these four levels of pain is for you to be able to come awake to yourself right in the midst of a painful experience and sense the quality of pain that you are feeling, and to a very large extent creating, right in that very moment. When you do that, you are then in a better position to respond appropriately, to learn the lessons of the pain, and make any necessary change. It is incredibly valuable to be able to tell the difference between homeostatic pain and chronic pain, and it requires practiced attention to do so. It is also valuable to be able to feel when the acute pain of a traumatic incident has subsided, leaving only transformational pain. There is an art to having pain, *a vitally important life skill which can and must be learned.*

As long as we are committed to living fully in this world, then we are of necessity committed to growth, to evolution, and to change: to pain. All of the big changes of our lives (and many of the little) carry some hurt with them. The first and biggest change of all — the movement from our mother's womb — can only occur, even under the best of circumstances, with a great amount of pain. The aches of an empty tummy, of 'where's Mommy?,' of a wet diaper, a new tooth, a growing limb, the bumped bottom of learning to walk, the scraped knee of learning to run, the bloody nose of learning to climb — there is no healthy child who thrives without the cries of pain that come with testing and exploring this world, and with stretching toward and learning/becoming something new.

Nor are any of us spared the infinite pains of budding adolescence, the gnawing tensions of urgent, yet tenuous dreams, or the exquisite ache of lovers coming closer still. We should not hope to be spared the rending pain that we feel as we contemplate, or participate in, our primitive human hates and our mindless environmental fiascos. Hope though we may, we shall not be spared the eternal hurt of friends and family passing away.

When we were toddlers, we fell down, went boom, cried for a while, then got up and tried again, lessons learned. As adults we spend vast amounts of our personal energies attempting to avoid any change whatsoever so that we will not get hurt. When, inevitably, we do fall down, we cry for a while and then remain chronically stuck and unmoving as we judge, blame, and criticize ourselves for failing, and devise strategies for avoiding any such painful loss of control in the future. As if we could.

Life is always changing. Sometimes it hurts. Every pain brings an important lesson, so that we may grow to live and love this life more fully.

If pain is a healthy human function which can teach us vitally important lessons, then the firewalk could be the premier pain university on the planet. For those of us who have walked many times, and have thus been through a few 'really bad burns,' the benefits have been abundantly clear. One should not assume that we are all masochists, and that we are people who are hooked on pain or who even like pain. I certainly do not, and I have not witnessed a single person at any of my firewalks who was attracted to or enthused about the idea of getting burned. However, along with many others I have come to appreciate, mostly through the firewalk, that pain is an essential ingredient in life. I have also learned, mostly through my more painful firewalking moments, ways to optimize the experience of pain, both diminishing its unpleasantness and better receiving its lessons.

When I lead firewalks now, I try to build a healthy context for the possibility of getting burned. What does not work at all is for a person to get burned and then to feel like a jerk who has just done some idiot thing and gotten what he deserved. A runner, for instance, who pulls a hamstring, or a dancer who sprains an ankle, or a skier who breaks a leg, have healthy contexts for their injuries and are treated with compassion, respect, and possibly even admiration by those around them because we have culturally placed a value on those activities. Since we have no cultural understanding of the value of firewalking, most people who come to a firewalk are lacking a healthy context for any pain sustained. The difference between a healthy and unhealthy context can make a big difference in how the pain is experienced (what level) and how quickly it heals.

So I talk about the possibility of getting burned, assuring the group that it can happen, that it most often does not happen, and that when it does happen it is *very* rarely a 'rush you off to the hospital' sort of burn. (I only know of that happening once.) I refer to firewalking burns as 'ouchies' and I characterize 'ouchies' as generally benign affairs, stinging for a short time and then passing, with some valuable lessons left behind. I point out that if it were not for the possibility of getting burned there would be no firewalk at all, and that it is the extreme heat of the fire and its clear potential for burning flesh which gives the evening much of its meaning. I caution people that while I certainly have a lot of experience with firewalking and a lot of insight into the nature of burns, I definitely do not have it all figured out, nor can I guarantee anybody's safety, including my own. Though I believe anyone can walk on fire, I warn them that on a given night, for a given person, for a given psycho-emotional moment in that person's life, it may or may not be wise to walk on hot coals. And, I assure them that they are the only ones who can tell for themselves whether or not tonight is a good night for firewalking.

Finally, I tell them that if they are not prepared to run the risk of getting burned, they should not even consider walking on hot coals. As in life, there are no guarantees. *If we are unable to deal with the worst that could happen, we really have no business pursuing the best.*

Later in the evening, after I have introduced the concepts of energy, excitement, and contraction, we do a little experiment, which I invite the reader try out. This is a way to experience just what an 'ouchie' feels like and how to best resolve it. Simply raise your hands in front of you, about four feet apart, palms facing, and then really **CLAP** your hands as hard as you possibly can. You have to *really* clap hard to get the effects of this experiment, so do your best!

If you have clapped your hardest clap then — Ouch! — you know pretty much what an 'ouchie' feels like. Now, if you have an 'ouchie' and you simply stay relaxed, and calm, breathing easily, listening to the pain passively, almost like listening to music, then you will notice that it buzzes, tingles, and vibrates for a while, and then gradually it passes. That is the natural course of an 'ouchie' — to hurt for a while and then fade away.

If, on the other hand, you have an 'ouchie' and your mind goes crazy with thoughts such as: "I did it wrong. I'm such a jerk. What a disaster. I know it's going to get worse. I'll never walk again. I never should have listened to that guy. I'm stupid, stupid, stupid, etc., etc.," as our minds so often do when our bodies are in pain, then you may very well turn an 'ouchie' into a blister. Firewalking blisters are primarily chronic creations. They are acute/transformational pains which the mind has negatively impacted, interfering with the natural course of the pain. Under hypnosis, people have created blisters *without* any pain or heat stimulus at all — only pure mind. It is just that much easier to do when a strong physical stimulus is present.

Try clapping your hands together again, very hard — Ouch! You have just traumatized thousands and thousands of cells in the soft tissues of your hands, causing an acute pain. The pain is telling you to stop the behavior or risk more serious injury. The pain is also *the healing in process.* That is, the actual sensory experience of body cells busily mending is very often painful. Recall Becker's current of injury — a stream of electromagnetic activity which occurs at the site of an injury, shifting polarities

as the body heals. I am suggesting that in the same way that
fear/energy always arises when we need it to meet a threat or
challenge, so *energy always arises and moves to a place in need
of healing. The sensory experience of this great influx of energy
and of all the healing work that is being done is usually one of
pain.* The injury hurts and hurts as the body heals, and then
slowly the pain subsides, and finally there is no pain at all —
the healing process is completed.

There are conscious ways to override or short-circuit the
experience of pain, as Jack Schwarz does, and in cases of very
severe acute pain the body automatically, and mercifully, takes
away our awareness of pain. We know now that the brain produces
a great variety of chemicals, collectively called neuropeptides,
some of which are as effective as morphine in relieving the body
of pain. It is currently being demonstrated on many fronts that
this vast pharmacopoeia is interactive with human thoughts and
feelings, which helps to explain the abilities of people such as
Jack Schwarz and firewalkers. It provides some biological explanation
and foundation for the powers of love, laughter, and positive
thinking. It is characteristic of the exquisite design of the human
body/mind that such chemicals are produced spontaneously,
according to need.

There are so many similarities in the nature and functioning
of pain and fear, and their relationship to energy and consciousness,
that I have come to view them as essentially the same thing,
pain being an intensification of fear/energy which is localized
somewhere within the body. Thus, we normally move through
life in a state of balance. Inevitably, we encounter and perceive
challenges to our balanced well-being. In the moment that we
perceive a challenge, *energies of adaptation* are automatically
generated and released to meet the challenge. (A good measure
of mental, physical, and emotional health is whether the energetic
response is appropriate to the specific challenge.) In some cases,
the body is energized *fearfully* toward fight, flight, and/or growth.
In other cases, the body is energized *painfully* toward the work
of mending a specific injury. In many cases there are no clear
lines of distinction. There are fears which cause real pain and
organic damage, and there are pains which cause a great deal of
fear and anxiety. At all times we are dealing with a movement
of energy in response to a perceived threat.

Homeostatic, acute, and transformational pain correspond precisely to fear/excitement. They are all natural, healthy, living movements of adaptation energy in response to the demands of an ever-changing environment. We *must* have such moments of fear and pain if we want to survive, grow, and thrive.

Chronic pain and fear/contraction are aberrations of our natural adaptive processes. They are the energies of adaptation invested with the creative/destructive powers of human consciousness, and they cause enormous amounts of human suffering. (Some would go so far as to say our habits of chronic contraction are the *only* cause of our suffering. Animals feel pain and fear, but do they suffer as humans do?) These habits are at the same time our evolutionary springboard, for it is in wrestling with the demons of chronic contraction that we will eventually come to truly feel and understand our co-creative powers and begin to use those powers responsibly and for the good of all. If pain is a teacher, then chronic pain is a grand master.

I view 'ouchies' initially as acute/transformational pains. There is very clearly some acute pain from "putting your foot where you shouldn't have put it." I see even more transformational pain, which reflects the individual's consciousness, and shows some degree of misalignment between the person's body, mind (intention and belief), and spirit. It may be the transformational pain of intensive purification, the energy of the fire impacting the body to work a strong healing. (I always worry a little when people announce during their intentions that they have come to be healed by the fire. Such people are almost guaranteed to get 'ouchies.') Or it may be the transformational pain of learning to appreciate and successfully deal with pain, or the transformational pain of greatly expanded conscious awareness.

However an 'ouchie' begins, the real challenge is then to keep it from becoming chronic, to keep it from hurting far more intensely than necessary and then turning into a blister. This, of course, cannot be prevented if the individual is due for the special lessons of chronic pain. Nonetheless, I offer firewalkers the ways which I have observed to be most effective for resolving pain, whether it is the pain of a firewalker's 'ouchie' or any other pain which a person may encounter in life.

———————————————————

Understanding that pain is essentially the same as fear/energy

is a very good beginning for successfully dealing with pain. Just
as the first step with fear is to say yes to it, and to see it as a
potentially positive force in life, so my work with pain begins
with the understanding that it has its place in a happy and
healthy life. Resisting pain, struggling to avoid it, stoically denying
it, using drugs to deaden it; or seeing pain as punishment, divine
retribution, or the price of one's stupidity; or feeling victimized
by pain, and hating the person or thing which 'caused' it; feeling
hopeless, helpless, incurable — these are the ways and means
of chronic contraction and they only add to the intensity and
duration of one's suffering. We best resolve pain by saying yes
to it, and creating a healthy context for it; by learning to accept
pain, when it comes, as an alarm clock, as a growing edge, as
a teacher, and as a path to higher states.

*I tell people they must be responsible to their pain rather
than responsible for it.* Being responsible *for* one's pain means
taking the blame, or casting blame, or somehow judging and
criticizing one's actions. It assumes that we can actually fathom
the real 'cause' of an event, which we cannot. Even if one is
coming from the point of view that "I create my reality therefore
I created this pain," (I prefer to say, *"contribute* to the creation
of reality" to avoid assigning absolute cause), it is still very
difficult to avoid casting a negative field of chronic contraction
around a pain when saying "I did this to myself!" To be responsible
to one's pain is to delete the need to know what 'caused' it and
to commit all of one's energies to fully resolving it — being
awake to the pain, learning any lessons, and helping it to heal
and pass on.

Feeling responsible *for* one's pain also tends to focus an
event in the past (I walk*ed* wrong; the fire *was* hot; I *wasn't*
clear enough), whereas *being responsible to the pain focuses
one's creative energies in the present moment, which is where all
of our power to create change and promote healing resides.*
What I found intriguing about the hypnosis experiments which
began this chapter was not that they showed a particular method
for healing burns (one experimenter had his patients *cool* the
areas of their burns, while the other had his patients *raise* the
temperatures), but that they demonstrated the healing power
of people who are acting responsibly *to* their injured bodies.
Taking responsibility does not mean taking the blame; it means

demonstrating one's ability to respond to a situation. What hypnosis, biofeedback, meditation, and placebo research have all shown us is that we have a wide range of abilities for positively and successfully responding to pain. (And we are probably still in grade school as far as our eventual abilities will go.) So I try to get people beyond thinking about how they caused their 'ouchies' — 'What went wrong?' — and into working creatively with any pain in the present moment.

I also stress the importance of creating an environment that is as healing as possible when one is sick or injured. I have often thought that if I were to take some of my more serious 'ouchie' cases and usher them right into a waiting ambulance, which would whisk them off to a hospital, sirens blaring, while officious people tch-tched over their wounds (and their stupidity), then I would be creating some *very* serious burn victims. Instead, the person who has had an intensely hot walk rejoins the circle, continues singing and dancing, watches other people joyfully walking, and perhaps even walks again. According to feedback I have received from countless walkers, *the burning goes away.* Once we begin as a culture to really understand the contribution of consciousness to the healing process, it will mean *totally* remaking our hospital system. In the meantime we have to create this for ourselves, doing everything we can to provide a positively supportive environment when we are in pain.

When you have the 'ouchies,' this means being only with loving, compassionate, positive, supportive people, and staying away from critical, harping, skeptical, negative people. If you are lacking the former in your life then, like the animals, you must go into isolation until your body is healed. The absolute worst is to be around somebody who will in any way make you love yourself less while you are in the state of pain. Remember the experience of the Kaufmans: people tend to get better when in an environment of unconditional love, when they can really feel that someone is happy with them just the way they are. I suspect the reason that love is so overlooked or dismissed as too simple by a world desperate for healing is that it can be overwhelming to even consider responding to all of the people in one's life with unconditional love; it is much easier to think in terms of miracle drugs and techno-fixes. Sometimes I close my eyes and imagine a world in which everyone is practicing such love. Can anyone doubt the enormous amounts of pain which would *instantly* disappear?

I have also found breath to be an amazingly powerful way of resolving 'ouchies,' and other pains. I actually discovered this years earlier as a technique for getting through dentistry without an anesthetic. It involves keeping the breath going, very lightly, like a very quiet panting, never holding the breath, or stopping it, or in any way contracting it. (This is much like the Lamaze breath which women are taught for resolving pain during natural childbirth.) I find that this never fails to lighten my experience of a pain, be it physical, mental, emotional, or spiritual, and that it illuminates any impending lessons and promotes the needed healing. I believe that it works by sustaining a continuous flow of energy throughout one's system and by transforming any experience of acute and chronic pains. This approach is easy to learn and, with the exception of certain lung and throat problems, can be used effectively with most any of our illnesses and disorders.

Ultimately, all of the ways of 'boiling energy,' and of best resolving fear, are also ways of effectively resolving pain. Love and breath, singing and dancing, connecting with others, making love, laughing, praying, maintaining a positive attitude, practicing forgiveness, serving others, expressing oneself creatively, touching and being touched with tenderness — these are our most potent healers, the very best ways for dealing with any and all of our illnesses and pains. Obviously, some common sense is called for in knowing which energy boiler to use: one does not dance on a broken leg or make love after a heart attack. At times when the body is seriously ill, our most important work will be internal: breathing, praying, affirming, etc. — sustaining a quiet, calming, but ever steady radiance of light energy from within. There are other times when two hours of wild dancing, or several hours of "Candid Camera" are just what the doctor ordered. As with fear, what matters most during our times of pain is that we do whatever we can to keep our energy moving, flowing, radiating, growing, evolving, and *adapting*.

Life is always changing. When we do not perfectly mesh with a change, we hurt. Every pain is a valuable potential lesson, guiding us through a balanced life, *transforming* us, teaching us to live this life more fully, and opening our hearts to greater love.

twelve

DANCING WITH
THE FIRE

*At the core of sacred ceremonial is the communication with
Deity. The ceremonies come into being out of the felt need of
the people. Somebody or some group needs something, wants
something — tangible or intangible — and the sacred ceremonial
process was discovered to be the most effective way to get results.
All of manifest creation is energy in various vibrational patterns.
All energy in the universe comes into form and changes form
(transforms) through patterns, through systems .   . Sacred
ceremonial is humanity's most highly developed meta-system
for the conscious transformation of energy.[1]*

*There is another story of a Chinese sage who was asked,
"How shall we escape the heat?" — meaning, of course, the heat
of suffering. He answered, "Go right into the middle of the fire."
"But how, then, shall we escape the scorching flame?" "No
further pain will trouble you!" .... The same idea comes in*
The Divine Comedy, *where Dante and Virgil find that the way
out of Hell lies at its very center.[2]*

A woman came to one of our firewalks and walked several
times, having a very joyful and empowering experience. Three
months later the car in which she was being driven had a collision,
throwing her through the windshield and full force into a tree.
She suffered tremendous pain and mercifully went unconscious.
As she was being attended in the hospital, she became aware of
the doctors saying, "We're losing her; she's not going to make
it." Her immediate thoughts were, "No way, I walked on fire!"
She recovered, left the hospital *that* night, and now experiences
more joy and power in her life than ever before.

What are we to do with such a story? We could certainly
dig for more details; try to find out 'exactly' what was wrong
with her; ask why the doctors thought she was dying, and if

183

they misdiagnosed; ask if they did something which suddenly turned the tide; or find out the 'exact' nature of her recovery. We could skeptically demand proof; we could reasonably doubt that she was seriously injured; we could steadfastly deny the possibility that walking on fire in any way 'caused' her healing; or we could refuse to even consider such a bald-faced anecdote. We could authoritatively intone, "spontaneous remission," shrug our shoulders, and forget the whole thing.

Or we could look to the indisputable facts of her story: she walked on fire; she considered the firewalk a valid demonstration of her personal creative powers; she went through a life-threatening accident; she heard the possibility that she could die; she countered with, "I am a powerful being — I will live!"; she is alive and healthy now; she is confident, capable, *excited* and feels a great source of inner power as she faces the challenges and difficulties of her life. She is certain the firewalk was critical to her process, that she would not have survived the accident without it, and that she is still deriving inspiration from its memory.

Though hers is the most dramatic, Penny and I have heard dozens and dozens of such post-firewalking stories. A salesman finds cold-calling much easier when he is remembering his firewalk; a student gets excited before exams instead of panicking; a couple meets at a firewalk and a few months later steps into 'the fires of marriage'; quite a number of people quit jobs they really did not like and/or started pursuing their most outrageous dreams. The common element in all of these experiences is that the individual has allowed the firewalk to stand as a source of inspiration and guidance for future living. From this perspective it does not really matter what is *actually* happening at a firewalk — how hot the coals are, should people really get burned, does walking on fire change one's energy in some positive way, does the physical impact of firewalking somehow *cause* healing or *cause* transformation, etc. — what matters is that *for many people the act of walking on fire becomes an extremely powerful metaphor for living at their fullest and for stretching beyond set limitations.*

A metaphor is a pattern of thought in which a meaning ordinarily used for one thing is applied to another. The use of metaphor is very basic to the human thought/creative process; it is a primary way which thinking creatures such as ourselves have for organizing and understanding our experiences, and it is fundamental to the generation and release of our co-creative energies. Metaphor runs through the heart of every myth and story, the heart of every poem, song, fable, totem, legend, parable, allegory, and fairy tale, the heart of all of our scriptures and psalms, and through all of the lessons of our greatest teachers. Furthermore, our ability to think metaphorically is intrinsic to our ability to grow and evolve; metaphor works at the deepest levels of our psyche, creating connections and aligning energies.

Joseph Campbell tells a wonderful story illustrating the nature of metaphor. As an acknowledged expert on myths, he was being interviewed once by a tough-minded skeptic who started out by asserting that "Myth is a lie!" Campbell explained that, in fact, "Myth is metaphoric. A mythology is an organization of symbolic images and narratives that are metaphoric of the possibilities of human experience and fulfillment in a given society at a given time." To this the man replied, "Nah, it's a lie." Campbell says they went back and forth like that for half an hour, getting nowhere, when he suddenly realized that this man did not know what a metaphor was. So he asked the man to give him an example of a metaphor. After some reluctance and hesitation, the man finally offered up, "Harry runs so fast people say he runs like a deer." Campbell said, "No, that's not a metaphor. The metaphor is 'Harry *is* a deer'." 'That's a lie!" said the man. 'No," said Campbell, "That's a metaphor."[3] Thus, metaphor is perfectly and vitally true without being literally true, in that metaphor illumines truth, reveals truth, connects us to truth, and enables us to *feel* truth.

When Shakespeare tells us, "All the world's a stage," he is speaking metaphorically, taking the lessons and meanings of a play and applying them to life. When a President proclaims, "We can now see the light at the end of the tunnel," he is providing a metaphor of perseverance, encouraging his people to feel the light of hope while in the midst of darkness. When a little-leaguer steps up to the plate, imagining Babe Ruth in Yankee Stadium, he is deriving inspiration and empowerment through the use of metaphor. When lovers stand on the shore, watching a pair of swans drifting through the water as one, their hearts are touched and moved through metaphor. When we stand in the midst of an October forest, leaves falling all about us, and we begin to feel a bittersweet sadness for people and places left behind, it is the metaphor of autumn which is stirring us so.

It is possible to wake up 'feeling like a million bucks,' go off to work 'walking on air' and ready to 'climb the highest mountain,' feel the 'strength of a lion,' and be a real 'eager beaver.' If somebody says, "Well, looking a little tired today, old girl," it is likely that an entirely different set of metaphors will arise from within: you are now 'feeling over the hill,' like you have 'been through a wringer,' the 'weight of the world on your shoulders,' and your 'feet mired in quicksand.' The common mistake is to think that such thoughts and images are strictly caused by events and circumstances. In fact, the metaphors we live by carry a great measure of creative energy. They are very strong elements within the co-creative process, and lie very much within the realm of personal choice.

Understanding this, while honoring our capacity to contribute to the creation of reality through conscious thought, leads us to the importance of consciously choosing positively supportive metaphors. To the extent that we can control the thoughts and images we are holding, we can directly affect our perception of reality. It is possible, and clearly preferable, to perceive reality in ways that leave us uplifted, inspired, awed, grateful, whole, compassionate, loving, creative — excited. It is the role of metaphor to carry us to such states, or to their opposites.

As powerfully creative as metaphor is, it becomes even more powerful when invested with purposeful action. The American Indian teacher, Brook Medicine Eagle, advises: "If you need to take a great leap in your life then go and stand on a large boulder and jump; if you are filled with a terrible anger that you want to be free of then dig a hole in the ground, scream your pain into the earth, and bury it; if you are feeling distant, disconnected and apart from some other person then think of the person while walking across a long bridge."[4] This actualizing of metaphors — making them real through action — is the essential human process of creating and enacting effective ritual.

It is one thing to imagine oneself being able to overcome limitations; it is so much more to actually walk through a bed of hot coals and not burn. It is one thing to imagine oneself connected to the spirit of Christ; it is so much more to partake of Easter communion. It is one thing to feel love and support for one's country; it is so much more to stand with fifty thousand other patriots and join in the singing of the national anthem. Such rituals are ways of actually *living* our chosen metaphors. All effective ritual serves as a bridge between our inner world and the outer one, between the subjective and the objective.

As Dolores LaChappelle has written: "Ritual is essential because it is truly the pattern that connects. It provides communication at all levels — communication among all the systems within the individual human organism; between people within groups; between one group and another in a city and throughout all these levels between the human and the non-human in the natural environment."[5] Through the practice of effective ritual, our co-creative energies are aligned, synergized, and amplified, to the benefit of the individual practitioner, to the benefit of the group, and to the benefit of the whole environment.

For instance, a group of people may gather together with a very sincere desire to feel harmonious, connected, and acting as one. If they were to proceed in a random fashion, behaving as a group of separate individuals, then after several hours, if they are very lucky, they may begin to experience some degree of group cohesiveness. If, on the other hand, they begin by standing in a circle, holding hands, imagining a flow of energy around the circle, and then raising their voices together in a beautiful chant, they will, in the space of a few minutes, achieve a very strong sense of connectedness. I have done this with hundreds of groups and it *always* makes a tangible difference. The intention to be as one, embodied within the metaphors of one circle, one energy flow, and one voice, *and then physically acted out*, is a simple yet very effective ritual for co-creating wholeness.

The American Indians knew this, and passed a peace pipe around a circle to begin any meeting of conflicted parties. One can only wonder what would happen if our courtrooms and boardrooms and congressional debates were to begin with such 'wholeness' rituals. Of course, there is rarely an *intention* to be whole at such gatherings, so we cannot expect 'wholeness' rituals to appear. Rather, when the intentions of two or more conflicted parties are to remain in conflict, with one party eventually winning over the other, the metaphors of 'us versus them,' of ongoing competition, of good and evil, and of survival of the fittest, give rise to entirely different rituals. United circles give way to squares and rectangles with 'them' on one side and 'us' on the other; holding hands gives way to 'who enters the room first' and 'who sits where;' affirmations of unity give way to exclamations of differences; harmonized singing gives way to shouting back and forth, filibustering, and *self*-serving speeches. The end results of such 'separation' rituals are always to effectively create further separateness, strengthen differences, and deepen hostilities. Though most modern men and women would deny it, we are already practicing extremely effective rituals. (Team sports and the military are both filled with powerful ritual.) The tragedy is that they are structured to co-create such a disconnected world.

There are three aspects to any effective ritual. The first (surprise!) is intention. *To be effective, ritual must be an expression of a clear intention of the individual or group.* The last step that I take before firewalking, after the coals have been raked into a path, is to have the whole group silently focus (while holding hands) on the creation of a successful firewalk, reaching for a clear, unified group intention. To participate in a firewalk, or any other ritual, with people who do not really want it to work, or people who do not really know what they want, is foolish and possibly dangerous. Ritual is a physical expression of intent; to want one thing while participating in a ritual of differing intent is self-defeating. As anyone who has ever been forced to go to church knows, participating in rituals against one's will is not only ineffective but tends to sour one to the very idea of ritual, thus debasing a vital human activity.

The second aspect of effective ritual involves (surprise again) belief. We must believe that our actions can make a creative difference. *On some level the individual must believe that performing the ritual will actually have an impact upon reality, affecting some degree of purposeful change.* This change may range from the raindancer who believes her dancing will cause rain to fall, to the voodoo queen who believes her incantations will cause another's death, to the confessioner who simply believes that she will feel better having confessed her sins, to the family which believes that saying grace before a meal instills good values.

Ritual without belief becomes ineffective and empty. There is a hollow insincerity to such ritual, a sterile 'going through the motions.' If I have seemed rather obsessive in my railing against

the skeptical mind, it is because I have experienced on far too
many occasions the power of skeptical disbelief to flatten and
diminish ritual. For one to whom ritual is a living, flowing
dance of human creativity, skepticism is *deadly* serious, a righteous
pin in search of childish balloons. (For unless we have the faith
of children ...) When there is a skeptic in the circle, brow
furrowed against all this nonsense, the energy of the whole
circle is sluggish, the dancing stumbles, and the co-creation is
less than it could have been (which the skeptic takes as proof
that it was all indeed nonsense, failing to understand the power
of his anti-contribution). To the extent that we have become a
skeptical, disbelieving culture, we have either filled our world
with empty rituals (strengthening the arguments against ritual)
or given up ritual altogether.

The final aspect of effective ritual is that we understand and
appreciate the involvement of metaphor. *Ritual is the actualization
of metaphor,* and to ignore the role of metaphor is to practice
ritual ignorantly. As Joseph Campbell puts it: "When we say
'Our father, who art in heaven,' it has nothing to do with a
father or a heaven! It is metaphoric. The 'father' idea is metaphoric
of a psychological relationship. It gives us the relationship to the
ultimate mystery that is experienced in the way of a father-child
relationship."[6] It is when we lose sight of the underlying metaphors
that ritual begins to fail us, degenerating into superstition or
fanaticism. The structured forms of ritual without the inner
heart of metaphor become meaningless in the truest sense of
the word, leading to rigid, unthinking followers who perform a
ritual a certain way "because it has always been done this way,"
or "because this is the one and only way to do it." For ritual to
remain a truly living, vital, and effective dance, each participant
must have an awareness of the metaphors involved.

When we remember the gifts of the magi, then Christmas
gift giving is a precious and marvelously potent ritual. When we
lose touch with the metaphor, the practice becomes a commercial
perversion. If, following Brook Medicine Eagle's advice, we were
to jump from a large boulder as a metaphor for our ability to
successfully leap forward in life, then we would indeed enhance
that ability. It is when the practice of jumping off rocks becomes
dogma — automatic and unthinking — that a living ritual has
hardened into superstition. Likewise, when we are embodying

a metaphor as we walk through a bed of hot coals (connecting with the earth's elements; walking through fears, etc.), it is a vital, important and wonderfully empowering ritual. To view it in strictly literal terms — stepping on coals of 'x' temperature for 'y' duration, and this happens for that reason — is to deritualize the firewalk, purging from it the human heart and greatly diminishing its mystery and its impact.

When, on the other hand, we believe that we are capable of consciously contributing to the creative process, then metaphors become vividly real, and ritual becomes a primary pattern for co-creating. There are three basic steps (beginning with belief in the co-creative process) which must be followed in the creation and performance of effective ritual. The first step is to identify a want or need (such as, "I must make a big change in my life"), the second step is to think of it in metaphorical terms (it feels like leaping into an abyss), and the third step is to create and perform a physical resolution of the metaphor ("I successfully jump from a great height"). To the extent that we conscientiously fulfill each of these steps, ritual becomes a vital part of our lives.

If your lover leaves you and you want to *really* be done with her, you could ritualize your separation by gathering all of her pictures and any other objects of memory, throwing them all in a garbage bag, and then *dropping her* in the dumpster. Quite often it is the rituals we personally create which have the most power, for they resonate more clearly with our personal situations. It is the individual's 'here and now' full participation in a ritual — through belief, clear intent, understanding metaphor, and purposeful action — which gives the ritual power. It is not some outside or higher authority. Indeed, it is *always* the individual practitioner who creates the ritual, even if it is an old tradition; without the individual's creative consciousness there is no meaningful ritual, though there may well be ritualized behavior.

Of course, we live in a culture which has little capacity or appreciation for meaningful ritual. It is a culture which has witnessed, and largely sanctioned, the death of God, the decline of religious practice, the desecration of sacred lands, the skeptical dismissal of primitive rites and ceremonies, the violent extermination of all Western pagan and witchcraft traditions, the loss of meaningful mythology, and a widespread embarrassment at the mere thought of participating in any sort of ritual. This is clearly a function of the rise of skeptical values, especially in the economic, political, and scientific arenas, and to the extent that it has freed the world from mindless superstitions and rigid fanaticism, such skepticism has been healthy, maybe. However, in depriving ourselves of meaningful rituals we have surely lost a major means of becoming whole and connected — within ourselves, to one another, and to the Earth and her elements.

As is so often the case, most of the damage is done when we are young. For we are a culture which provides no coming-of-age rituals for our children — no rites of passage to mark, assist, and celebrate the transitions from childhood to adolescence, and from adolescence to adulthood. (Bar mitzvah and confirmation have been forced, empty, and ineffective rituals for most everyone I have ever spoken with.) While we may scientifically explain the facts of genital reproduction, we do nothing to consecrate and joyfully affirm the child's awakening sexuality. Most young women are shocked, appalled, or embarrassed by their first menses — contracted attitudes which can lead to lifetimes of monthly pain. For young men, two of the major signs of 'coming of age' are the right to drink and a driver's license; is it any wonder that drunken driving is a vital male teenage activity? Our children are hammered with "What do you want to be when you grow up," while being given little substantive guidance in actually *growing*. The radical clothing and strange hair styles, the music that only the young can enjoy (a phenomenon stretching back to the 1920s), the defiance of authority, the running away from home, the adoption of a separate language, the use of intoxicants, the grouping into gangs and cults, the need to participate in high-risk behaviors, the attraction to suicide: when we suppress a vital human need such as ritual, then we must expect it to arise in aberrant ways. If we do not provide healthy and meaningful rites of passage for the young, they will continue to create their own, and with all the inevitable folly of youth.

In the Native American cultures (and most all primitive societies) the child who was coming of age would go alone into the woods or off to a mountain or desert to 'quest for vision.' Days and nights would be spent in solitude, fasting, praying, and ritualizing. This is when many children would receive the names which they would be called for the remainder of their lives. Or they would receive a dream, or a vision, which would

describe their life's work, their purpose for being born. Or they
would meet their totem — an animal or earth elemental who
would be their guide, companion, and source of power in life.
There is no substituting for such experience — the child who
returns from a 'vision quest' has become a woman/man, not by
virtue of having reached some arbitrary age or class, but *through
having actually made the transition, internally and externally, to
a deeper way of being in the world.* Through participation in
the ritual the child has grown more whole. As Jean Houston has
written: "(Ritual) offers ways in which your transitions are
illuminated. When occurring in time and space that are prepared
and understood as sacred, ritual has the power to help you
move to the next stage of your life journey. Once arrived, you
know by the difference in yourself and your surroundings that
you are there."[7]

When Penny and I were married, we designed our own
ceremony, wrote our own vows, and took care to invite those
friends and family members who we felt would be able to give
themselves fully to the rituals involved. Though we had been
living together for seven years before our wedding, we both felt
tangibly changed by the ceremony, and our relationship clearly
passed through a major transition. To me there is no question
that the rituals made a creative difference, and that our marriage
would be/feel/look very different had we been married in a civil
ceremony, void of any meaningful (to us) ritual. To have created
a sacred space, to have surrounded ourselves with loving and
consciously supportive friends, to have publicly declared our
love and our intentions to be as one, to have heard the beautiful
blessings of our minister, to have felt such emphatic agreement,
as if the whole Earth were singing Yes! — *of course* such rituals
make a creative difference. How could they not!? Is it possible
that the rising divorce rate is directly related to the diminishing
appreciation and understanding of the wedding ceremony?

I am reminded of the scientist who suggested I come into his
laboratory, lie upon a table, and have varying temperatures of
heat applied to the soles of my feet as a way of testing the
firewalk. What do we say to such a person? How do we begin
to explain that his rituals of experimental technique within
sterilized spaces tend to create an entirely different set of results;
that his metaphor of "removed observer analyzing chosen subject

through changing variables" is light years away from the fire-walking metaphors? Will he believe me if I say that over the years the 'burn or not burn' question has become of secondary importance; that what really matters for me now is the ritual; that *the firewalk's greatest contribution to our culture is to bring people together for the co-creation of beauty, wonder, and meaningful ceremony?*

What has given me the most satisfaction in leading the firewalks has been watching people who had never participated in a meaningful ritual, who had no conception at all of what a ritual was, and who were in fact strongly biased against such things, come away from that half hour of singing and dancing in the dark, their eyes sparkling with a whole new realm of possibilities. The firewalk touches very old and deep places within us. "The need for ritual, encoded in the old, reptilian brain, is insistent in its demands for expression. The reptilian brain also needs security and repetition, the old mammalian midbrain needs emotional charges, and the cognitive neocortex needs intellectual stimulation. If you court all these parts of your brain, your body will listen to you! A ritual engages the fullness of your whole being."[8] Having participated in a firewalk, people have been fully engaged and thus are awakened to their connectedness and inspired to create more ritual in their lives.

Along with this new awareness of the importance of ritual, I have also seen firewalkers become more appreciative of the natural world and their place within it. Totally urbanized folk start thinking about the importance of dirt, or the phases of the moon, or the turning of the seasons. Participation in the firewalk seems to lead people to a deeper awareness of the Earth and her elements, and to the feeling that somehow we are a part of it all. "Ritual is essential because it is truly the pattern that connects," writes Dolores LaChapelle. To this she adds: "Most important of all, during rituals we have the experience, unique in our culture, of neither *opposing* nature nor *trying* to be in communion with nature; but of *finding* ourselves within nature, and that is the key to sustainable culture."[9] Indeed, we might ask, with Elizabeth Cogburn, "Is sustainable culture even *possible* without meaningful sacred ceremony?"[10]

This is probably the firewalk's greatest gift of all: that we begin to experience, deeply and viscerally and without question, that we are integrally connected to the living being that is our planet; that we humans are, in every sense of the word, *one* with nature. Even more important, we come awake to the truly *co*-creative process, an unfolding evolutionary spiral of creation that is the lifework and responsibility of humans, surely, and also of whales, dolphins, monkeys, horses, cats, dogs, spiders, dragonflies, carrots, onions, trees, angels, fairies, water, dirt, wind, and fire; all is alive and all life is connected. Even more importantly, we are able to feel the Earth as a living creature, given to the living dances of conception and birth, and of growing and learning and becoming more; a living creature of which we are, *through energy*, a vital part. Our changes are this creature's changing; we/the creature are spinning through an evolutionary leap, at this very moment, into a whole new way of living and experiencing — an entirely new sense of self.

This is the vision of Teilhard deChardin, Buckminster Fuller, and so many others (as well as many primitive cultures). It is a vision described and well-supported in Lovelock's *Gaia*, Russell's *The Global Brain*, Jantz's *The Self-Organizing Universe*, and Leonard's *The Transformation*, to name a few.[11] It revolves around the understanding that the Earth is a living system (called Gaia by many, from Greek mythology) evincing qualities of intelligence, consciousness, and self-evolution. It has been pointed out that by the year 2000 there will be as many humans on the planet as there are brain cells in the human brain, and it is suggested that if humanity is the brain/nerve system of Gaia, then she is moving through a change comparable to the appearance and maturation of intelligence in humanity. It is a vision which encompasses most of the wonders of modern technology — the evolved means for creating greater connectedness between the individual 'cells' of her brain/nerve system. It is a vision which allows for the vast degrees of upheaval and disintegration which our world is currently passing through — the unavoidable cathartic breakdowns which so often precede breakthroughs. Finally, it is a vision which gives meaning and healthy purpose to the human: we are essential players in a cosmic drama some four billion years in the making.

However, it is *not* a vision which gives humans dominion over nature. This planet is much more than a vast collective of resources for humans to control for their own well-being. We have a major role to play in the evolution of Gaia, much as the brain plays a major role in the human organism. But a brain without a skeleton, a stomach, a heart, lungs, skin, etc., would not be a whole, viable human being. Likewise, to consider humanity apart from nature is a grave misunderstanding, and one which has delivered us to the brink of destruction. We humans must begin to see things *as* a whole, viable planet: to consider things from a planetary perspective; to make decisions as Gaia's brain; to act as Gaia's body.

This requires more from us than just rejecting the 'bad' ways of modern man to return to the 'old' ways of the past. Acting *as if* we were separate from nature has caused great suffering but, in truth, we have never actually been disconnected, any more than a living brain could be disconnected from a living body. *We must assume that our path has been Gaia's path all along.* We must assume that our prodigal journey has all been part of a plan, and that an intelligent presence has been operating throughout human history. The road to computers, laser surgery, rapid transportation, long-distance communication, and (soon!) a renewable, non-polluting source of energy, passed through strip mining, acid rain, sweat shops, polluted oceans, and military technologies. Our challenge is to continue down that road while striving for greater balance, shifting from industrialization to planetization, from human engineering to Gaian engineering.

Ritual can awaken these planetary sensitivities within us, guiding us through these critical transitions. The firewalk has certainly done so for Penny and me. When we first began, we would do firewalks anywhere we could light a fire and get a group of people together. During our first year we firewalked in all sorts of crazy places, including a couple of times in the middle of Manhattan, surrounded by T.V. cameras, extremely skeptical reporters ("It would be a better story if someone got burned," said one photographer), and a gathering of some of New York City's more obnoxious onlookers, screaming, "Burn, baby, burn!" Eventually we came to feel the extreme contradictions in our actions. We saw that casting the firewalk before skeptics was a futile and dangerous enterprise. More importantly, we realized that practicing meaningful sacred ceremony on hostile, non-sacred land was just stupid. To be sure, there was something very heady about going into such places and doing it anyway, proving that we were audacious and powerful enough to pull it off despite the environment. Yet, the concept of doing something 'despite the environment' is the very attitude which the practice of effective ritual must eventually overcome.

Our ongoing experience has led us to the understanding that doing something 'with the environment' makes a whole lot more sense, and is much easier and much healthier to put into practice. We have come to appreciate and believe very strongly in the active presence and contribution of 'place,' and that the Earth is clearly an important player in all of our dramas, giving her own special energies to the co-creation. We now approach each firewalk as a combined effort, a merging of human with environment, which is more successful the more intimately we can merge.

People will often characterize the firewalk as an example of 'mind over matter,' and I always cringe, for, like the concept of 'man over nature,' it is just another version of doing something 'despite the environment': "My superior human intellect has commanded the fire not to burn; my powerful mind has commanded my flesh not to blister!" Better to say that firewalking is a demonstration of 'mind in matter' — me, you, the soil, the wood, the fire, the moon, the stars, the nighttime breeze — there is one mind, one intelligence, one consciousness flowing through all of life, connecting all of life, creating all of life, and firewalking is one manner of surrendering to its expression. There is human consciousness and there is nature consciousness, and different though they may be, they derive from the same source, and communication, cooperation, and co-creation (remember Findhorn) is possible. After so many millennia of growing up, the human and nature are now approaching the altar, consenting to be wed, with Gaian consciousness to be the offspring.

My own theory about the origin of the firewalk is that it arose quite spontaneously within primitive cultures which were already merged with the concept of 'mind in matter.' To those who were intimately connected with the forces of nature, 'dancing with the fire' probably came as naturally as swimming in the water. They would be aware in both cases of clear limitations and real dangers, and they would be equally aware of the possibilities for ecstatic play and co-creative practice.

We must assume that, for the best of reasons, most of

humanity left the garden to pursue the lessons and possibilities of civilization. Gradually we lost much of the awareness that we still observe in primitive cultures, such as the ability to accurately predict weather patterns or the 'knowing' of the properties of plants and herbs. Generation by generation we grew away from the vast consciousness that is nature, steadily disconnecting, ultimately becoming 'strangers in a strange land.' The celebration of the firewalk slipped away, in some places remaining as a practice for the masters and adepts, in other places disappearing altogether, impossible even to imagine.

Indeed, most meaningful, sacred ceremony slowly disappeared and no, sustainable culture is *not* possible without meaningful, sacred ceremony. The signs of human miscreation are everywhere as our rituals of separation and destruction tear at the very fabric of our world. We are threatened and challenged from all directions, without pause and with ever-growing intensity. Each day seems to bring more bad news, more reason for despair, more evidence of a civilization in decline.

Yet, there is even more evidence of an all-encompassing planetary transformation, and of an evolutionary shift to Gaian consciousness. There is a growing realization of human capabilities, of untapped human reserves coming to the surface, along with an understanding of our essential involvement in the divining of creation. There is intense exploration into the rites and ceremonies of wholeness. There is networking and deep ecology; there is birth without violence and there are global meditation days. There is a building international awareness of the undeniable linkage between our political systems, our economies, our air and water, and our people. For those attuned to Gaia's heartbeat, it is a time of great excitement. There is all of the stress of massive change, yes, and there is more energy boiling toward evolutionary breakthrough than the world has ever known.

Into the midst of this massive leap, Gaia has offered an ancient ritual — that old evolutionary mutant, the firewalk. It is a very potent ingredient in this co-creational soup, as it is such a powerfully apt metaphor for the challenges before us. *Who is not being asked to 'walk on fire' each and every day; who does not have far too many challenging situations looming ahead, threatening dire consequences, and all too often seeming to be impossible?* We each have our health firewalks, our relationship firewalks, our job firewalks, our financial firewalks — each area bringing its own set of difficulties and worries, its challenges and threats, its fires to be mastered. As a planet we stand before some awesome firewalks: a few dozen festering wars, the twin demons of cancer and AIDS, economic disarray, growing ecological emergencies, and almost fifty years of living with the fact that simple human stupidity could unleash a fire mighty enough to burn this entire planet to a cinder.

Mostly, what we would like to do is take a few steps in the opposite direction, hoping that if we avoid these fires for long enough they will just go out. Yet a small, quiet voice keeps whispering within that it will not happen that way, that what is required of us now is that we find the courage to step into the fires, creating resolution through our actions. All of the dangers of this age are of human creation; all of the solutions must also be. *Somehow a solution resides in the heart of each fire.* Ultimately, all of our paths lead, with Virgil's, into the center of the heat.

The firewalk offers an effective and compelling model for resolving challenges, both personal and planetary: squarely and honestly face the fire; affirm your connection to the Earth, to her elements, to your fellow travelers; join in the rituals of wholeness; say yes to your fears and let their energies boil into excitement; listen to your own inner guidance, open to a clear intention and, when your moment arrives, step forward. Even better yet, let go into spontaneous and ecstatic dancing.

Maybe you will be badly burned. Maybe you will create a miracle. Surely you will discover something new about yourself and just as surely your discovery will support the evolving consciousness of our world. What matters most is that you participate, that you *dance*, that you face the fires of this age, willing to be *in*volved, to be an instrument of the work, and to serve as a channel for the possible human.

NOTES

Chapter 1

1. Fred Alan Wolf, *The Body Quantum* (New York: MacMillan, 1986), p. 285.
2. Lewis Carroll, *Through the Looking Glass* (New York: Bramhall House, 1984), p. 251.
3. This is not her real name. Though I have been unable to locate "Kathy" to discuss this episode with her, I have confirmed it with others who were there. I continue to feel awed by the courage which she displayed that night.

Chapter 2

1. Ken Carey, *Vision* (Kansas City: Uni*Sun, 1985), p. 34.
2. George Leonard, *The Transformation* (Los Angeles: J.P. Tarcher, 1972), p. 37.
3. James Jeans, *The Mysterious Universe*, (New York: Macmillan, 1930), p. 59.
4. Peter Russell, *The Global Brain* (Los Angeles: J.P. Tarcher, 1983), p. 198.
5. Albert Einstein, in Fritjof Capra, *The Tao of Physics* (Berkeley: Shambhala, 1975), p. 42.
6. *The Turning Point* and *The Tao of Physics* by Fritjof Capra, *The Dancing Wu Li Masters* by Gary Zukov, *Stalking the Wild Pendulum* by Iztak Bentov, *Taking the Quantum Leap* by Fred Alan Wolf, and *The Silent Pulse* by George Leonard, to name a very few.
7. Barbara Marx Hubbard and Ken Carey, *Manual for Co-Creators of the Quantum Leap* (Gainesville: New Visions, 1986), pp. 1-4.
8. Ibid., pp. 1-5.
9. Leonard, *The Transformation*, p. 236.

Chapter 3

1. Chris Griscom, *Ecstasy Is A New Frequency* (Santa Fe: Bear & Co, 1987), p. 124.
2. Richard Katz, *Boiling Energy* (Cambridge: Harvard University Press, 1982), chapters 3-7.
3. Laurens van der Post, *The Lost World of the Kalahari* (New York: Harcourt Brace Jovanovich, 1977), pp. 231-243.
4. Jim Doherty, *Science Digest*, August 1982, pp. 67-71.
5. Richard Leavitt, *Fate*, September 1974, pp. 88-96.
6. Jeffrey Mishlove, *The Roots of Consciousness* (New York: Random House, 1975), pp. 157-160.
7. Joseph Chilton Pearce, *The Crack in the Cosmic Egg* (New York: Julian Press, 1971). Pearce's other four books also contain numerous references to the firewalk.

Gilbert Grosvenor, *National Geographic*, April 1966, pp. 481-485.

Andrew Weil MD, *Health and Healing* (Boston: Houghton Mifflin, 1983), pp. 246-249.

Omni, September 1985.

8. Tolly Burkan, *Dying To Live* (Twain Harte: Reunion Press, 1984).

Chapter 4

1. Lawrence LeShan, *Alternate Realities* (New York: Ballantine Books, 1976), p. 183.
2. T.H. Huxley, in Larry Dossey, *Space, Time & Medicine* (Boulder: Shambhala, 1982), p. 225.
3. Da Free John, *The Transmission of Doubt* (Clearlake: The Dawn Horse Press, 1984), p. 147.
4. Weil, *Health and Healing*, p. 248.
5. Ibid.
6. Richard Bach, *Illusions* (New York: Dell Publishing, 1977), p. 100.

Chapter 5

1. C.G. Jung, *Psychological Types*, (New York: 1933), pp. 616-617.
2. Roberto Assagioli, MD, *The Act of Will* (New York: Penguin Books, 1973), p. 91.
3. Evelyn Underhill, *Mysticism* (New York: New American Library, 1955), p. 437.
4. Jimmy Cliff, from the song of that title.
5. Otto Rank, in Ira Progoff, *The Death and Rebirth of Psychology* (New York: McGraw, 1973), p. 261.
6. Larry Dossey MD, *Space, Time and Medicine* (Boulder: Shambhala, 1982), p. 210.
7. Ibid.
8. LeShan, *Alternate Realities*, p. 26.

Chapter 6

1. William James, *Talks to Teachers on Psychology* (New York: W.W. Norton, 1958), p. 191.
2. Gary Zukav, *The Dancing Wu Li Masters* (New York: William Morrow, 1979), p. 328.
3. Epictetus.
4. Herbert Benson, MD, *The Relaxation Response* (New York: William Morrow, 1975).
5. Herbert Benson, MD, *Beyond the Relaxation Response* (New York: Berkeley Books, 1984).
6. Benson, *Beyond the Relaxation Response*, p. 8.

Chapter 7

1. Da Free John, *The Transmission of Doubt*, p. 313.
2. William Blake, *The Marriage of Heaven and Hell* (Miami: University of Miami Press, 1963).
3. Fritz Frederick Smith, MD, *Inner Bridges* (Atlanta: Humanics, 1986), p. 22.

4. Laurence Beynam, *Body, Mind and Spirit*, September/October 1987, p. 44.

5. Guy Murchie, *Seven Mysteries of Life* (Boston: Houghton Mifflin, 1978), p. 408.

6. Harold S. Burr, *Blueprint For Immortality* (Spearman, 1952).

7. Leonard Ravitz, in H.S. Burr, *The Fields of Life* (New York: Ballantine, 1972), p. 92.

8. David Eisenberg, *Encounters With Qi* (New York: Penguin Books, 1985).

9. John W. Thompson has compiled a very extensive collection of energy research, conclusions and documentation in *The Human Factor* (Farmingdale: Coleman Publishing, 1983).

   Also, Dr. Richard Gerber's *Vibrational Medicine* (Santa Fe: Bear & Co., 1988) provides a wealth of energy research documentation along with a compelling synthesis.

Chapter 8

1. Hans Selye, *The Stress of Life* (New York: McGraw Hill, 1956), p. 307.

2. George Leonard, *The Ultimate Athlete* (New York: Avon, 1974), p. 220.

3. Da Free John, *Easy Death* (Clearlake: The Dawn Horse Press, 1983), p. 13.

Chapter 9

1. van der Post, *The Lost World of the Kalahari*, pp. 241-243.

2. Katz, *Boiling Energy*, p. 100.

3. Ibid., p. 42.

4. Ibid., p. 121.

5. Ibid., p. 122.

6. Ibid., p. 42.

7. Ibid., p. 42.

Chapter 10

1. Sri Aurobindo, *The Essential Aurobindo*, ed. Robert McDermott (New York: Shocken Books, 1973), p. 45.

2. George Leonard, *New Realities*, September/October 1988, p. 58.

3. Brian Swimme, *The Universe is a Green Dragon* (Santa Fe: Bear & Co., 1984), p. 169.

4. Joseph Chilton Pearce, *Exploring the Crack in the Cosmic Egg* (New York: Julien Press, 1974).

5. Jean Houston, *The Possible Human* (Los Angeles: J.P. Tarcher, 1982).

6. Ibid., p. 214.

7. Rupert Sheldrake, *The New Science of Life* (Los Angeles: J.P. Tarcher, 1982)

8. *The Findhorn Garden* (New York: Harper & Row, 1975).

9. While there is now a large, thriving community at Findhorn, centered around a still thriving and beautiful garden, the Findhorn community's approach to the garden has gone through many changes over the years. Much of the magical approach that I am describing was connected to Findhorn's early founders and has become less apparent as those specific individuals have moved away.

10. Barry Neil Kaufman, *Son-Rise* (New York: Harper & Row, 1976), and *Love Is To Be Happy With* (New York: Fawcett Crest, 1977).
11. Jack Schwarz, *The Path of Action* (New York: E.P. Dutton, 1977) and *Human Energy Systems* (New York: E.P. Dutton, 1980).
12. The Perelandra Garden in Jeffersonton, Virginia is one ongoing demonstration of the lessons of Findhorn. See: *Behaving As If The God In All Life Really Mattered* and *The Perelandra Garden Book*. Both books by Machaelle Small Wright, published by Perelandra, Ltd.

Chapter 11
1. Stephen Locke, MD, and Douglas Colligan, *The Healer Within* (New York: New American Library, 1986), p. 212.
2. Ibid., p. xv.
3. John Wheeler, in Fred Alan Wolf, *Taking the Quantum Leap* (San Francisco: Harper & Row, 1981), p. 192.

Chapter 12
1. Elizabeth Cogburn, "Warriors of the Beauty Way," *In Context*, Spring 1984, p. 43.
2. Alan Watts, *The Wisdom of Insecurity* (New York: Vintage Books, 1951), p. 90.
3. Joseph Campbell, from a lecture given on the occasion of his 85th birthday at the San Francisco Palace of Fine Arts, March, 1984.
4. Brooke Medicine Eagle, spoken to a group while traveling down the Colorado River, through the Grand Canyon, October 1987.
5. Dolores LaChapelle, "Ritual Is Essential," *In Context*, Spring 1984, p. 41.
6. Joseph Campbell, from lecture.
7. Jean Houston, *In Search For The Beloved* (Los Angeles: J.P. Tarcher, 1987), p. 42.
8. Ibid., p. 43.
9. LaChapelle, "Ritual is Essential," p. 41.
10. Cogburn, "Warriors of The Beauty Way," p. 43.
11. James Lovelock, *Gaia: A New Look at Life on Earth* (London: Oxford University Press, 1979).

    Peter Russell, *The Global Brain* (Los Angeles: J.P. Tarcher, 1983).

    Eric Jantsch, *The Self-Organizing Universe* (Oxford and New York: Pergamon, 1980).

    Leonard, *The Transformation*.

SUGGESTED READING

While little has been written about the actual practice of firewalking, my understanding of it and its deeper implications owes a great deal to the following authors and books:

Acharya, Pundit. *Breath, Sleep, The Heart and Life*. Clearlake Highlands, CA: The Dawn Horse Press, 1975.

Achterberg, Jeanne. *Imagery and Healing: Shamanism and Modern Medicine*. Boston: Shambhala, 1985.

Bach, Richard. *Illusions: The Adventures of a Reluctant Messiah*. New York: Dell Publishing, 1977.

Becker, Robert. *The Body Electric: Electromagnetism and the Foundation of Life*. New York: William Morrow and Company, 1985.

Benson, Herbert, M.D. *Beyond the Relaxation Response: How to Harness the Healing Power of Your Personal Beliefs*. New York: Berkley Books, 1984.

Capra, Fritjof. *The Turning Point: Science, Society, and the Rising Culture*. New York: Bantam Books, 1983.

Carey, Ken. *Vision*. Kansas City: Uni Sun, 1985.

Da Free John. *Conscious Exercise and the Transcendental Sun*. Middletown, CA: The Dawn Horse Press, 1977.

Da Free John. *The Enlightenment of the Whole Body*. Middletown: The Dawn Horse Press, 1978.

Da Free John. *The Transmission of Doubt: Talks and Essays on the Transcendence of Scientific Materialism through Radical Understanding*. Middletown: The Dawn Horse Press, 1984.

Devall, Bill, and George Sessions. *Deep Ecology: Living as if Nature Mattered*. Layton, Utah: Gibbs Smith, Inc., 1985.

Dossey, Larry, M.D. *Space, Time & Medicine*. Boulder: Shambhala, 1982.

Katz, Richard. *Boiling Energy: Community Healing Among the Kalahari Kung*. Cambridge: Harvard University Press, 1982.

Geba, Bruno Hans, M.D. *Breathe Away Your Tension: A Five Week Program of Body Relaxation*. New York: Random House, 1973.

Gerber, Richard, M.D. *Vibrational Medicine: New Choices For Healing Ourselves*. Santa Fe: Bear & Company, 1988.

Grossinger, Richard. *Planet Medicine: From Stone Age Shamanism to Postindustrial Healing*. Boulder: Shambhala, 1982.

Gunther, Bernard. *Energy Ecstasy and Your Seven Vital Chakras*. Los Angeles: The Guild of Tutors Press, 1978.

Henderson, Julie. *The Lover Within: Opening to Energy in Sexual Practice*. Barrytown: Station Hill, 1986.

Hubbard, Barbara Marx, with Ken Carey. *Manual for Co-Creators of the Quantum Leap.* Gainesville, FL: New Visions, 1986.

Houston, Jean. *The Possible Human: A Course in Extending Your Physical, Mental, and Creative Abilities.* Los Angeles: J.P. Tarcher, 1982.

Kaufman, Barry Neil. *Love Is To Be Happy With.* New York: Harper & Row, 1977.

Leonard, George. *The Transformation: A Guide to the Inevitable Changes in Humankind.* Los Angeles: J.P. Tarcher, 1972.

Leonard, George. *The Ultimate Athlete.* New York: Avon, 1974.

Leonard, George. *The Silent Pulse: A Search for the Perfect Rhythm That Exists in Each of Us.* New York: E.P. Dutton, 1978.

LeShan, Lawrence. *Alternate Realities: The Search for the Full Human Being.* New York: Ballantine, 1976.

Lovelock, J.E. *Gaia: A New Look at Life on Earth.* Oxford: Oxford University Press, 1979.

Locke, Steven, M.D. *The Healer Within: The New Medicine of Mind and Body.* New York: E.P. Dutton, 1986.

Murchie, Guy. *The Seven Mysteries of Life: An Exploration in Science and Philosophy.* Boston: Houghton Mifflin, 1978.

Murphy, Michael. *Jacob Atabet: a speculative fiction.* Millbrae, CA: Celestial Arts, 1977.

Pearce, Joseph Chilton. *The Crack in the Cosmic Egg.* New York: The Julien Press, 1971.

Pearce, Joseph Chilton. *Exploring the Crack in the Cosmic Egg: Split Minds & Meta-Realities.* New York: The Julien Press, 1974.

Russell, Peter. *The Global Brain: Speculations on the Evolutionary Leap to Planetary Consciousness.* Los Angeles: J.P. Tarcher, 1983.

Selye, Hans, M.D. *The Stress of Life.* New York: McGraw Hill, 1956.

Sheldrake, Rupert. *A New Science of Life: The Hypothesis of Formative Causation.* Los Angeles: J.P. Tarcher, 1982.

Siegel, Bernie S., M.D. *Love, Medicine & Miracles: Lessons Learned about Self-Healing from a Surgeon's Experience with Exceptional Patients.* New York: Harper & Row, 1986.

Thompson, John W. *The Human Factor: An Inquiry Into Communication and Consciousness.* Farmingdale, NY: Coleman Publishing, 1983.

Schwarz, Jack. *Voluntary Controls: Exercises for Creative Meditation and for Activating the Potential of the Chakras.* New York: E.P. Dutton, 1978.

Smith, Fritz Frederick, M.D. *Inner Bridges: A Guide to Energy Movement and Body Structure.* Atlanta: Humanics, 1986.

Swimme, Brian. *The Universe is a Green Dragon: A Cosmic Creation Story.* Santa Fe: Bear & Company, 1985.

Tarthang Tulku. *Kum Nye Relaxation, vols I-II.* Berkeley: Dharma Publishing, 1978.

Watson, Lyall. *Supernature.* New York: Bantam, 1973.

Watts, Alan. *The Wisdom of Insecurity.* New York: Vintage Books, 1951

Wenger, Win. *Beyond O.K.: Psychegenic Tools Relating to Health of Body and Mind.* Gaithersburg, MD: Psychegenics Press, 1979.

Weil, Andrew, M.D. *Health and Healing: Understanding Conventional and Alternative Medicine.* Boston: Houghton Mifflin Co., 1983.

Williams, Paul. *Das Energi.* New York: Warner Books, 1973.

Wolf, Fred Alan. *The Body Quantum: The New Physics of Body, Mind, and Health.* New York: MacMillan, 1986

ABOUT THE AUTHOR

Michael Sky is a firewalking instructor and holistic healer. Since 1976 he has maintained a private practice as a bodyworker/ therapist exploring breath, life-energy, and body image. His workshops in the exploration of human potential investigate the creative process, the nature of stress, fear, and pain, the bio-electric body, the new physics, and the importance of ritual. Michael has facilitated firewalking workshops for over 3000 people since 1984.

Michael holds a bachelor of arts degree in Chinese Studies (language and philosophy). He was taught by Tolly Burkan and Peggy Dylan-Burkan, the founders of American firewalking. He has also produced a video documenting the ancient ritual of the firewalk. He and his wife, Penny Sharp, are authors of the nationally distributed newsletter, *Dragonfly*, and are residents of Eastsound, Washington.

Michael Sky has produced a powerful
fifteen-minute video of a typical firewalk —
also entitled *Dancing With The Fire* — which
conveys all of the joy and wonder that is
present whenever people come together in this
ancient dance.

Available on VHS from:
MACROMEDIA
P.O. Box 1223
Brookline, MA 02146
$29.95 + 2.50 postage

TO WRITE TO THE AUTHOR:

Michael Sky
P.O. Box 1085
Eastsound, WA 98245